A C++ Primer for Engineers:
An Object-Oriented Approach

McGraw-Hill Series in Computer Science

SENIOR CONSULTING EDITOR

C. L. Liu, University of Illinois at Urbana-Champaign

CONSULTING EDITOR

Allen B. Tucker, Bowdoin College

Fundamentals of Computing and Programming
Computer Organization and Architecture
Computers in Society/Ethics
Systems and Languages
Theoretical Foundations
Software Engineering and Database
Artificial Intelligence
Networks, Parallel and Distributed Computing
Graphics and Visualization
The MIT Electrical and Computer Science Series

FUNDAMENTALS OF COMPUTING AND PROGRAMMING

*Abelson and Sussman: *Structure and Interpretation of Computer Programs*

Astrachan: *A Computer Science Tapestry: Exploring Programming and Computer Science with C++*

Bergin: *Data Abstraction: The Object-Oriented Approach Using C++*

Heileman: *Data Structures, Algorithms, and Object-Oriented Programming*

Kamin and Reingold: *Programming with Class: A C++ Introduction to Computer Science*

Kernighan and Plauger: *The Elements of Programming Style*

Ponnambalam and Alguindigue: *A C++ Primer for Engineers: An Object-Oriented Approach*

Smith and Frank: *Introduction to Programming Concepts and Methods with Ada*

*Springer and Friedman: *Scheme and the Art of Programming*

Tremblay and Bunt: *Introduction to Computer Science: An Algorithmic Approach*

Tucker, Bernat, Bradley, Cupper, and Scragg: *Fundamentals of Computing I: Logic, Problem Solving, Programs, and Computers*

Tucker, Cupper, Bradley, Epstein and Kelemen: *Fundamentals of Computing II: Abstraction, Data Structures, and Large Software Systems*

*Co-published by the MIT Press and The McGraw-Hill Companies, Inc.

A C++ Primer
for Engineers:

An Object-Oriented Approach

K. Ponnambalam
University of Waterloo, Canada

Tiuley Alguindigue
Engsoft, Canada

Boston, Massachusetts   Burr Ridge, Illinois   Dubuque, Iowa
Madison, Wisconsin   New York, New York   San Francisco, California   St. Louis, Missouri

WCB/McGraw-Hill

A Division of The **McGraw·Hill** Companies

A C++ PRIMER FOR ENGINEERS: AN OBJECT-ORIENTED APPROACH

2 3 4 5 6 7 8 9 0 DOC DOC 9 0 9 8 7

P/N 050501-2
Part of ISBN 0-07-913140-9

This book was set in Times Roman by Publication Services, Inc.
The editor was Eric M. Munson;
the production supervisor was Paula Keller.
The cover was designed by Christopher Brady.
Project supervision was done by Keyword Publishing Services Ltd.
R. R. Donnelley & Sons Company was printer and binder.

Library of Congress Cataloging-in-Publication Data

Ponnambalam, K.
    A C++ primer for engineers: an object-oriented approach / K.
Ponnambalam, Tiuley Alguindigue.
      p.   cm.
    Includes index.
    ISBN 0-07-913140-9
    1. C++ (Computer program language)   2. Object-oriented programming
(Computer science) I. Alguindigue, Tiuley.   II. Title.
QA76.73.C153P67   1997
005.13′3—dc21   96-49674

http://www.mhcollege.com

ABOUT THE AUTHORS

K. PONNAMBALAM is a faculty member at the Department of Systems Design Engineering, University of Waterloo, Canada. He received a Bachelors degree in Engineering from Madras University, a Masters degree from the National University of Ireland, and a Doctoral degree from the University of Toronto. He has been involved in creating and teaching computer programming and mathematical modeling courses in various universities for over a decade. He has authored many publications in leading research journals. His research interests include software engineering, risk and reliability analyses, and large-scale numerical optimization.

TIULEY ALGUINDIGUE received her Bachelors degree in Systems Engineering from Universidad Metropolitana in Caracas, Venezuela, and her Masters degree in Industrial Engineering, specializing in Information Systems, from the University of Toronto. She has taught programming courses and Object Oriented Programming at Universidad Metropolitana and in several companies where she has worked in system development using Fortran, C, Pascal, C++, NATURAL, PowerBuilder, and Optimatt. In the past she had worked as software engineer for Software AG of Canada and Powersoft, and is currently the Chief Software Engineer for Engsoft.

To Our Parents
for the Past and the Present

To Our Children
for the Present and the Future

CONTENTS

PREFACE

Why write yet another C++ book? Why and what should engineers know about Object-Oriented Programming (OOP)? This preface will attempt to answer these two questions by indicating the intended audience for the book and what they gain from reading it. To know the answer intimately you need to read the book and complete the exercises!

Who Should Read This Book?

The book is written at a freshman or junior level (First or Second year in University). If you are *one* of the following, you should consider reading the book:

 (i) An undergraduate engineering student at a University looking for a first book on C++ or OOP
 (ii) A student on a Diploma in Computer Engineering course at a Polytechnic or Technical College looking for a first book on C++ or OOP
(iii) An instructor for any of the above
(iv) An engineer who usually programs in Fortran, C, or similar languages and wants to get a quick introduction to C++ or OOP
 (v) You are interested in problem solving using computers and are curious about C++ or OOP.

What Should You Know?

The book assumes that you have passed high school and have some knowledge of mathematical subjects such as algebra. Although it *does not* assume a computing background, familiarity with the basics of DOS or Windows or UNIX would help in using your C++ compiler for editing, compiling, and executing your programs.

Why Is This Book Unique?

This is one of the first books to introduce C++, Object-Oriented Programming (OOP), and practical Object-Oriented Modeling to an audience with no background in computing. If you become thoroughly familiar with the concepts covered in the book, you can think of yourself as an intermediate-level programmer; just at the lower rung of the vast middle class of programmers. You will have developed skills in Object-Oriented Modeling and Design which a large number of intermediate programmers have yet to master. This will give you an edge over most of your peers!

The book emphasizes engineering problem solving and follows the evolution of ideas of programming from (i) using a single function to solve the entire problem (Chapters 2 and 3), to (ii) using a structure chart and functions to modularize (Chapters 4 to 6), to finally (iii) using object-oriented programming (Chapters 7 to 11), all using the principles of problem decomposition and top-down design. Class invariants, pre- and postconditions are explained in practical examples and are emphasized throughout. The book also introduces program complexity (not just algorithm complexity as traditionally introduced in computer science texts) based on simple metrics and demonstrates how OOP reduces program complexity without losing the advantages of modularity. The book contains review questions and exercises at the end of each chapter. The starred exercises are more advanced than others in the same chapter. To save space, detailed solutions (five-step design methodology and C++ code) to many exercises are provided only on the accompanying diskette. Answers to even-numbered review questions and sample solutions to the two exercises are in Appendix F. We have also included an introductory chapter on Java, a new and currently becoming popular object-oriented programming language. There is enough in the book to make it not just another C++ or OOP book!

Who Should *Not* Bother Reading the Book?

  (i) Programmers looking for cute C++ tricks
 (ii) Those interested only in C++ programming and not problem solving
(iii) Instructors of higher-level computer science courses
(iv) Anyone looking for a comprehensive coverage of C++ or OOP

What Are Our Qualifications?

The authors have taught Fortran, PL/1, APL, Pascal, Turing, and C++ over the past ten years (incidentally, we have never taught C before!), with C++ dominating the past four years. The book is the result of teaching C++ and OOP to first-year engineering students for four years at the University of Waterloo. At first we used C++ just as another programming language without using any of its OOP features. The second year we used C++ and OOP but not much was done using inheritance, a new concept to reuse already available code. The third year we covered inheritance but did not emphasize object-oriented modeling. In the fourth year we devised our own ways to introduce object-oriented modeling, design, and programming, synthesizing ideas with well-known OOP methodologies. As our knowledge and skills evolved we were able to take a much more daring approach and the students not only kept pace but taught us much of what we have covered in the book.

What Is Object-Oriented Modeling?

In order to use C++ and OOP effectively you have to understand and use object-oriented modeling techniques (OMT). Many comparable definitions for object-oriented modeling techniques exist, proposed by stalwarts like Booch, Coad and

Yourdon, Desfray, Rumbaugh, among others. Our presentation has been influenced by all those ideas, thus following the current trend of unifying these definitions or at least providing equivalents. In particular, we have benefited through use of the modeling techniques of Rumbaugh and colleagues and the notations and diagrams of Coad and Yourdon. In addition, our ideas on class invariants, pre- and postconditions are simplifications of the work of Desfray. It would be fair to say that our work has been influenced quite heavily by the works of Booch and the C++ "inventor" Stroustrup [Please refer to the Annotated Bibliography for relevant publications]. The next paragraph describes briefly the principles of OMT.

OMT concerns the modeling of objects, their classification, their interrelationships, their functionality, and their dynamic behavior. The three sub-models of OMT are the Object Model, the Functional Model, and the Dynamic or State Model. The Object Model concerns objects, their classification, and their static relationships. The Functional Model is very similar to the old procedural models and it concerns the transformation of data. Lastly, the Dynamic or State Model studies the state of the program, its objects, and their dynamic transitions from one state to another. In this book, the State Model is not explicitly discussed and is lumped with the Functional Model. In Chapters 1, 7 and 8 we introduce these modeling ideas a little at a time. Next, we briefly discuss objects which are the central figures of OMT.

Engineers have been using OMT for many years in all disciplines except in software building. Suppose you have to build a building, an electrical circuit, or a bicycle. First you have an overall idea of the object. You choose each object's (for example, bicycle's) attributes such as the wheel size and the number of gears, and decide what services it will provide, for example (how much) the bicycle will carry, (how fast) it will move, (how sharp it can) turn, etc. In addition, the object you are building may be composed of other objects (a bicycle has a handlebar, seat, frame, wheels, pedals, etc.), some of which may already exist. You simply acquire those objects and assemble the bicycle. The fundamental principle of OMT is to identify objects, their attributes, and the services they provide, and classify them using some commonality. When a new object needs to be built you can attempt to use some existing objects and build the new object without starting from scratch. These ideas have been quite acceptable to engineers for a long time but were hardly used in computer programming. Note that the idea of using a library of functions is not equivalent as the functions do not carry data but simply operate on data supplied to them.

With OMT and OOP it is now possible to apply some well-known engineering ideas to software development. Problem solving requires modeling real-world objects in computers to simulate their behavior. With OMT you can model your object to resemble the real-world object as closely as you want and, with OOP (and C++), you can implement the model in software. Unfortunately, to say much more on OMT or OOP will need an entire book and we stop our explanations here!

Summary

The book helps you learn programming in a systematic way (top-down design and a five-step methodology) using the principles of structured programming and OOP, and the programming language C++. The problems are mostly from the domain of engineering. The book does not assume a computing background for the reader. If you have any comments and questions please send us an email at `ponnu@uwaterloo.ca`. Thanks!

Instructions to Instructors

Please read the preface before proceeding! We assume 12 weeks of 3–50 minute periods of lecturing, and 3 hours of Computer Lab with one of them used as a tutorial class. The students are expected to work outside lab hours as well. See the Instructors manual (you can get it from the publisher) which contains necessary lecture material (including the complete set of overhead slides for 36 lecture hours) organized into weeks. Depending upon what you think is possible (the background of students at freshman level varies widely) or what you want to achieve in the course, the three possible levels at which this book can be used are given in the table below. Note that the book has 10 chapters on C++ but the tenth chapter is really a reference and has not been extensively used in teaching by us. Some chapters overlapping over more than one week are shown with shading.

The chapters on pointers can be left to the end when you are teaching C++ with Object-Oriented Programming. Pointers are simply implementation devices and not a high-level concept. We are assuming that you are teaching a high-level programming course with problem solving as the main objective! In the table, the details

Week	Basic C++ (like C)	Basic C++ and OOP	More adventurous
1	1. Problem solving using computers	1. Problem solving using computers	1. Problem solving using computers
2	2. C++ Programming Basics	2. C++ Programming Basics	2. C++ Programming Basics
3	2. . . . + Pointers	3. Selections and Repetitions	3. Selections and Repetitions
4	3. Selections and Repetitions	3. . . .	4. Functions to Aid Modularity
5	3. . . .	4. Functions to Aid Modularity	5. Arrays for Grouping Data of Same Type
6	4. Functions to Aid Modularity	5. Arrays for Grouping Data of Same Type	5. . . .
7	4. . . .	5. . . .	7. Encapsulation of Data and Functions in Classes
8	5. Arrays for Grouping Data of Same Type	7. Encapsulation of Data and Functions in Classes	7. . . .
9	5. . . . + Pointers [Chapter 9]	7. . . .	8. Inheritance to Aid Reusability
10	6. Structures for Grouping Data	7. . . .	8. . . .
11	9. Pointers for Efficient Implementation	9. Pointers for Efficient Implementation	9. Pointers for Efficient Implementation
12	9. Pointers for Efficient Implementation	9. . . .	9. . . .

covered in the last two weeks on pointers also depend on what has been taught earlier and hence are different for each of the three levels. You can consult the Instructor's manual for more details.

Our observation from the past four years of teaching C++ and OOP is that today's youngsters are quite capable of coping with the material in the book. This does not mean that there will not be the customary 5% of students who seem to have trouble with some of the basic computing skills, irrespective of the level of the course or the language taught. In the past, the authors have taught Fortran, Pascal, and Turing, all supposedly easier to use than C++, and had also found that, to their dismay, a few of the students had had great trouble with the required skills. On the positive side, even those students who faced problems with C++ programming skills seldom had any problem with object-oriented modeling or following the five-step methodology we use for problem solving. Lastly, compared with Fortran or Pascal, C++ is a larger language and hence it is not possible to cover all the features of the language in 12 weeks. However, the features covered in the book are sufficient to solve even some sophisticated problems, as you will see from the case studies and exercises.

Practicing engineers will find Chapter 10 (Miscellaneous Topics in C++) useful, especially the section on how to use existing Fortran or C functions with their new C++ programs which extends the idea of reuse to legacy code!

Annotated Bibliography

Ellis, M., and Stroustrup, Bjarne, *The C++ Annotated Reference Manual,* Addison-Wesley, 1990. The base document used for drafting the ANSI ISO C++ standard currently under review.

Stroustroup, Bjarne, *The C++ Programming Language,* Second Ed., Addison-Wesley, 1991. C++ examples in many books probably originated here. He also talks about object-oriented design which is quite helpful.

Stroustrup, Bjarne, *The Design and Evolution of C++,* Addison-Wesley, 1994. A historic note on C++ and object-oriented programming languages in general. Talks about the future C++ and many ideas from here are already implemented in the ANSI ISO C++ draft standard.

Barton, John J., and Lee R. Nackman, *Scientific and Engineering C++,* Addison-Wesley, 1994. Presents good examples on how advanced and the not so advanced C++ can be used for solving practical engineering problems such as nonlinear systems, finite-element applications, etc.

Booch, Grady, *Object-Oriented Analysis and Design with Applications,* Second Ed., Benjamin-Cummings, 1994. A pioneering work on the subject. Easy reading.

Desfray, Philippe, *Object Engineering: The Fourth Dimension,* Addison-Wesley, 1994. Use this for understanding some detailed issues of object-oriented modeling such as class invariants, pre- and postconditions. A European view of object-oriented analysis and design.

Pressman, R.S., *Software Engineering: A Practitioner's Approach,* 3rd Ed., McGraw-Hill Publ., 1992. An introductory book on general software engineering principles.

Rumbaugh, J., et al., *Object-Oriented Modelling and Design,* Prentice-Hall, 1991. Object-oriented modeling is explained best here. Lots of engineering examples in exercises.

Coad, P., *Object Models: Strategies, Patterns, and Applications,* Yourdon Press, 1995. The notations used here are available in most Computer-Aided Software Engineering (CASE) tools. Many examples of object modeling.

Cline, M. P., and G. A. Lomow, *C++ FAQs: Frequently Asked Questions,* Addison-Wesley Publ., 1995. A nice reference. After reading our book, this book is easier to understand.

Microgold Software Inc., With Class 2.5 Scripting Tool, 1994. An easy-to-use tool and allows you to use popular notations. Generates code in many programming languages.

Gamma, E., R. Helm, R. Johnson, and J. Vlissides, *Design Patterns—Elements of Reusable Object-Oriented Software,* Addison-Wesley Publ., 1995. Read this book before you venture into any large-scale programming. Contains a catalog of design patterns (class relation diagrams and sample implementations) for many common problems.

ACKNOWLEDGMENTS

It is a pleasure to be able to acknowledge the help we have received from various persons and institutions that affected the writing of this book, some directly, others indirectly. If we have failed to mention anyone whose name should be here please forgive us for our oversight and inform us so that we can include it the next time. While we acknowledge the help of others we of course accept full responsibility for any errors.

First and foremost, we acknowledge the first year engineering students and the teaching assistants of the Department of Systems Design Engineering, University of Waterloo, who tried the early versions of this book and provided the many useful suggestions for its improvement. Without their encouragement, and their desire to try a new language which was not considered at that time to be suitable for a new computing student, this book would not have materialized. We have also modified and used some of the student solutions developed during the past years which are gratefully acknowledged. Thanks are also due to the faculty and the undergraduate studies committee of the department for allowing this new "experiment." C++ is now the language used for the first year engineering students in nearly the entire Faculty of Engineering at University of Waterloo which we believe to be one of the results of the innovation-minded culture developed here by faculty, students, and staff!

Todd Veldhuizen was our first and foremost critical reader. He also suggested the examples in the Templates section. Thank you Todd. Jiri Vlach was the first non C++ programmer to have read our book and his comments as well as his companionship are gratefully acknowledged. Jane C. Ho and Marlo Raynolds helped in the development of some of the answers to the exercises and the source code in the book. Bob Bowerman and Jesse Perla helped us with the many nuances of C++ and the different C++ compilers we used during the last few years. Dan Stashuk was a reviewer and now an instructor using our book. Thanks for his many comments and suggestions and for testing out our overhead slides for instructors. We acknowledge the comments and suggestions of our reviewers and readers (in alphabetical order): Otman Basir, Mike Batchelder, Sanjeev Bedi, Ben Calloni, Thomas Denney, Li-Ping Fang, George Freeman, Israel A. Morles, Dan Stashuk, Todd Veldhuizen, and Jiri Vlach.

On the publishing side we are thankful to Eric Munson of McGraw-Hill, and Alan Chesterton of Keyword Publishing Services Ltd for their help. Eric's constant encouragement and emails during the time of the project (over 3 years) gave us enough impetus to finish the work. Thank you. Alan ironed out the creases in our presentation and also made sure that our suggestions on the manuscript were passed on to the typesetter and we gratefully acknowledge his help.

Arnold Heemink of TUDelft arranged for a sabbatical in The Netherlands and some of the final stages of the book were completed there. We thank him and his family for their generosity.

Lastly, our children Maria-Saroja, Kumary, and Canmanie have had to endure much nonsensical talk about computers and C++ ("Are you teaching C++ because you have finished teaching A++ and B++?"), and our families in India and Venezuela and our friends in many countries had to put up with less of our time and effort due to our ever busy schedules. Thank you! Nandri! Gracias! Dank U wel!

A C++ Primer for Engineers:
An Object-Oriented Approach

CHAPTER 1

Problem Solving Using Computers

Computers are today among the most important tools used in problem solving in various domains including engineering. In the near past, most significant engineering projects have generally been solved by interdisciplinary teams consisting of engineers, scientists from many disciplines, mathematicians, and specialists from the humanities. We can expect the same in the future. Some selected engineering achievements are the moon landing, computer aided tomography (CAT), large electrical power systems and their control, cleaning up Niagara Love Canal, computers with user-friendly interfaces, etc.

The reasons for the need to use interdisciplinary teams to solve complex problems are (i) the understanding that many projects cross traditional disciplines and (ii) the delegation of work to specialists who are able to solve problems in their own specialty better than others. However, such an interdisciplinary team has to integrate well to solve the problem. In general, problem solving for large engineering projects requires *decomposition* into many *subproblems and domains* and their eventual *integration,* a strategy also required in problem solving using computers. This strategy is called the *top-down design* process and is described in this chapter.

Computers and their hardware–software combinations and notes on structured and object-oriented programming languages are introduced next. Then, a discussion of the top-down design process is followed by sections on problem solving methodologies. The methodology introduced here is sufficient for most of the book, although some additional principles will be introduced in other chapters as it becomes necessary.

COMPUTERS

Computers are systems made up of electrical and mechanical components, with the mechanical components limited mainly to secondary memory devices such as floppy drives, CD-ROM drives, and hard drives which primarily consist of rapidly spinning

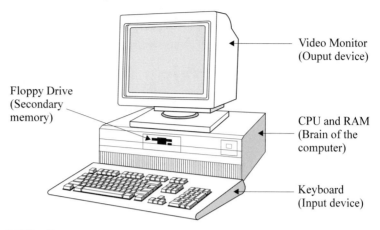

Video Monitor
(Ouput device)

Floppy Drive
(Secondary
memory)

CPU and RAM
(Brain of the
computer)

Keyboard
(Input device)

FIGURE 1.1
A personal computer.

disks. The bulk of the computer is made up of electrical components such as the main memory (also called random-access memory, RAM) and the central processor unit (CPU) which together are the brain of the computer. Common input devices are the keyboard and mouse and common output devices are a video monitor and a printer. So far we have talked about components which are classified as *hardware*. All are managed by *software* to produce the complete computer. The innermost layer (kernel) of the software is the basic input/output system (BIOS). The BIOS is usually a machine language program (explained later), often stored in read-only memory (ROM). The next level of the software is the operating system, or disk operating system (DOS), and all our programs reside on top of the operating system. MS-DOS® and UNIX are examples of common operating systems in use today. Programs such as MS-Windows 3.1® for DOS or X-Windows for UNIX provide friendlier interfaces to the underlying operating system. A diagram of a personal computer (PC) is shown in Fig. 1.1.

Conceptually the hardware of the computer can be sketched as in Fig. 1.2. The arrows indicate the direction of data flow. Data between the CPU and RAM flows in both directions at high speed, using wires called the *bus*. Next we will briefly describe the main memory (RAM) and the central processing unit (CPU).

Main memory

Memory is where information is stored during processing. The information could be data or instructions for the computer. The atomic unit of memory is the bit (which is a small cell that can store only 0 or 1) and the molecular unit of memory is the byte which is a larger cell consisting of 8 bits. For example, to store the information content of a single character using the ASCII system, say A, we need 1 byte, stored as decimal 65 or 0100 0001. Fortunately, in this book and for most high-level programming, we rarely have to worry about low-level or machine-level details such as this.

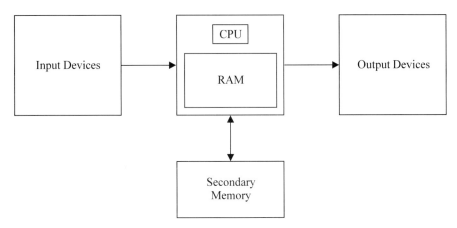

FIGURE 1.2
Conceptual diagram for a computer.

The memory is organized in sequence with the exact location given by its *address,* usually denoted as a hexadecimal number (a number whose base is 16, unlike the base 10 numbers that we normally use). Again, we rarely need to read hexadecimal numbers, but what is worth knowing is that each type of information that we store requires different numbers of bytes. For example, characters require 1 byte (in ASCII), and the requirements of other data types are discussed in Chapter 2.

Central Processing Unit (CPU)

Information processing in computers is done by the CPU. The main components of a CPU are the control unit and the arithmetic logic unit (ALU). The control unit controls all activities between the arithmetic logic unit, the instruction registers, and the RAM. The main job of the ALU is to perform additions, subtractions, multiplications, and divisions, all of which are controlled by the control unit using instructions from the instruction registers. The instruction registers temporarily store the program instruction transferred from RAM by the control unit. The instructions are in machine language. The next section describes the various processes involved in producing a machine language instruction.

High-level language to machine language

C++ is a high-level language which humans can understand and use to communicate with the computer. However, the computer (CPU) understands only a machine language instruction and therefore the high-level language must be translated into machine language. A compiler is a special computer program that carries out this translation. Compilers depend on the machine and the operating system. The sequence of operations required to produce a machine executable program is described in the next section.

Source file to executable file [edit–compile–link–execute process]

Operating systems (such as DOS or UNIX) allow you to store the source files containing your C++ programs in secondary memory. Creating source files depends

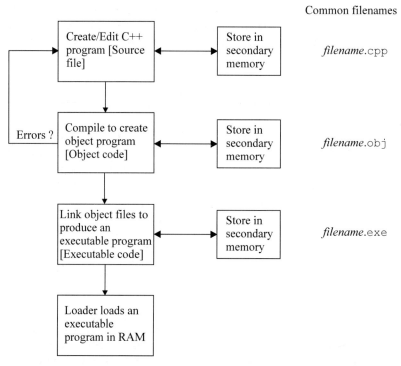

FIGURE 1.3
Edit–compile–link–execute cycle.

on the compiler and operating system you use. Many compilers for personal computers provide an integrated development environment (IDE) where the sequence of editing (or creating) a source file, compiling, linking, and executing can all be done in a single program. Fig. 1.3 shows the sequence which converts a source file to an executable file. This is often a cyclic process. Errors found during the process include compile errors, link errors, and executable errors and these are discussed in detail in Chapter 2.

PROGRAMMING PARADIGMS

Patterns or models are called paradigms. According to Stroustrup, the four important programming paradigms—procedural, data hiding, data abstraction, and object-oriented—can be defined as follows. In the *procedural* paradigm you select the procedures needed and choose the best algorithm you can find for each one. An algorithm is simply the steps to follow in order to solve a problem in a finite time. In the *data hiding* paradigm you select the modules needed and partition the program such that data is hidden in the modules. In the *data abstraction* paradigm you select the data types needed and supply the required set of operations for each type. Lastly, in the *object-oriented* paradigm you select the classes needed and supply the required set of methods (operations) for each class, using inheritance to exploit commonality among classes. The two paradigms covered in this text are procedural and object-oriented. These are described in detail in the next two sections, respectively.

PROCEDURAL PROGRAMMING LANGUAGES

Procedural programming languages such as Fortran, BASIC, C, and the original Pascal provide constructs to solve a problem based on processes or things to do, as described in detail in the next section. The program statement is the main construct. The development of the procedure (or function or subroutine) was the major step forward in the design and implementation of programs to solve complex problems. Following the top-down design process (described in detail later in the chapter), the problem is divided into smaller problems, each of which does something or processes something. For small programs, there was no other paradigm.

Program Statements and Functions

The most indivisible part of a procedural language is the program statement which instructs the computer to do something. That is, a program is simply a list of instructions. In these languages, when programs solving complex problems became harder to understand, functions were invented to solve the subproblems. Each function supposedly has a single purpose and a clearly defined interface to other functions in the program. This was the major idea of structured programming.

Structured Programming and Limitations

In structured programming and procedural languages, the emphasis was on performing an action. For example, get two numbers, add them, print the result, and so on. The data was not given a prominent place. For example, in a program that keeps track of student records, the data representing the students' grades is read and passed on to many functions, such as the one that calculates the average, checks for failures before deciding on promotions, and so on. All these functions had access to the data (that is, the students' grades) and hence the risk of accidental corruption increased.

Secondly, we cannot build models for real-world problems using only functions. We also need to consider the data processed by these functions. For example, suppose we have to model a municipal water supply where there are components such as reservoirs, pumps, pipes, valves, and so on. Each of these components has certain attributes and provides specific services. With the procedural paradigm, there is no quick way to decide what functions we should have and what data structure should be used. There is no one-to-one relationship between the real-world object and the software. Functions are the only mechanism for extensibility in procedural languages. Although new data types can be devised using features like RECORD in languages like Pascal, these data types carry all the disadvantages we have discussed so far, like no protection from accidental corruption, not enough resemblance to real-world objects, etc. Object-oriented programming languages attempt to overcome this problem.

OBJECT-ORIENTED PROGRAMMING LANGUAGES

In this section, we will briefly review object-oriented programming (OOP) and the C++ language. Although the fundamental concepts on which OOP is based simply reflect good programming practice, the new ideas of OOP have provided systematic ways to use OOP for program design and implementation. Also, practicing OOP with procedural programming languages is difficult, if not impossible. Languages such as C++ provide language constructs to overcome the shortcomings of procedural programming languages.

Object-Oriented Programming and Design

Limitations in previous approaches to programming brought about the new ideas of Object-Oriented Programming (OOP). Both OOP and older methods require problem decomposition, but the methods of analysis, design, and programming are fundamentally different. In traditional structured programming languages, data (the characteristics or attributes of things) and functions (methods or services provided by things) are programmed as separate entities. For example, a program may have a data type `student_grade_record` which contains the data and a global function (a function that can stand alone and be used for processing data) `print_student_grade_record()` which can print any student record. In OOP both data and functions are united in objects which are instances of classes. Secondly, in traditional programming languages users are not prevented from accessing implementation details. That is, in the above example the global function `print_student_grade_record()` will not only be able to print any student record but will also be able to modify the data in the student record, unless data is passed to it using safe mechanisms. On the other hand, in traditional programming languages it is not easy to insulate the user from the need to know the implementation details. In order to overcome these shortcomings, in OOP problems are analyzed and modeled using objects; this process is called Object-Oriented Analysis (OOA). Connecting OOA with OOP is Object-Oriented Design (OOD) which provides guidelines and notations for analyzing and modeling problems in an object-oriented manner.

Object-Oriented Modeling

Programming is used to realize the model of real-world problems (or systems) in a computer which can be used for analyzing and solving. OOP languages can help in modeling real-world objects as software objects. A related concept is that of abstraction. Humans use abstraction to deal with complexity. For example, a person using a television set rarely worries about all the details of what a television is but is only concerned with the limited functions of a few switches and controls. In essence, the user abstracts the essentials according to his or her own view and relegates the inessential details to somebody else. Types and levels of abstraction (and hence models) may vary. For an airline reservation clerk, an airplane is nothing but an object with seats to be filled. For an air traffic controller, an airplane is just a blip on the radar screen with its position and velocity. For the airline accountant an airplane is nothing but dollars! Each has abstracted the same object in a different way by picking out the essentials and ignoring non-essential details. Suppose in a computer we have a single object called `plane_007`. This object may have data (number of seats, length, maximum speed, etc.) and provide various services. However, not all users of the object require all of the data. A reservation clerk does not normally need to know the maximum speed, for example. In order to prevent unnecessary and unauthorized access to data, data hiding and encapsulation is used in OOP. The concept of classes is used to abstract and classify objects and to provide data hiding and encapsulation; it is discussed in detail later.

Reusing existing models and code reduces repetition. Reuse also takes advantage of already tested code and leads to higher reliability. In OOP, the concept of inheritance allows and extends the idea of reusability. Inheritance involves deriving new classes from already existing classes. For example, if there exists a class called `plane` which contains some basic data and services, we can derive new classes called `executive_jet`, `cargo_plane`, etc. by specializing the original base class `plane`. Therefore, `cargo_plane` is a new class with constraints such as the number of seats equal to zero. However, `cargo_plane` should not do something that a `plane` would not do. The derived classes are subclasses of the original base class and these are discussed in some detail later.

Therefore, the major principles on which OOP is based are data hiding and encapsulation, and inheritance. Both these ideas lead to high modularity which can lead to higher reliability and possibly lower costs in developing software.

Data Abstraction and Encapsulation

With structured design we tend to forget that data is the reason for doing something. If there are no `student_grade_records`, there is no need to read them, update them and print them. Data *is* the reason for the programming. Programming models real-world objects as software objects. Objects are entities that have data and functions united in a single unit.

Humans manage complexity by abstracting essentials. Consider a television set. The knobs (or buttons) are the interfaces that humans use to input their desires. The picture tube is where the output is. *What about all those detailed implementations of the TV?* Hidden from the user! Users only need to worry about input and output. The knobs and picture tube are the sole interfaces between humans and the TV.

Abstraction depends on the viewpoint of the user and the context in which the problem is solved. Consider an airplane and its many abstractions to different users.

Airplane

Reservation clerk	Seats
Air traffic controller	Radar blip
Frame manufacturer	Frame
Engine manufacturer	Body to hang engines
Accountant	$ $ $

Classes are blueprints for objects. `plane_007` is an object that is instantiated (created in computer memory) using the `plane` class. This object may have data (maximum number of seats, maximum speed, weight, etc.) and provide services like `fly()`, `carry()`, and so on. The objective of OOP is to identify first objects and then classes using the principles of data abstraction and encapsulation. Classes can be further streamlined using inheritance as discussed next.

Polymorphism and Inheritance

The word polymorphism means having more than one form. In OOP it refers to the fact that a single operation can have different behavior in different objects. Polymorphism is implemented in C++ using function and operator overloading. When a function or operator is overloaded, it can operate differently on different types of data. The appropriate version of the function or operator is selected by the compiler.

For example, the addition operator "+" can be given different meanings depending on the context:

`1 + 2 = 3` describes a scalar addition.
`"John" + "Doe" = "John Doe"` describes a string concatenation.
`C = A + B` may describe a matrix addition.

The same "+" operator is used to describe the "addition" operation on different types of data.

Inheritance allows the derivation of new classes from existing base classes. Inheritance facilitates the extensibility of the language through the reuse of code. Reusing existing code reduces repetition and increases reliability. Inheritance is one of the primary mechanisms for reusing code in OOP. In summary, the OOP paradigm is based on data hiding, encapsulation, and inheritance.

More on Object Modeling

Natural language provides clues for object-oriented modeling; for example, common names express concepts (e.g., a tiger, a city), proper names indicate objects (e.g., Shircan, Waterloo), adjectives qualify attributes (e.g., ferocious, small), verbs indicate processes, actions, services (e.g., roars), prepositions and articles connect objects to show dependency and relationships (e.g., the teeth of Shircan are sharp). Problem decomposition is the key step in modeling complexity. OOP provides the concepts of class and inheritance to help us implement the problem decomposition steps in the computer. Next we give a brief introduction to C++.

INTRODUCTION TO C++

C++ is a superset of C, which is a well-known and widely used programming language. C++ is a hybrid object-oriented programming (OOP) language. That is, what you can do with C or FORTRAN 77 can be done in the same manner in a hybrid language, without using OOP. Unlike Smalltalk or Java, C++ is not a pure OOP language. In pure OOP languages everything is an object, whereas in C++ there are both objects and global functions.

C++ is fast and efficient and many competing compilers (and integrated development environments) are available for all platforms. It is portable. A draft ANSI/ISO C++ Standard is already available. C++ is a strongly typed language with static or compile-time type checking which means that new data types cannot be introduced at execution time. C++ allows multiple inheritance, unlike Smalltalk.

HISTORY OF C++

C++ (Fig. 1.4) is derived from the language "C With Classes" which itself is derived from C and Simula 67. Simula 67 traces its ancestry back to ALGOL 60 whose parent was good old FORTRAN. C is derived from BCPL which is derived from

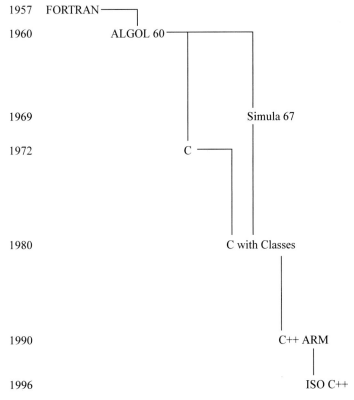

FIGURE 1.4
Essential details of C++ evolution.

ALGOL 60. However, the current ANSI/ISO standard C++, based on C++ Annotated Reference Manual (ARM), is also influenced by the following languages: Ada, ANSI C, ML, and Clu. The most significant languages that influenced C++ are C and Simula 67. The concept of classes was introduced by Simula 67, which was a language specially defined for large-scale simulation of systems.

In the next section the top-down design process is described in detail.

TOP-DOWN DESIGN PROCESS

A key step in problem solving is breaking a hard problem into problems that are relatively easier to solve, as shown in Fig. 1.5.

This is also called the *divide and conquer* strategy. A practical point to note is that the number of subproblems at any problem box is normally small, say from 2 to 4. If you have too many subproblems at any one box you are probably including details too early in the decomposition. Consider the complex problem of moon landing. A major subproblem is to have an appropriate transportation device which we call a rocket. It is true that for the moon rocket to work, the bolts, nuts, rivets, and o-rings that are used to construct it have to work and they too need to be designed. However, they are details that should be avoided at the beginning; they should be considered only after the problem has been decomposed from a large system to many smaller ones. The ability to see the forest before you see the trees is a key skill to acquire in problem solving. Fig. 1.6 shows a possible decomposition of the "moon rocket problem."

Designing from the top and implementing from the bottom is a commonly used problem solving strategy.

It is true that in the history of technology nuts and bolts were invented and understood long before rockets. However, with the current state of knowledge and technology we are able to visualize larger problems before the smaller ones. In order to implement a solution, however, we must often start from the bottom of the hierarchy and work to the top. This same process is also common for solving problems in computers: Design from the top and implement from the bottom. Of course, in many complex problems a mixture of both strategies is used. Implementing from the top is also possible when solving problems in computers. This is called rapid prototyping.

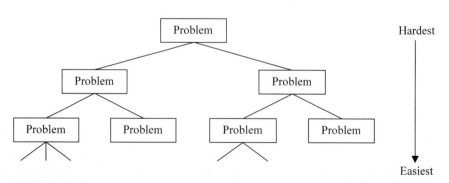

FIGURE 1.5
Problem decomposition or the divide and conquer strategy.

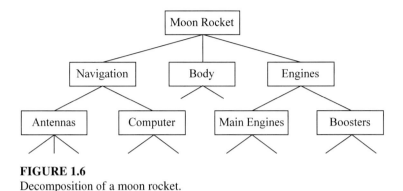

FIGURE 1.6
Decomposition of a moon rocket.

The systematic application of a problem solving strategy which includes the top-down design process differentiates the programmer (or software engineer) from a hacker. A hacker takes the problem and runs, literally, to the computer to solve it. A programmer takes the problem and applies the problem solving strategy; to the programmer a computer is just another tool in addition to paper, pencils, etc. In the next section we use an example to describe problems, data, and algorithms and the problem solving methodology used in the book.

PROBLEMS, DATA, AND ALGORITHMS

A simple example will be used to *overview* data, algorithms, and the problem solving methodology. We will also discuss some basic software engineering principles such as complexity, modularity, and maintainability. In this example, we are interested in calculating an average grade for a student and updating the student record. An algorithm is defined as the steps to follow to determine a solution to a problem in a finite time.

The problem is calculating the average grade. Grades in individual subjects are the necessary input data. The steps required for calculating the average is the algorithm. Additional steps required to solve such problems include reading data and writing the output. Although the example is simple and can be easily done on the back of an envelope, it will become tedious if we have to do this for thousands of students in a university. Therefore, we are interested in using a computer which should be able to do the job in a few seconds. What sort of methodology should be used to systematically solve this problem?

Problem Solving Methodology

The systematic methodology we will use consists of five steps. Depending upon the complexity of the problem, the details expected in each step will vary. The explanation of the five steps follows next.

1. Problem analysis

Understanding the problem, the necessary inputs, and the required outputs is the analysis step. The results of this step are a problem statement and a description of the inputs and outputs.

Problem statement. Understand the problem and produce a *concise* problem statement.

Input/output analysis. Analyze what is required as input data and what is required as the output.

2. Design

This step consists of

 (i) problem decomposition using the top-down design process;
 (ii) developing the object/class design to organize modules in object-oriented programming;
(iii) studying a simple hand example of the problem to understand the necessary data transformations; and
(iv) algorithm design to generalize the steps followed in solving the hand example.

Apply steps (i) to (iv) iteratively until satisfied. At the end of this section we will discuss how to recognize a satisfactory design.

We will follow the evolution of programming in this text, which means we give priority to algorithm design in the early chapters. Object design is postponed until Chapter 7 where we learn object-oriented modeling and design. If you do not fully understand all the steps now, do not worry. As you explore the case studies in the next few chapters the problem solving methodology should become clearer.

In more detail, the four components of the design step are:

Decomposition. Divide the larger problem into smaller and smaller subproblems. Here, the decomposition may be *process*-based or *object*-based, as will be explained later.

Class design. Develop classes from your understanding of the objects involved in the project. Note that process-based design can be used to design methods or functions within an object or class.

Hand example. Solve a small example by hand using paper and pencil. If the problem is too big to solve with paper and pencil then you have not decomposed it far enough. Go back to the previous step, decomposition, and attempt to decompose the subproblems further. The smallest and easiest to solve will be at the bottom of the hierarchy.

Algorithm design. Develop a generalized algorithm (pseudocode) for the problem (subproblems) solved in the hand example. Check that your algorithm is correct for the hand example.

3. Coding and debugging

Coding. Implement the design in the chosen computer language (for this text, C++). Hackers ("hit and run" or unskilled programmers) start at this step, which is but a small step in a systematic problem solving methodology.

Debugging. Debugging is the process of finding and correcting errors in the design and in the source code. For large problems, debugging or module (program solving a subproblem) testing is done here. Module testing may be done to verify the correctness of the code.

4. Integration

This step is the opposite of problem decomposition. For convenience, we divided the large problem into many small problems. However, to solve the original problem we must integrate the many resulting modules, each of which only solves a subproblem. For small problems this step may be trivial and may be included in the previous step of coding and debugging. For large problems, where several programmers are involved, this step is crucial and often daunting. You may follow a depth-first strategy (that is, go down a single leg of the top-down design process) or a breadth-first strategy (develop all the modules at the same level of decomposition) or a mixture of both, to integrate the different modules. Debug and correct errors, some of which will probably only appear during integration.

5. Testing and validation

Testing. Test the program with the hand example to verify that it is correctly implemented. Generate test cases and debug. More on this in Chapter 3.
Validation. This checks that the program provides what was originally asked for.

Although the above steps are listed sequentially, there can be iterative loops between any two steps, especially among steps 2 to 5 for most small to medium-sized problems. Large problems may require going back to the first step as well, because it is very likely that understanding what is to be solved constantly changes as the design and implementation proceeds.

How to Recognize a Satisfactory Design

It is hard to recognize a good design unless we have defined a set of criteria that we must satisfy. Some of the quality attributes for a good design are: functionality (how suitable the design is and how correct the solution is), reliability (running successfully, and the ability to recover from failures), efficiency (minimum use of time and memory resources), usability (how easy to use it is), maintainability (testability and the ability to modify it easily), portability (works in computing environments other than the one it was developed in), and reusability (how much of it can be reused in other problems). Because this is an introductory text we will consider a smaller set of the above features in a simplified fashion to understand a potentially good design. In the order of highest to lowest preference, we can attempt to produce a design with the following quality attributes: correctness (functionality), simplicity, high comment ratios (which is a program or code-level characteristic), modularity and testability (to satisfy maintainability and reliability—a design that is easy to test is hopefully more reliable). Note that often modular design tends to be simpler to maintain, more reusable, and less complex.

Maximize cohesion and minimize coupling.

A good design should maximize cohesion and minimize coupling. Cohesion refers to the number of kinds of outputs a module produces. If there are too many unrelated varieties of output, the function is not cohesive and should be broken into more sub-modules. Coupling is defined as the number of inputs a module requires from other modules plus the number of outputs a module produces for other modules. These are sometimes called fan-in and fan-out, respectively. A good design minimizes fan-ins and fan-outs and hence minimizes coupling. A good design is functionally cohesive and, if there is coupling, it is done only through a well-defined parameter list. Parameters are defined in Chapter 4. To a large extent object-oriented programming helps to minimize coupling and maximize cohesion. We discuss some of these features with examples in Appendix E. Unfortunately, it is not possible to discuss these issues further until one has gained at least an introductory level of experience in programming.

Application

Let us now apply the methodology to the problem of calculating the average grade. We will assume that there is something called a `student_grade_record` and that each student has a `student_id`, `grades` in individual subjects, and an `average` (Fig. 1.7).

In the figure, the first line is the `student_id`, the second line consists of `grades` in five subjects separated by spaces and the last line contains the grade `average`. The -1 indicates that it is yet to be calculated. Although the record looks much simpler than an actual student record, it does contain the most important information you will see in student records.

1. Problem analysis

Problem statement. Calculate the average grade and write the `student_grade_record` with the `average`.

Input/output analysis. The input data is the `student_grade_record` which includes the `student_id`, the `grades`, and the `average` ($= -1$ if yet to be calculated). The output is `student_grade_record` with the calculated `average`.

2. Design

Decomposition. We are going to show two methods of problem decomposition. The first is based on processes (that is, things to do) and has been the traditional method in software design. It mainly uses a functional model where the function sim-

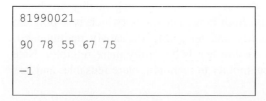

FIGURE 1.7
An example of the student grade record.

ply transforms input to output using a given algorithm or method. The second, newer method is based on objects where the object is something that has data (or *attributes* or characteristics) and provides services through *methods* or *member functions*. The model showing the objects, their static interrelationships and their classification is called the *object model.* The complete *object-modeling technique* (OMT) includes the object model, a *functional model* (corresponding to the methods of the objects), and a *dynamic model* which involves modeling the sequential or temporal changes that objects go through. In this book, we will deal with object models and functional models only.

Process-based decomposition. Generally, we start with a coarse level of detail and then refine it. This divide and conquer approach should be continued until the subproblems are easy enough for algorithm design and coding. You may notice that this is one of the quality attributes of a good design, resulting in simple to understand and highly modular code. The decomposition can also be presented in text form without diagrams. A possible decomposition is shown in Fig. 1.8.

Object-based decomposition. This method produces an object model, a first step in object-oriented methodology. Objects are things that have attributes (or data) and provide services (methods or member functions). A class is a blueprint that can be used to create (or *instantiate*) objects. In this small problem the only object that we are interested in is the student record. The corresponding object diagram is shown in Fig. 1.9.

The top part of this object diagram shows the name of the object, the middle part contains the data and the bottom part lists the services provided by the object. The corresponding class, that is, the blueprint for creating the object, could be as shown in Fig. 1.10.

Note the differences between the class and the object. The object has data stored in memory. The class simply conceptualizes it. The object is a real thing. The class is an idea. The top part of the class contains the class name, the middle part contains the class data attributes, and the bottom part contains the services provided

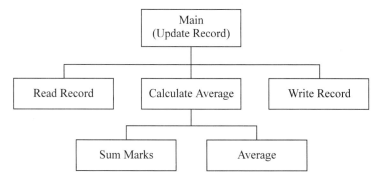

FIGURE 1.8
A process-based decomposition.

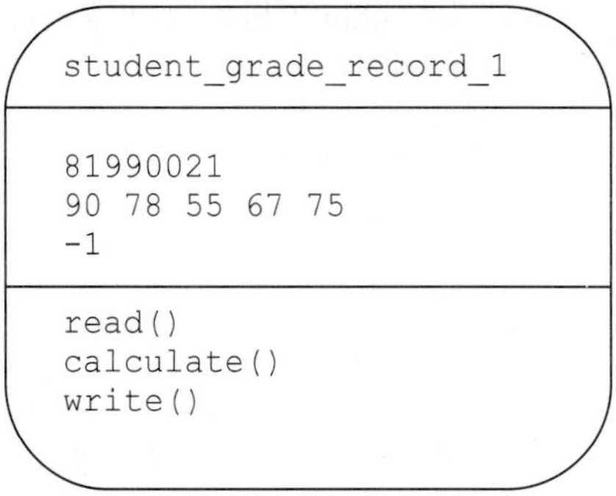

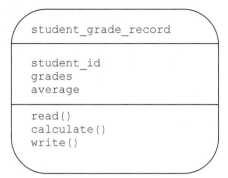

FIGURE 1.9
An object-based decomposition.

FIGURE 1.10
A `student_grade_record` class.

by the class. Another choice for class decomposition is shown in Fig. 1.11 where the `student_grade_record` class was derived using a base class and derived class relation. The arrow indicates that `student_grade_record` is derived from `student_record`. Sometimes, the base class is called the superclass and the derived class is called the subclass.

The advantage of the second decomposition is that a new class, for example `student_medical_record`, can be created using the base class `student_record`. It will reduce some of the repetitive work such as storing the `student_id` which may be common to many types of student record such as grade, medical, employment, sports, etc. These are simple examples, but the power of class decomposition will become clear when used to solve complex problems.

Object-based decomposition is not used until Chapter 7. Until then, process-based decomposition will be used. Such training can be handy when designing the individual member functions in objects. Note that member functions are part of the functional model in the overall object-oriented methodology.

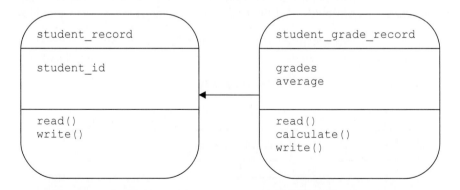

Base class `student_record`   Derived class `student_grade_record`

FIGURE 1.11
An alternative derivation of `student_grade_record` class.

So far, we have seen how to break the problem into subproblems using either a process-based or an object-based decomposition. The next step is to formulate or identify algorithms, for which we will use a hand example.

Hand example: The average grade can be found by the following two steps

$$\text{sum} = 90 + 78 + 55 + 67 + 75 = 365$$

$$\text{average} = \text{sum}/5 = 365/5 = 73$$

Algorithm design: The following is a simple algorithm that can be used to translate the numerical part of the problem solving process into a program. You should avoid details to start with; as you refine the algorithm further you can add more details.

> when the average is -1 (or not calculated)
> sum = grade1 + grade2 + $\cdots$ + grade5
> average = sum/5

3. Coding and debugging

Here we will show three different ways of solving the above problem in the computer. The algorithm to calculate the average is the same but we have many choices for the design of the program structure. The various program structures are shown in Figs 1.12, 1.13 and 1.14 and the actual programming details are omitted for now.

Fig. 1.12 shows the common structure found in most programs for two decades until about 1970. The advantage of this structure is its simplicity. However, for complex problems this structure becomes error prone as well as wasteful. The data `student_grade_record` is available to all parts of the program and hence there are many opportunities to make unauthorized or inadvertent changes to the data with dangerous consequences. If the average calculation is necessary in many parts of the problem, then the program using this structure will have those steps repeated in many places in the program. Because of this difficulty, the structure shown in Fig. 1.13 was advocated from 1970 to about 1985.

This figure is called a structure chart. The structure divides the original problem into three subproblems which are solved in individual *modules* `read()`, `calculate()`, and `write()`, respectively, and the `main()` module integrates

```
                 main()
 //Main Program
 ...
 //Read student record
 ...
 //Calculate average
 ...
 ...
 //Write student record
 ...
```

FIGURE 1.12
Solution 1. A simple program structure.

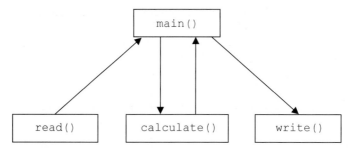

FIGURE 1.13
Solution 2. A structured program.

the three. The `main()` module receives data (`student_grade_record`) from the `read()` module, passes it to the `calculate()` module, gets the updated record, and passes it to the `write()` module for output. The advantage of this structure is its modularity (modules have a single and specific piece of work to do). It reduces program duplication, which is one of the disadvantages of Solution 1, and increases program clarity. On the other hand, program complexity increases due to the many transfers of data shown by the arrows. Also, the data `student_grade_record` is still unnecessarily exposed (meaning that the data is accessible) in the `main()` module whose only purpose here is to pass information back and forth. Solution 3, presented in Fig. 1.14, is the currently preferred method and uses object-oriented programming.

The diagram shows the relationship between the `main()` function and a single object `student_grade_record_1`. In this structure, the data and the modules that do the work of reading, calculating, and writing are united in a single unit called an *object*. The `main()` function has a relationship (shown by the line and the label has-a) to this object but cannot peek into its private data such as `grades`. However, the `main()` function can ask the `student_grade_record` to read, calculate, and write through the publicly available interface functions `read()`, `calculate()`, and `write()`, respectively. These member functions have direct access to the mem-

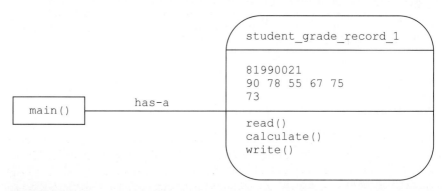

FIGURE 1.14
Solution 3. An object-oriented program.

ber data such as `student_id`, `grades`, and `average` (that is, member data is visible to member functions) and therefore no data passing is needed to get the work done. Although at first this structure looks unnecessarily complicated, it has combined the advantage of simplicity in Solution 1, for example no data passing, and the advantage of Solution 2, namely its modularity, with the same number of functions as in Solution 2. This structure has also overcome the disadvantage of both Solutions 1 and 2, namely unnecessary data visibility. These issues were discussed in some detail in the section on object-oriented programming languages and will also become clearer as we progress through the book. Note that maintainability is said to increase with modularity but decrease with high coupling. Coupling between modules happens, for example, when they share the same data. Object-oriented programming is expected to increase maintainability while not increasing complexity. The algorithmic complexity of all three solutions remains essentially the same for the problem at hand. See Appendix E for more details on these comments which will become clear after some experience in programming.

4. Integration

For the time being no details are shown here.

5. Testing and validation

Testing and validation should be performed using various choices of data for a given module or code segment. Generating test cases during design and coding is preferable (for example, add comments that indicate possible test cases while coding). The preconditions (explained in Chapter 4) can also help in the generation of test cases, especially for function testing. In general, test cases can be divided into three types: (i) valid cases that are normally encountered and specifically include boundary cases; (ii) special cases that are not normally encountered; and (iii) invalid cases that are meaningless. Testing only verifies that the program works for test cases. Validation requires going back to the problem analysis (or to the user who supplied the problem) and checking that the solutions provided by your program answer the questions asked.

We suggest that from now on any non-trivial problem should be solved using the above five steps, namely (1) Problem analysis, (2) Design, (3) Coding and debugging, (4) Integration, and (5) Testing and validation. Appropriate diagrams will be provided wherever necessary. It is quite natural to show the many refinements undertaken in any of the steps.

SUMMARY

OOP is a new approach to programming and is helpful in representing real-world objects as software objects. By uniting data and functions in objects, OOP (and hence C++) has provided a convenient and reliable way to model real-world objects. A class is a blueprint for objects. Many features have been added to C to provide a versatile OOP language in C++. A systematic problem solving methodology is available and should be used.

EXERCISES

1. In your opinion, what is a programming language used for? Possible choices are:

    1. To instruct machines (computers)
    2. To communicate with other programmers
    3. To help you design high-level concepts
    4. To help you design algorithms
    5. All of the above

2. Identify three objects that may be relevant to the following professionals. For example, a doctor is interested in the following objects: patient record, drug catalog, handbook of diseases.

    1. Veterinarian
    2. Postal clerk
    3. Lawyer

3. Identify three objects that you expect to use within an engineering problem that needs to be modeled with a computer program. For example, in a graphing problem the objects would be points, lines, rectangles, etc. Some examples of engineering problems are: electrical circuit design, robot design, and bridge design.

4. A car is an object. Identify at least three attributes and three functions of a car.

5. Do the same as in Exercise 4 for trucks and buses.

6. Find out the common attributes and functions of cars, trucks, and buses and design a base class called the vehicle class. Derive cars, trucks, and buses from the vehicle class.

7. List in detail the five steps used in our problem solving methodology.

8. You are programming a credit card authorization machine that can accept credit cards and obtain approval for transactions. It can read cards issued by major credit card companies. You are currently interested in contacting the appropriate credit card company and providing the card number read. Apply the first two steps of the problem solving methodology to design all the operations that you think are reasonable for such a problem.

*9. You are writing the program for the "brain" of a robot that will do the job of vacuuming a living room. There may be obstacles such as a sofas, light stands, speakers, and a piano, whose dimensions are not known. The robot can feel each object but otherwise is "blind." Apply the first two steps of the problem solving methodology.

*10. You have to write a program that will help a robot ride a bicycle. Apply the first two steps of the problem solving methodology to solve this problem. You can assume that the robot will ride the bicycle on a large piece of a flat ground with no obstacles. The bicycle has pedals, wheels, handlebar, one brake, and a seat. There is a simple transmission. The robot can act on all the required directions, has physical characteristics like a human, and is nimble.

CHAPTER 2

C++ Programming Basics

In this chapter we will see some fundamentals of C++ programming, including variables, input/output(I/O), comments, data types, arithmetic operators, and some library functions. Although some C++ program statements resemble mathematical formulae more than other languages such as BASIC or Pascal, most fundamental ideas are very similar. Secondly, C++ is a larger language (in the sense of having more features) when compared to older languages like FORTRAN-77 or BASIC. For example, there are additional operators that at first look formidable and confusing. But, just as with other programming languages, practice will make you comfortable with C++ language features.

A C++ PROGRAM

A C++ program is constructed using a mix of one or more functions and one or more objects. Let us see an example C++ program and learn the many components of program construction.

```
//Filename first.cpp
//Your first C++ program.
#include <iostream.h>

int main()
    {
    cout << "Let us have fun writing C++!";
    return 0;
    }
```

This first program is simply a single function called `main()`. You may remember that functions were devised to help organize large programs. A function is normally designed for a single purpose and has a clear interface with other functions of the program. When the function is a member of an object it is a member function. However, functions can be standalone functions as in this example.

Functions

The main() func-
tion is where the
computer starts
executing a C++
program.

Every function has a name. In the example here, `main` is the function name (as in Fig. 2.1). The parentheses `()` following the name can optionally have a set of arguments (none here) which are used to pass values to the function. In the above program, `return 0` is used to indicate that the function executed normally. When a function returns no value to the calling program we can add the word `void` preceding the function name. However, the ANSI standard requires that `main()` always return an integer, so adding the word `void` before `main()` will not be possible in future.

The curly brackets `{...}`, which must be used by every function, indicate the body of the function or a block of program statements. The function name `main()` indicates that the program control, in the absence of global declarations (explained later in Chapter 4), will always start at this function and hence this function will be present in all programs.

Program Statements

A program statement is one of the fundamental units of most programming languages and so it is in C++. Statements instruct computers to do something. In our first program we have a single statement

```
cout << "Let us have fun writing C++!";
```

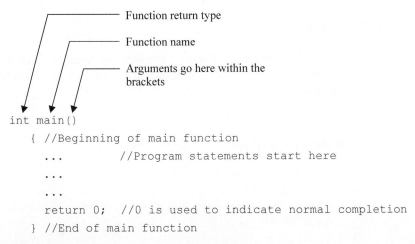

```
                          Function return type

                          Function name

                          Arguments go here within the
                          brackets


int main()
    { //Beginning of main function
    ...          //Program statements start here
    ...
    ...
    return 0;  //0 is used to indicate normal completion
    } //End of main function
```

FIGURE 2.1
A C++ function.

with a semicolon at the end which signals the end of the statement. Do not leave out the semicolon. If you do, the compiler will complain of an error. In general, white spaces (spaces, carriage returns, linefeeds, tabs, vertical tabs, and formfeeds) are ignored completely. However, in quoted materials, most white space within the double quotes will be reproduced as it is. For example, in `"Let us have fun writing C++!"` the spaces between the words are reproduced as they are. Carriage returns and linefeeds are an exception to this. Use white space everywhere in order to make your program easily readable. For example, the following is the same program as before. Note how hard it is to understand the program once you have removed the white spaces. Use white space to make programs easier to understand for yourself and for other readers.

```
//Filename fir2nosp.cpp
//An alternative for first.cpp.
#include <iostream.h>
int main(){cout<<"Let us have fun writing C++!";return 0;
//Returns a zero value to the
//calling program or operating system
}
```

Use ample amounts of white space to make your program more readable.

cout FOR OUTPUT

The output of our first program is:

```
Let us have fun writing C++!
```

This output is due to the single program statement in our first program. The name cout indicates a special C++ object which outputs the contents it receives to the standard output device (such as the monitor). In this context, the left shift operator << directs anything on its right, either the contents of a variable or a constant, to the object on its left (cout). For example, quoted material such as Let us have fun writing C++! is passed to the object cout to be output. Do not worry how cout << works at this time as we will deal with objects and operator overloading (two concepts used in this case) later on. Just learn to use them for now! In Chapter 5, you will find an example of how to write output to a file instead of to the screen.

C programmers should avoid using printf(...) for outputs. cout is more versatile.

COMMENTS FOR CLARITY AND UNDERSTANDING

Comments are ignored by the compiler and thus are not an executable part of the program. Comments are very important in programming languages because they make programs understandable to anyone reading the code. But note that comments are for humans and should be used to clarify the purpose of a program statement. Therefore, do not just repeat the program statement in the comment. The more comments, the clearer (hopefully) is the program. Comments are not only for others who may read the program but also for you, the author of the program. After some time has

Comments are for you and other readers! Write them such that readers can understand the working of your program.

elapsed, even you would find it hard to understand your own program without the help of comments!

C++ provides two comment styles. One allows you to write a comment anywhere. A double slash `//` marks the beginning of a comment and the comment ends at the end of the line. For example,

```
//This is a comment and the comment ends at the end of the line.
```

This style is especially good for clarifying each statement with a short comment by the side of it. For example,

```
ahyp = sqrt(a*a + b*b);    //Calculates the hypotenuse of a
                           //triangle with sides a and b.
```

The other style is useful for long multiline comments. This was the only style available in C.

```
/*This is a.....................................................
.....................................multiline.............
comment...............................................ending here*/
```

That is, you enclose your comments between two character pairs, namely `/*` and `*/`. Anything enclosed between the character pairs `/*` and `*/` will be considered a comment. So beware! Write comments as you write the program, when your memory is fresh. Do not wait to add them later as they are seldom added. Do not forget the double `//`. Note that there is no space between `//` or `/*` or `*/`. Try compiling a small working program like `first.cpp` with only a single `/` in a line and try to understand the error messages the compiler produces!

Although only `/*` and `*/` are required for multiline comments, it is often considered good practice to distinguish long commented sections from code by placing a single asterisk (`*`) at the beginning of each line:

```
/*
* Putting an asterisk at the beginning of each line of a
* multiline comment allows people looking at the code to
* determine with a quick glance what is comment and
* what is code.
*/
```

PREPROCESSOR DIRECTIVES

So far, for good reasons, we have not talked about the first line, `#include <iostream.h>`. The reason is that it is not a program statement. As you can see, it came even before the function name and is outside the function's body. Any line that starts with a `#` sign is called a *preprocessor directive*. The first line tells the compiler to process another file called `iostream.h` before the source file (here, the program `first.cpp`). The file `iostream.h` is a source file provided by the compiler manufacturer containing the declarations needed for I/O operations, such as those needed for the object `cout`. Try compiling without this line and see what happens! Incidentally, all files ending with .h are called *header files*. In Appendix C often-used header files are listed for your reference.

IDENTIFIERS

Names given to variables, functions, classes, objects, etc. are considered as user-defined identifiers. Identifiers can be as long as you want, but, in most compilers, only the first 32 characters will be recognized. You can use uppercase or lowercase letters (they are distinguished as different in C++, unlike in some other languages) and you can use underscore (_) or digits 0 to 9. Digits cannot be the first character of a variable name. Do not use special characters such as +, -, etc. or reserved words such as int, float, etc., for identifiers. Consult a reserved words list (see Appendix B) if in doubt! In the text, we will use the more common terminology of variable name, function name, and class name rather than variable identifier, function identifier, and class identifier, respectively.

C++ is case sensitive.

VARIABLES FOR PROCESSING DATA

Data is represented in C++ programs by variables. Variables have unique names and types, and hold values that you assign them. The type of the variable determines the way the variable is stored in the computer memory and the type of value it can contain. The three fundamental variable types are integer, character, and floating or real variable. The values held by these are called integer constants, character constants, and floating constants, respectively. Integer constants or integer numbers are whole numbers that do not contain a fractional part. Some examples are: 254, 521, and 30,000. The above are 10-based or decimal numbers. Do not write decimal-based integer numbers with zero as a starting digit; for example, write 8 and not 08. In C++, numbers starting with zero are interpreted as octal (base 8) integer numbers.

Floating constants or real numbers are numbers that may contain a fractional part written after a decimal point. Floating point variables can be written in two ways: 3.1415 is the same as 0.31415E01, and the second form is called exponential notation. The numbers immediately after the decimal point are the mantissa and the number after the E is the exponent. Note that 0.31415E01 is the same as 0.31415×10^1 and 0.31415E-01 is the same as 0.031415. Character constants are usually from the ASCII character set where each character is assigned an integer number ranging from 0 to 127. For example, the number 65 corresponds to the character A, and 97 corresponds to the character a. See Appendix A for the ASCII table used in most computers.

Variable Names

Variable names are unique, just like the address of a house. Recall that a variable name is a kind of identifier and hence follows the same rules for naming identifiers.

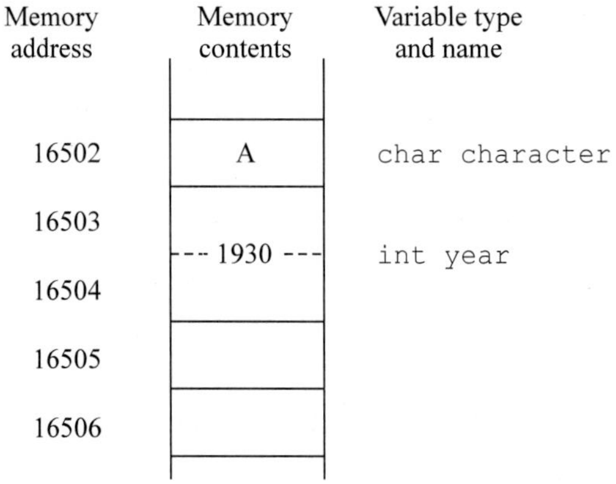

Memory address	Memory contents	Variable type and name
16502	A	char character
16503		
16504	--- 1930 ---	int year
16505		
16506		

FIGURE 2.2
Memory arranged as bytes, showing their addresses and their contents.

Some examples of variable names are:

> var1, temp1, studentnumber, student_record, YourAge, x_y_z

Meaningful variable names make programs self-documenting.

Note that a variable name should reflect the purpose of the variable. For example, studentnumber is self-explanatory, but not x_y_z. Usually, names in all upper-case are reserved for constants such as

> M_PI, AVOGADRO, LIGHTSPEED

Variable Types

Write parentheses following a C++ name to indicate that you are referring to a function and not a variable.

Different kinds of data are held differently in the computer. For example, characters are typically held in a single byte of memory (byte = 8 bits), wchar_t is a 16-bit character type (we will ignore this type from now onwards), integers are often held in 2 bytes, and floating point numbers in 4 bytes. See Fig. 2.2 which shows memory arrangement in bytes, their unique addresses (locations) and contents.

However, for simplicity, we will use just a rectangular box to indicate memory contents, as we seldom need to worry about the actual address or the order in which variables are stored. This convention is shown in Fig. 2.3.

Although a bit is the most fundamental unit of a computer memory, for most practical purposes, a byte is used to describe the memory segments. There are many variable types, as shown in Table 2.1. The actual memory requirements to store a particular type vary from machine to machine. Those given in the table are for Intel-based PCs.

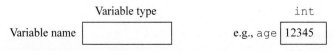

FIGURE 2.3
Convention for showing memory contents.

TABLE 2.1

Variable type	Keyword	Range	Memory requirement	Digits of precision
Single character	`char`	−128 to 127	1 byte	—
Integer	`int`	−32,768 to 32,767	2 bytes	—
Floating point	`float`	3.4e−38 to 3.4e+38	4 bytes	7
Longer integers	`long`	−2,147,483,648 to 2,147,483,647	4 bytes	—
More accurate floating point	`double`	1.7e−308 to 1.7e+308	8 bytes	15
Even more accurate floating point	`long double`	3.4e−4932 to 1.1e+4932	10 bytes	19
Larger character set	`unsigned char`	0 to 255	1 byte	—
Positive integers	`unsigned int`	0 to 65,535	2 bytes	—
Longer positive integers	`unsigned long`	0 to 4,294,967,295	4 bytes	—

Note that `signed int` is equivalent to `int`. Because of the differences in memory requirements, it is sometimes important not to over-type your variable. That is, if you do not need double precision (15 digits of accuracy) then do not use `double` floating point variables. Table 2.1 is only a guide and the specifications may vary between computers and compilers. The following program gives an example of how to define variables.

For efficient memory usage use appropriate variable types.

Defining Variables

C++ is a strongly typed language like Pascal and unlike BASIC; that is, variables have to be defined or declared before they can be used. The following example shows how different types of variables can be defined in a C++ program.

```
//Filename variable.cpp
//Demonstration of how to define different variable types.
#include <iostream.h>

int main()
   {
   char characterA, tabchar;
   int studentnumber;
   float average;
   long mean;
   double converfac;
   long double factor;
   unsigned char characterA_again;
   unsigned int total_students;
   unsigned long population_canada;
   return 0;
   }
```

All variables must be defined or declared before they can be used.

The above program does nothing but define variables of different types. When you *define* a variable, the appropriate type of storage is allocated in that variable's name. When you *declare* a variable type no storage is yet allocated. We will learn about variable declarations, a feature not emphasized in this text, in Chapter 4.

INITIALIZATION AND ASSIGNMENT OPERATION

Variables can take on values either through initialization or through the assignment operation. Defining a variable allocates storage for the variable. The assignment operation puts the value on the right of the assignment operator (namely, the equal sign =) in the memory space allocated for the variable on the left of the assignment operator. Defining and assigning a value to a variable in the same program statement is called initialization. Variables can be defined or initialized anywhere in the program. It is preferable to define or initialize a variable just before its first use. Initialization and assignment examples are presented in the program below where characters preceded by a backslash are special characters or escape sequences like the newline character \n.

```
//Filename initass1.cpp
//Demonstration of initialization versus assignment.
#include <iostream.h>

int main()
   {                      //Beginning of main function
   char character;        //Define character as
                          //a character variable
   char BELL = '\a';      //Define and initialize
                          //character variable BELL to beep
                          //Will work only in DOS!

   /*
    * Note that backslash creates what is called an escape sequence
    * and hence BELL stores the value that creates the
    * beep and not the letter a.
    */

   int class_size;        //Define an integer variable called
                          //the class_size

   character = 'A';       //Assign the variable character the
                          //the value of character A. Note the
                          //single quote! Single quote for single
                          //character and double quote
                          //for string constants (see Chapter 5).

   class_size = 100;      //Assigns a value of 100 to class_size
```

```
character = '\n';        //Assigns the newline escape sequence
                         //to character variable character.
/*
 * Note that we can define anywhere in the program and not
 * necessarily only at the beginning. But see the Scope of
 * Variables section in Chapter 3 for more information.
 */

cout << BELL << BELL << character
     << class_size << character;

// Note that we can cascade out (<< ... << ...) many outputs with a
// single cout statement as in the above lines

 return 0;
}                        // End of main function
```

Understanding how each variable is stored in computer memory will help you understand programming better. Fig. 2.4 shows memory allocation for the variables used in a simple program. It presents necessary information for different variables and their contents at various stages of the program.

In the first program statement following the brace a character variable `character` is defined and initialized. In the second program statement, an integer variable `class_size` is defined. The original character variable and its contents remain the same in memory. In the third program statement the integer variable `class_size` is assigned a value of 100. In the fourth program statement, the character variable `character` is assigned a new character value \n. In examples that come later on and when you describe the memory allocation, the memory cells need not be presented at each program statement. Draw the cell once and just change its contents as necessary.

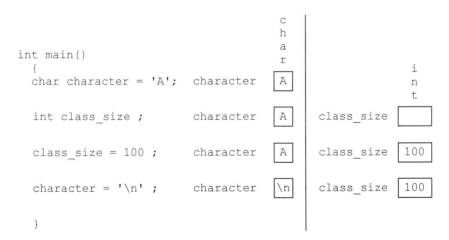

FIGURE 2.4
Correspondence of program statements, variable definitions, memory allocations, and memory contents.

POINTER VARIABLES (OPTIONAL)

We will briefly introduce pointer variables, but we will not use them in the text until Chapter 9 which is devoted completely to pointer variables and on how to use them for managing memory efficiently. A pointer variable is a variable that holds pointer constants or addresses of computer memory locations divided into bytes. See Fig. 2.5 showing a pointer variable `charptr` holding `16502` which is the address of the memory location where a character constant A is stored. Pointer variables are defined as follows:

```
...
char* chptr;
int* intptr;
float* flptr;
...
```

and, as can be imagined, point to (that is, contain the start address of) different types of variables, respectively. The following C++ statements are used to get the results shown in Fig. 2.5 (not necessarily at the memory locations 16502 to 16506 which may vary!).

```
...
char character = 'A';
int year = 1930;
char* chptr = &character;   //Gets and stores the address of the
                            //variable character
```

The ampersand (&) in front of a variable name is used to get the memory address of the variable. After the above statements, it is possible to assign a new value to the memory addressed by `chptr` in the following manner:

```
*chptr = 'B';   //Assignment with indirect addressing
```

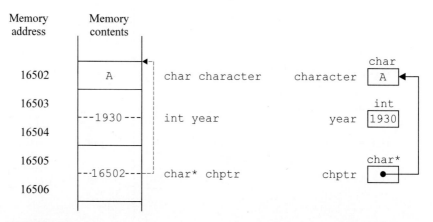

FIGURE 2.5
Memory contents in bytes, pointer variables, and the usual convention for showing memory contents.

where the notation *variable name is called indirect addressing, as opposed to direct addressing as in

```
        character = 'B'; //assignment with direct addressing
```

Once again, indirect addressing will not be used in the text until Chapter 9.

cin FOR INPUT

We have seen so far how to output results from a program with cout. We will now see how to input values to a program using the object cin. The example reads input values from the screen. You will find an example of how to read from a file instead of from the screen in Chapter 5.

```
//Filename cinex.cpp
//Inputting data with cin.
#include <iostream.h>

int main()
   {
   char characterA;
   int age;
   float average;

   cout << "Enter the character A:\n";   //Backslash n is used
                                         //for newline

   cin >> characterA;
   cout << "Enter your age:\n";          //Enter an integer number
                                         //(you can lie!)

   cin >> age;
   cout << "Enter your average:\n";      //Enter a real number
   cin >> average;

   /*
    * To check that our input values are correct, print them
    * out. The additional check one can do is to check that all the
    * input values are within the range expected from your input
    * analysis. For example, you can check that the average is between
    * 0 and 100, etc. In the next chapter this step
    * will be discussed.
    */

   cout << "This is character A: " << characterA  << "\n";
   cout << "Your age is: " << age << "\n";
   cout << "Your average is: " << average << "\n";
   return 0;
   }                                  // End of main
```

The following is an example of the interaction between the computer and the user.

`Enter the character A:`	*Computer prints on the monitor screen.*
`A`	*User types A and presses enter.*
`Enter your age:`	*Computer prints on the monitor screen.*
`36`	*User types 36 and presses enter.*
`Enter your average:`	*Computer prints on the monitor screen.*
`99`	*User types 99 and presses enter.*

The computer prints the following on the monitor.

```
This is character A: A
Your age is: 36
Your average is: 99
```

ARITHMETIC OPERATORS

Operators are symbols used to express different kinds of operations on variables or constants. The objects involved in an operation are called operands. In C++, there are three kinds of arithmetic operators: unary, binary, and ternary. The unary operators operate on a single operand; binary operators operate on two operands, one operand on each side of the operator; and ternary operators operate on three operands. The ternary operator will be explained in Chapter 3.

Basic Arithmetic Operators

A + or − operator may be used either as a unary operator or a binary operator

Basic arithmetic operations in C++ involve only the unary or binary operators. A C++ expression is similar to an algebraic expression involving one or more variables or constants, and one or more basic arithmetic operators. Unary and binary operators are discussed next.

Unary Operators

Unary operators + and - are used on single operands only. For example, -b changes the sign of the value contained by variable b. A legal C++ statement is

```
a = -b;  //Variable a is assigned the negative of variable b
```

Binary Operators

In addition to the unary operators + and -, the basic arithmetic operations addition, subtraction, multiplication, and division can be performed using the binary operators +, -, *, and /, respectively. These operators work on both integer and floating point data types. Basic arithmetic operations are done much the same way as in alge-

TABLE 2.2

Operator	Algebraic expression	C++ expression	Example	Result
+	$a + b$	a + b	1+2	3
−	$a - b$	a - b	3-2	1
*	$a * b$ or $a \times b$	a*b	1*2	2
/	a/b (or) $a \div b$ (or) $\dfrac{a}{b}$	a/b	3/2	1
%	$a \bmod b$	a%b	2%3	2

bra except that one should be aware of the order of calculations in C++ arithmetic expressions, or *precedence*.

A set of examples using common arithmetic operators are shown in Table 2.2. The order of calculations or precedence for basic arithmetic operators are as follows. FIRST: *, /, %; SECOND: + −. If arithmetic operators have the same precedence then calculations are carried out from left to right; this is called the *associativity* of the operator. All operators in Table 2.2 have left to right associativity. The full list of operators, their precedence, and their associativity are presented in Appendix D.

A division with integer numbers on both sides of the / gives a result that is an integer (3/2 is 1 not 1.5; similarly, 7/4 is also 1). If you want a result with fractions then use real numbers. For example, 3.0/2.0 or 3.0/2 or 3/2.0 results in 1.5. Note that 3 + 5 * 2 is not 16 but 13 because, in the same expression, multiplication has higher precedence than addition; that is, the multiplication was carried out before the addition in the above expression. However, you can use parentheses to change precedence (or the order of calculations in the computer) because expressions in the (innermost) parentheses are carried out first. For example, (3+5) * 2 will give 16. Another example: 8 / 4 * 2 - 3 + 1 is done as if you had written (8/4)*2 - 3 + 1. Multiplication and division have the same precedence but division was carried out first because it was the first operation from the left. For clarity and surety always use an ample number of parentheses!! The remainder or modulus operator % works as follows: 2 % 3 gives 2, 3 % 3 gives 0. That is, it gives the remainder of the division. This operator works on integer operands only.

Example of a modulus operation: 2%3 is done as:

$$3 \overline{\smash{\big)}\, 2 \atop \underline{0} \atop 2}$$

0–Quotient
2–Remainder

Use an ample number of parentheses to avoid errors in arithmetic expressions.

Compound Operators

Compound operators are composed of two operators used jointly with no operands in between, for example +=, -=, etc. These operators are available in C but these are unfamiliar symbols to programmers who have used only Fortran, BASIC, or Pascal.

Earlier we saw the assignment operator which simply assigns values to variables. For example, the statement character = 'A' assigns A to the variable character. Similarly, the statement age = 18 will assign a value of 18 to the integer variable age, and so on. But suppose you want to add 100 dollars to your bank balance every month. You may want to use a statement like

```
your_balance = your_balance + 100.0;
```

TABLE 2.3

Operator	Required expression	C++ expression
+=	total = total + 10;	total += 10;
-=	expense = expense − 100;	expense -= 100;
*=	salary = salary * 0.05;	salary *= 0.05;
/=	x = x/.9;	x /= .9;

where `your_balance` on the right of the assignment operator is the balance from last month.

The same can be written more concisely in C++ as

```
your_balance += 100.0;  //Equivalent to your_balance =
                        //your_balance+100.
```

Table 2.3 gives some of the compound operations that you can do with assignment statements.

Increment and Decrement Operators

Often we are interested in either adding or subtracting 1 to or from an existing variable. In C++ we use increment or decrement operators. For example, `i = i + 1` can be written as `i++` and `i = i −1` can be written as `i--`. These are called postfix notations and the following are prefix notations: `++i` and `--i`. The following examples illustrate the difference. Suppose

```
total_weight = total_weight * ++number_of_students;
```

The above expression is equivalent to the following two statements:

```
number_of_students = number_of_students + 1;
total_weight = total_weight * number_of_students;
```

Try not to use these operators in an obscure way that will hinder the easy understanding of your program.

The above example uses prefix notation. The following example uses postfix notation.

```
total_weight = total_weight * number_of_students++;
```

The above expression is equivalent to the following two statements:

```
total_weight = total_weight * number_of_students;
number_of_students = number_of_students + 1;
```

Therefore, the difference is in the order of the increment or decrement operation. Their use depends on the need and your preference.

LIBRARY MATH FUNCTIONS

There are many library mathematical functions in C++ that are ready and easy to use. For example, to find the sine of an angle just use the `sin()` function as shown in the next program.

```
//Filename:sine.cpp
/*Use the built-in library function to calculate the sine of an argument
in radians*/

#include <iostream.h>    //Header file for input and output
#include <math.h>        //Header file for mathematical functions

//const double PI = 3.145926535; //A constant declaration
                                 //for illustration only.
//we are using M_PI from math.h instead of the above.

const long aLongconstant = 254L; //The constant 254 is stored
                                 //as a long type constant
int main()
   {
    double angle = 90.0,        //Angle in degrees
       sine_of_angle;           //Multiple variables
                                //can be defined in a
                                //single statement.

    sine_of_angle = sin(angle*M_PI/180.0); //Angle in degrees was
                                           //converted to radians
                                           //before passing it as an
                                           //argument to built-in
                                           //function sin().
    cout << "The sine of angle " << angle
         << " is " << sine_of_angle << "\n";
    return 0;
    }                                      //End of main
```

Therefore, the way to use built-in mathematical functions is to pass input value(s) as arguments to the function and receive the result in the name of the function you are calling; this result can be assigned to another variable, as in the above example, or can also be directly output using the cout operator. Do not forget to include the appropriate header files such as <math.h>, <stdlib.h>, among others.

Avoid building your own functions. There may be library functions available to do the same work.

Constant Declaration

Note the program statements const double PI = 3.1415926535 and const long aLongconstant = 254L in the above program. When you want certain variables to have a constant value throughout the program and you want to avoid changing their values by mistake, use the constant declaration statement as above. Constant declaration can come anywhere in the program and once declared and initialized, the value cannot be changed later in the program. In our program the constant declaration was commented out as we used a more accurate π value available in M_PI constant of the math.h header file. Check math.h for useful constants before you declare them. Also note that the trailing L in 254L indicates that the constant 254 should be treated as a long type constant.

MANIPULATORS

When you want to print characters and numbers in an orderly or tabular manner, you may have to use the stream manipulators. They manipulate the way in which data is displayed. We will use an example to understand the need and syntax.

```
//Filename: Manipul.cpp
//Example using manipulators
#include <iostream.h>
#include <iomanip.h>

int main()
    {
    //First pair of cout use no manipulator
    cout << "Student_Number" << "Student_Name" << "GPA" << "\n";
    cout << "93123456" << "Jane Doe" << "3.5" << "\n";

    //Second pair of cout use manipulators setw() and endl
    cout << setw(15) << "Student_Number" << setw(15) << "Student_Name"
        << setw(15) << "GPA" << endl;   //Right justifies
                                        //the variables
                                        //in a field of 15 characters

    cout << setw(15) << "93123456" << setw(15) << "Jane Doe"
        << setw(15) << "3.5" << endl;   //endl is the newline
                                        //manipulator
    return 0;
    }
```

Explore the following manipulators, flags, and stream functions:
setfill()
setiosflags()
setf()

showpoint
scientific
fixed
left
right

get()
getline
put()
flush()

The first pair of cout statements give the following result:

```
            Student_NumberStudent_NameGPA
            93123456Jane Doe3.5
```

and the second pair produce

```
        Student_Number    Student_Name          GPA
              93123456        Jane Doe          3.5
```

We hope that the example clarifies the need and shows how to use the setw() manipulator, which right justifies a variable in a field of w characters. Another manipulator is setprecision(d) which can be used when you want to output any floating point number with "d" digits of precision. For example, if you are outputting average salary, you do not want more than two digits of precision. Use:

```
        cout  << setw(15) << setprecision(2) << average_salary;
```

The end-line manipulator endl in the above program replaces the newline character '\n'.

MIXING DATA TYPES AND TYPE CASTING

Although you can use different data types in the same C++ expression, it is important to understand some pitfalls. For example, if you are using integers (see the range given in Table 2.1) and an intermediate result in an expression is outside the range of an integer type then you may get meaningless answers. Let `int salary = 10000`. If we calculate

$$salary = (salary * 10) / 10;$$

the result is *not* stored as 10,000 because the intermediate result 100,000 due to `salary*10` is too big for integer variables. The safe way to do this would be to use type casting, that is, change the type (at least for the intermediate result) to `long` so that the intermediate result would be kept intact. For example, use

```
salary = (long(salary)*10)/10; //In C,it is ((long)salary*10)/10
```

When two operands of different data types are used in the same expression, the lower type operand is converted to that of the highest type variable automatically.

Often in floating point calculations we may require the intermediate calculation to be done in double precision. If originally the variable `radius` was declared as type `float`, then cast it as

```
float perimeter = 2.0*M_PI*double (radius);
```

The conversion of `radius` to type `double` is only temporary and is effective only in that expression. Note that when two operands of different data types are used in the same expression, the lower type operand is converted to that of the highest type variable automatically. Converting to a lower type from a higher type can result in incorrect values and so it can only be done by using a cast operator or by assigning the value to a variable of the lower type, which sometimes causes errors (see the next section for an example). The order of lowest to highest is: `char`, `int`, `long`, `float`, `double`, and `long double`.

ERRORS AND DEBUGGING OF ERRORS

You followed the five-step design process to the letter. You wrote the C++ code on paper. You went through it carefully to make sure it was to your satisfaction. You added white spaces and comments when you coded it in the computer. Then, as a first step towards an executable code, you compile the program and, to your dismay, it does not compile and tons of error messages are spewed out. You have every right to be frustrated and all programmers go through this quite routinely. In fact, if a program compiles and runs at the first attempt be careful with the result it produces; it probably is not correct! The process of removing the errors is called debugging.

Debugging is a cyclic and continuing process that observes, identifies, and modifies the program to remove errors.

Errors that are caught by the compiler are called compile-time errors. These errors are due to omission and wrong syntax in your C++ program statements or, sometimes, due to peculiarities of some operating systems or compiler environments. Not including appropriate header files is an example of an omission error. Missing semicolons, wrong spelling of reserved words (compiler flags them as missing

C++ syntax:

The sequence of symbols and words that a C++ compiler can translate to an object code.

declarations), unmatched brackets, etc. are syntax errors normally caught by the compiler. Error messages are usually provided with line numbers. Beware that many of the error messages are difficult to understand and that sometimes correcting one syntax or omission error at the start of a program will remove subsequent error messages. Compile-time errors are relatively easy to correct. Note that some operating systems and compilers produce error messages for problems that others do not recognize as problems. The following is an error message we got when we compiled the program first2.cpp in Visual C++ (1.0) under Windows 3.1®.

```
Initializing...
Compiling...
c:\book\source\basics\first2.cpp
error C2470:
c:\book\source\basics\first2.cpp(3) : fatal error C1083:
 CL returned error code 2.
FIRST2.EXE - 2 error(s), 0 warning(s)
```

First, to understand what this error means use the compiler online help or the compiler manuals. To get help most often all you need to do is place the cursor on the error message and press F1. For error C1083 we got the following help message.

Fatal Error C1083

Cannot open *filetype* file: '*file*': message

```
The specified file could not be opened.
This error may be caused by not having enough file handles. Close some open
applications and recompile.
If an include file could not be opened check that the INCLUDE environment
variable is set correctly, and that the name of the file is spelled
correctly.
```

This is a common error message you get due to the peculiarity of MS-Windows 3.1®. All we needed to do was simply close all Windows programs except the C++ compiler and recompile. The error messages vanished.

Syntax Errors

To understand syntax errors and the error messages peculiar to your computing environment do the following. Take a working program (you can use one from the diskette accompanying the book) and introduce errors one at a time or a few at a time and then compile. Following is the error message we got when we compiled the sine.cpp program presented earlier, commenting out the line #include <iostream.h>. Not including appropriate header files is a common mistake and here the compiler could not understand the cout operator. The error is indicated as happening at line number 24 (the number in the brackets after the name of the file) although the true error is omitting the #include <iostream.h> at the top of the program.

```
Compiling...
c:\book\source\basics\sine.cpp
c:\book\source\basics\sine.cpp(24) : error C2065: 'cout' : undeclared
identifier
c:\book\source\basics\sine.cpp(24) : error C2121: '<<' : bad right
operand
 CL returned error code 2.
SINE.CPP - 2 error(s), 0 warning(s)
```

Further errors were added and the program was compiled. The program with errors is presented below, including the line numbers for easy reference. The compile-time error messages and their explanation follow the program.

```
1.//Filename:sine.cpp (Buggy version!)
2./*Use the built-in library function to calculate the sine of an
argument in radians*/
3.
4.//#include <iostream.h>    //Header file for input and output
5.//#include <math.h>        //Header file for mathematical functions
6.
7.int main()
8.  {
9.  const double PI = 3.14159265    //Constant definition.
10.                                  //No changes are possible
11.                                  //to PI beyond this
12.                                  //statement.
13.    double angle := 90.0,         //Angle in degrees
14.        sine_of_angle;            //Multiple variables
15.                                  //can be defined in a
16.                                  //single statement.
17.
18.
19.    sine_of_angle = sin(angle*PI/180.0); //Angle in degrees was
20.                                         //converted to radians
21.                                         //before passing it as an
22.                                         //argument to built-in
23.                                         //function sin().
24.    cout << "The sine of angle " << angle
25.        << " is " << sine_of_angle << "\n";
26.
27.    return ;
28.
29.                      //End of main
```

The messages received at compile time are:

```
Compiling...
c:\book\source\basics\sinerr.cpp
c:\book\source\basics\sinerr.cpp(13) : error C2144: syntax error :
missing ';' before type 'double '
c:\book\source\basics\sinerr.cpp(13) : error C2599: 'angle' : local
functions are not supported
```

```
c:\book\source\basics\sinerr.cpp(14) : error C2059: syntax error : ';'
c:\book\source\basics\sinerr.cpp(19) : error C2065: 'sine_of_angle' :
undeclared identifier
c:\book\source\basics\sinerr.cpp(19) : error C2065: 'sin' : undeclared
identifier
c:\book\source\basics\sinerr.cpp(19) : error C2065: 'angle' : undeclared
identifier
c:\book\source\basics\sinerr.cpp(19) : error C2064: term does not
evaluate to a function
c:\book\source\basics\sinerr.cpp(24) : error C2065: 'cout' : undeclared
identifier
c:\book\source\basics\sinerr.cpp(24) : error C2121: '<<' : bad right
operand
c:\book\source\basics\sinerr.cpp(27) : warning C4508: 'main' : function
should return a value; 'void' return type assumed
c:\book\source\basics\sinerr.cpp(30) : error C2060: syntax error : end
of file found
 CL returned error code 2.
SINERR.EXE - 10 error(s), 1 warning(s)
```

The error messages outsize the length of the program! Next, we describe how to get rid of these errors from your program.

Explanation of Compile-time Error Messages

We explain the error messages and their causes one error at a time. The following error is due to missing the semicolon at line number 9; note that this error was discovered by the compiler at line number 13.

```
c:\book\source\basics\sinerr.cpp(13) : error C2144: syntax error :
missing ';' before type 'double '
```

The following three error messages are due to the colon before the assignment operator (a Pascal-style assignment); note that, first, it is hard to identify the error from the description and second, this error and the previous error have propagated to more than one line.

Often a compile error at a line is due to errors from previous line(s).

```
c:\book\source\basics\sinerr.cpp(13) : error C2599: 'angle' : local
functions are not supported
c:\book\source\basics\sinerr.cpp(14) : error C2059: syntax error : ';'
c:\book\source\basics\sinerr.cpp(19) : error C2065: 'sine_of_angle' :
undeclared identifier
```

The next three error messages are due to not including the header file math.h; the compiler does not understand that "sin" is a library function and neither does it recognize the variable angle whose declaration was not accepted due to a previous error.

```
c:\book\source\basics\sinerr.cpp(19) : error C2065: 'sin' : undeclared
identifier
c:\book\source\basics\sinerr.cpp(19) : error C2065: 'angle' : undeclared
identifier
c:\book\source\basics\sinerr.cpp(19) : error C2064: term does not
evaluate to a function
```

The next two errors are due to not including the header file `iostream.h`.

```
c:\book\source\basics\sinerr.cpp(24) : error C2065: 'cout' : undeclared
identifier
c:\book\source\basics\sinerr.cpp(24) : error C2121: '<<' : bad right
operand
```

The next warning message is due to the missing zero after the `return`.

```
c:\book\source\basics\sinerr.cpp(27) : warning C4508: 'main' : function
should return a value; 'void' return type assumed
```

Although warning messages are not fatal they might be worth checking as they may indicate errors that are hard to find and understand. The next error message is due to the missing close curly bracket at the end of the function.

```
c:\book\source\basics\sinerr.cpp(30) : error C2060: syntax error : end
of file found
```

In summary, although at first beginners will have a hard time identifying the real errors at compile time, with practice it becomes easier to find compile-time errors.

Link Errors

Link errors are discovered at link time after successfully compiling the program. See Chapter 1 for an explanation of the edit–compile–link–execute cycle. Link errors are usually due to wrong environment setups or not including paths to libraries. You may need some help from experienced users to find some of these errors. However, once a setup is working, save it and you will seldom get link errors.

Execution-time Errors

Execution-time errors are also called run-time errors. The following program illustrates two kinds of execution-time errors which are due either to incorrectly initializing a variable or to not initializing it.

```
//File name:runerr1.cpp
//Demonstrates the two kinds of run-time errors

#include <iostream.h>
```

```
int main()
  {
  int x1=0;

  float y1=1.0/x1;  //Calculates the fraction of 3 in decimal notation

  cout << "1/3 in decimal notation is= " << y1 << endl;

  int x2;

  cout << "2 plus 2 equals= " << x2+x2 << endl;

  return 0;

  }
```

Forgetting to ini-
tialize and incorrect
initialization lead
to execution-time
errors.

The expected results of .333333 and 4 are not obtained. Instead the program aborts due to a divide by zero error for incorrectly initializing x1 to 0 instead of 3. After correcting this error the result for 2 + 2 equals a large negative number which is due to not initializing the variable x2. This incorrect result will depend upon the compiler used.

Logic Errors

Logic errors are errors that can be spotted only by an informed and watchful programmer who examines the results carefully, often using known results for known input. Finding logic errors is often a daunting task. Debuggers are tools provided with compilers to help you spot errors by tracing the program's progress at each statement or by jumping to an indicated statement using *break points*. Debuggers also help you watch all variables and their values and help you spot errors in the logic of the program statements. If you do not have a good debugger, use appropriate output statements to debug. These statements may be simple cout statements. Programmers print out necessary intermediate results and use these results to trace the program execution statement by statement. Once the debugging process is over, instead of deleting the cout statements you may want to "comment them out" using the comment syntax /*...*/. The following program illustrates errors due to mixing data types. A possible problem identified with a warning message issued by the compiler is ignored by the programmer.

```
//Filename: debug1.cpp
//Program for demonstrating debugging

#include <iostream.h>

int main()
  {
  int x=11;
```

```
int y = 1.0/x;     //Find the reciprocal of 11
cout << " The reciprocal of 11 is= " << y << endl;


}
```

The compiler issued the following warning and we ignored it.

```
c:\book\source\basics\debug1.cpp(10) : warning C4051: type conversion;
possible loss of data
```

The result we got at execution time is

```
                    The reciprocal of 11 is= 0
```

Obviously a wrong result! We added two `cout` statements after the initialization of `x`

```
cout << "x is= " << x << endl;
cout << "1.0/x is= " << 1.0/x << endl;
```

and got the correct result of `11` and `0.0909091`. So what happened? Where is the error? From the new and old `cout` statements we know that the error is not in the initialization and not in the arithmetic operation but somewhere in the line `int y= 1.0/x1;`. We see that we have declared `y` to be an `int` type and hence, after correctly calculating the reciprocal (the value `1.0` in the arithmetic expression `1.0/x1` indicates a `float` to the computer), the fractional part was truncated and only a zero was stored in `y`. Remember we ignored the warning message that said something about type conversion and possible loss of data, which was an indication of this type of mismatching problem.

Using the **assert()** Function for Debugging

This function tests the value of an expression. If the value of the expression is `false` `(0)`, it terminates the program by invoking the function `abort()`. For example, the following statement will ensure that the value of `x1` is not `0` before continuing with the execution of the program:

```
assert(x1 != 0)
```

If the condition `x1 != 0` is false, the program is terminated. The `!=` is a relational operator and Chapter 3 contains details on these and you may want to defer using them until then. A message containing the line number, assert condition, and the name of the source file using this condition is printed (might depend on the compiler). The `assert()` function is declared in `assert.h`, and the `abort()` function is in `stdlib.h`. When debugging is completed, assert conditions do not have to be removed. You can add the line

```
#define NDEBUG
```

to your program to indicate that assert conditions should be ignored. Note that some compilers may have a slightly different name for the `assert()` function. Check your compiler manual for the correct name.

In summary, debugging can be done by tracing the program line by line and comparing the actual value of variables to the result they are supposed to contain. When we identify an anomaly we probably have identified an erroneous program statement and we should attempt to correct the problem before proceeding to the next line. Depending upon the compiler environment, the debugging process can be made somewhat easier by using integrated debuggers that allow you to break at any line, watch any variable, and sometimes dynamically alter the value of a variable.

Unsystematic debugging leads you to spend a lot of time wastefully!

However, we have to give a warning at this point. Many beginners end up debugging in a very unsystematic manner. They identify errors wrongly, change them, create further errors and end up in a vicious circle of more errors and more debugging. Avoid quick fixes and try to understand the real problem before fixing. Secondly, keep copies of the different versions of your program while adding debug fixes until you have completely verified and validated a good working program. Print a paper copy of your program and go through it line by line. Another trick to find logic errors is to explain your program to another person. During that process *you* usually end up finding errors in your program logic. Debugging can be frustrating and taking a break from looking at the program also helps!

SUMMARY

We started with the understanding of the main() function in C++ and simple program statements including cout for output and cin for input. We also studied header files and preprocessor directives such as #include. The two types of comment styles in C++, and the many different variable types and the way to initialize and assign variables values, were also discussed. Arithmetic operators such as +, -, *, and / and arithmetic assignment operations such as +=, -=, *=, etc. are part of the basics of C++ programming. Increment and decrement operators ++ and -- are unique to C++ (and C). Library functions can be called as in other programming languages and manipulators are quite useful for formatting output. Lastly, type casting is used when mixing data types.

REVIEW QUESTIONS

1. A C++ program may contain many functions and objects. True or false?

2. If a C++ program has many functions, where would the computer start executing?

3. A function name is followed by { }. True or false?

4. Variable names are identifiers. What are identifiers?

5. There can be more than one main() function in a program. True or false?

6. Functions are modules used to organize programs. True or false?

7. The _____ marks the beginning of a function body and _____ marks the end of the function body.

8. A program statement is terminated by _____.

9. In C++ a newline character (\n) is automatically output for every cout statement. True or false?

10. C++ and C use cout to output variables and constants. True or false?

11. What are header files?

12. cout is an _____.

13. There are two ways to designate comments. What are they?

14. Using exponential notation, write the following numbers in at least two or three ways: (i) 0.0001, and (ii) 1000.000001.

15. Would using X as a variable name be confusing to (i) the computer, or (ii) the programmer? What is the alternative?

16. Mark the variable names that are not allowed in a C++ program: (i) potato, (ii) student number, (iii) x100, (iv) 1e01, and (v) _zap.

17. Why do we need different types of variables and why do we have to define them?

18. If we define int x, X; the variables x and X will have the same memory space. True or false?

19. Memorize the number of bytes used for defining char, int, float and double type variables in your computer.

20. Over-typing is good for efficient memory use. True or false?

21. Initialization means defining and assigning an appropriate value to a variable. True or false?

22. An assignment operation assigns the value on the _____ side of an _____ operator to the variable on the _____ side of the operator.

*23. What are pointer variables?

24. What is the object used to input a value to a defined variable?

25. Computers never make errors. Discuss.

26. What are syntax errors?

27. What are compile-time errors?

28. In C++ 2/3 means the same as 2%3. True or false?

29. Bugs in a program can be removed by cleaning the computer. Discuss.

30. Lower precedence operators are executed before higher precedence operators. True or false?

31. Precedence can be overridden by parentheses. True or false?

32. Associativity dictates the direction of evaluation in a mathematical expression. True or false?

33. Which one of the following is not a legal compound operator in C++? (i) +=, (ii) --, (iii) */, (iv) ++, and (v) -+.

34. If int x = 2, x++ is _____, x-- is _____, x += 1 is _____, and x /= 3 is _____.

35. The statement sqr(x) gives the square root of x. True or false? (Check available library functions.)

36. Write in C++ the expression x^y.

37. C++ constants, once defined, retain their value throughout the program. True or false?

38. The manipulator setw(w) sets the width of printed output to _____ spaces and _____ sets the precision of the output to d digits.

39. What is type casting and why is it needed?

40. If two operands have two different types in an expression then _____ type operand is converted to _____ type operand automatically.

EXERCISES

1. Write a program that prints out the following

```
//****************************************************************//
//                         Assignment 1                         //
//                                                              //
//                         Due:                                 //
//                                                              //
//                         Your Full Name                       //
//                         Your Student ID                      //
//                                                              //
//Program Name:   ******.cpp                                    //
//Program Description:                                          //
//                                                              //
//****************************************************************//
```

2. Write a program that generates the following output. Use initialization of variables.

```
100
T
3.1415927
```

3. Do Exercise 2 with assignment operations instead of variable initialization. Show the memory allocation.

4. Write a program that generates the following output using manipulators:

```
Annual Maximum Rainfall of Different Cities
-------------------------------------------


City Name        Rainfall (mm)
----------------------------
Waterloo         1000
Madras           1250
```

5. Use the built-in function `sizeof()` to determine how many bytes are used for all the basic data types available in your computer.

6. Write C++ expressions for the following mathematical formulas:

$$\text{(i) } y = x\sin(x) \qquad \text{(ii) } g = \frac{\mu}{\sigma^3} \qquad \text{(iii) } Q = \frac{(P - .2S)^2}{P + .8S}$$

$$\text{(iv) } V = \frac{1}{n}R^{\frac{2}{3}}\sqrt{S} \qquad \text{(v) } R = \frac{y(b + \cot\alpha)}{b + \dfrac{2y}{\sin\alpha}}$$

7. Apply the first two steps of the problem solving methodology (no C++ programming necessary) to

   (a) determine the length of the hypotenuse of a right triangle when given the lengths of the other two sides;
   (b) estimate the height of a building given the angle between the eye of the observer and the top of the building and the distance from the observer to the building.

8. Write a program that will accept an integer as an input, find its square, and pick out the last three digits of the squared number. Print out the number, the square of the number, and the number that is formed by the last three digits picked out. Write out clearly by hand all the steps you take to solve this problem in a systematic manner. (Example: 108, 11664, 664.)

9. Write a program that prints an arrow, a rectangle, a diamond, and a circle whose maximum dimensions do not exceed 10 lines along the vertical and 10 characters along the horizontal.

10. When n resistors are connected in series in an electrical circuit, the total resistance is given as $R_{total} = R_1 + R_2 + \cdots + R_n$ and if they are connected in parallel the total resistance is given by $1/R_{total} = 1/R_1 + 1/R_2 + \cdots + 1/R_n$ where R are resistor values. Write a program to get input values from the user and print out total resistance for both series and parallel systems.

11. The following table describes the movement of a particle in a two-dimensional x-y plane starting from the origin. Read each coordinate (in meters) from the user and immediately output the magnitude of the movement. For example, the magnitude at time $= 1.0$ is $\text{sqrt}(1 + 4) = 2.236068$.

Time(sec)	1.0	2.0	3.0
x	1.0	3.5	−4.0
y	2.0	−2.0	3.0

CHAPTER 3

Selections and Repetitions

Programs normally execute sequentially from top to bottom, one line at a time. However, there are situations where we are interested in diverting from a sequential execution to another part of the program or we want to repeat a certain block of statements many times. An `if` statement is used for diversions and `for`, `while`, and `do` loops are used for repetitions. The diversion from sequential executions or the repetition of a block of statements depends upon a certain condition being true or false. This condition is often written using relational operators, which compare two values and provide a true or false result. Logical operators `&&` (and), `||` (or), and `!` (not) are used to combine two or more relational operations.

Sequence, selection and repetition are three basic structures in structured programming.

STRUCTURED PROGRAMMING

The basic program structure we have seen so far involved the computer starting the execution of the program at the top and completing each program statement in a sequential order. This is shown schematically in Fig. 3.1(a) where each box indicates a program statement.

The figure also presents the other two basic structures in structured programming, namely, the selection and repetition structures. In the selection structure the program control may divert from its sequential nature and jump to a different part of a program, depending upon a test result being true or false. In the repetition structure, a program statement or a block of program statements may be executed many times in a loop when a test is true. The program control jumps out of the loop to the next program statement when the test is false. Structured programming means that we use one or more of the above structures either singly or nested; that is, any rectangular block may include the other basic structures such as sequence, selection or repetition. In structured programming, the program flow should be clear and

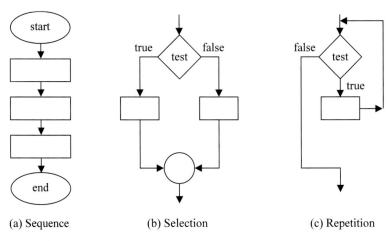

(a) Sequence   (b) Selection   (c) Repetition

FIGURE 3.1
Examples of program structures.

uncomplicated. In the next section, we describe the visibility boundary (access boundary) of a variable. Because we use { } to indicate a block of program statements (a single rectangular block in the diagram), we need to understand how this affects variable visibility (scope).

SCOPE OF VARIABLES

Understanding the scope or visibility of variables in C++ functions is of the utmost importance. The scope of a variable defines the visibility boundary of the variable (specifically, identifiers like the variable name); that is, where the variable is accessible in a program. A variable declared outside any function is known in all functions from the point where the function is declared until the end of the file; it has what is called file scope. Global variables are examples of variables with file scope. Curly brackets are used to block a set of statements. Blocks can be nested, and are commonly used in selection and repetition structures. A variable defined within a block is visible from the point where the variable is declared until the end of the block, indicated by }. These variables have what is called block scope. Local variables have block scope. The following example illustrates how blocks affect the visibility of variables.

C++ accepts identifiers with (i) file scope, (ii) block scope, and (iii) class scope (see Chapter 7).

```
//Filename scope.cpp
//Demonstrates the scope of variables

#include <iostream.h>
```

```
int g;              // g is a global variable that can be
                    //referenced by any function in this file.

int main()
   {
   int x=1;         //Only variable x is visible in the outer-
                    //most block. Compiler won't
                    //allow you to access y and z.

      {
      int y=2;      //Inner block. Variables x and y visible.
                    //Compiler won't allow you to access z.

         {
         int z=3,y ;   //Innermost block. All variables are visible.
                       // The variable y defined in the previous block
                       // becomes hidden until this block
                       // terminates. A new y is defined.

         }
                       // Now z is no longer visible.

      }
                       // Now y is no longer visible.
   return 0;
   }
```

Notice that if a variable with the same name is defined in a nested block, i.e., variable y, the first variable becomes hidden (that is, cannot be accessed) until after the end of the inner block.

In the next chapter, we will deal with "storage classes," the attribute of a variable that defines both the scope and the lifetime of a variable. Next we describe relational operators which are commonly used to test conditions for program diversion and repetition.

RELATIONAL OPERATORS

A relational operator compares any two values of built-in variable types, for example char, int, and float. The comparison results in either *true* (result equals 1) or *false* (result equals 0). Table 3.1 describes these relational operators with examples.

TABLE 3.1

Operator	Description	Example	Result
==	equal to	'a'=='b'	false (0)
>	greater than	'b'>'a'	true (1)
<	less than	'b'<'a'	false (0)
>=	greater than or equal to	1>=2	false (0)
<=	less than or equal to	1<=2	true (1)
!=	not equal to	1!=2	true (1)

==, >, <, >=, <=, != *are relational operators.*

*When a condition
with a nonzero
value is tested it
is interpreted as 1
(true). Only zero
results in 0 (false).*

First, a few important notes. Any value that is not 0 will be considered as true. For example (12) will be true and (0) will be false. Another tricky example: (12==12==12) results in false (0). Why? First, the relational operators have associativity from left to right. Hence, 12==12 results in true, that is, with a value of 1. Of course, 1==12 should result in false and that is what we get. This brings us to note another serious error most programmers make, which is writing one equal sign = instead of two equal signs ==, when comparing two values. The compiler will not find this error as it is a logic error and the results can be quite unexpected!

SELECTION OR DECISION MAKING

Often a program diversion depends upon the value of a relational operation resulting in true or false. We can use if statements, if...else statements, or switch statements to divert program execution to chosen program statement(s). In if statements, the body of the if statement is executed when a relational operation results in a *true* (1) value. Fig. 3.2 explains the program flow in an if statement.

The if Statement

The following example demonstrates the use of the if statement for program diversion. As shown in Fig. 3.2, a relational operation is associated with the if statement and the block following that statement is executed if the relational operation results in true.

if *(test expression)*
{statement(s)}

```
//Filename ifex1.cpp
//Demonstrates the use of if statement

#include <iostream.h>
```

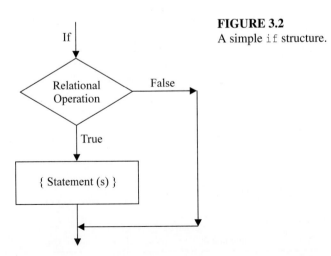

FIGURE 3.2
A simple if structure.

```
int main()
   {
   char note;
   cout << "Please press c to print letter c\n";
   cin >> note;
   if (note == 'c')      //If the condition is true
                         //the following block
                         //is executed
     {
     cout << "\nYou typed c " << endl;
     }
   return 0;
   }                        //End of main
```

To make the compiler catch missing equal sign in relational operation use, for example,
```
if ('c'==note)
   {
   ...
   }
```

The program simply prints c if c is entered. If the relational operation (note == 'c') results in false the program ends.

The if...else Statement

The simple if statement is sometimes not sufficient; often we want to do something different if the tested condition is false. In this case, the if..else statement can be used, as shown in the example below. The selection structure discussed at the beginning of the chapter corresponds to the if..else statement.

if (test expression) {statement(s)} else {statement(s)}

```
//Filename ifex2.cpp
//Demonstrates the use of if..else statement

#include <iostream.h>

int main()
   {
   char note;
   cout << "Please press c to print letter c\n";
   cin >> note;
   if (note == 'c')      //If the condition is true
                         //the following block
                         //is executed
     {
     cout << "\nYou typed c " << note << endl;
     }
   else  //If the relational operation result is false
         //the following is executed.
     {
     cout << "I can only print c!\n";
     cout << "Run the program again\n";
     }
   return 0;
   }              //End of main
```

if (test expression) {statement(s)}
else if (test expression) {statement(s)}
else {statement(s)}

The block following the `if` statement is executed when the relational operation results in true and the block following the `else` statement is executed when it is false. The following example demonstrates how `if..else` can be used in a nested form to make decisions in a multiple decision tree.

```
//Filename ifelse.cpp
//Demonstrates the use of multiple if..else statement

#include <iostream.h>
int main()
    {
    char note;
    cout << "Please press c or d or e\n";
    cin >> note;
    if (note == 'c')       //If the condition is true
                           //the following block
                           //is executed

     {
     cout << "\nYou typed c " << endl;
     }
    else if (note -- 'd')  //or else if this condition is true
                           //print d

     {
     cout << "\nYou typed d " << endl;
     }
    else if (note == 'e')  //or else if this condition is true
                           //print e

     {
     cout << "\nYou typed e " << endl;
     }
                                //If no condition is true or
                                //after printing any character the program
                                //control transfers here
    return 0;
    }                      //End of main
```

Check for semi-colons immediately after a relational operation or the else statement. They may cause logic errors.

If the letter received was `d` then after printing `d` the program control switches to the line after the `if..else` block which in the above program is simply the end of the main program. When you have problems such as the above, where you have to make multiple decisions, you may find the `switch..break` combination easier to use and clearer as explained below.

The `switch...break` Combination

The `switch` statement tests a value against a set of constants. The `break` statement is used to exit the `switch` statement. If the value tested does not match any of the

constants, the `default` option is used. The example given above can be rewritten
as follows.

```cpp
//Filename switch.cpp
//Demonstrates the use of switch and break statements

#include <iostream.h>

int main()
    {
    char note;
    cout << "Please press c or d or e\n";
    cin >> note;
    switch (note)          //Depending on the character entered,
                           //one of the following blocks
                           //is executed. Note no semicolon!

        {
        case 'c':          //If the note is 'c' then execute
                           //all the statements following until break
        cout << "\nYou typed c " << endl;
        break;             //Transfer control to the end
                           //of switch block

        case 'd':
        cout << "\nYou typed d " << endl;
        break;

        case 'e':
        cout << "\nYou typed e " << endl;
        break;
        }                  //End of switch block
    return 0;
    } //End of main
```

Missing the appro-
priate **break** *state-*
ment
is a common
error when using
the **switch...**
break *combina-*
tion.

In the above examples, if you miss out the `break` statements then each case will be
executed before program completion!! This feature may actually be useful in some
examples where you want the program to fall through all the cases.

Please note that in `switch` statements the branching is done depending
on the value (either `char` or `int` type) of a single variable such as `note` in the
above example, or an expression. What will happen if the character entered
is neither `'c'` nor `'d'` nor `'e'`? In the above program, the termination is
abrupt in the sense that the user would not know that he or she had keyed in the
wrong input. However, you can use the `default` statement as the last case
and inform the user of this mistake. Just above the end of the switch block
add

```cpp
default: cout << "Please run the program again and enter only c or d or e\n";
```

BOOLEAN VARIABLES

The ANSI C++ standard introduces a built-in Boolean type, called `bool`. However, if you are using an older compiler, it may not be supported. This can be easily overcome by using an enumerated data type, as in Pascal, in the following way.

```
//Filename: boolean.cpp
//Defining a boolean type variable

#include <iostream.h>

enum boolean {false, true};      //False has a value 0 and true = 1.
                                 //boolean is a new data type with the
                                 //value of 0 or 1.

int main()
   {
   boolean bolvar1, bolvar2;

   bolvar1 = false;              //Variable bolvar1 is
                                 //assigned a value 0
   bolvar2 = true;               //Variable bolvar2 is
                                 //assigned a value 1

   cout << "\nbolvar1 has a value of " << bolvar1;
   cout << "\nbolvar2 has a value of " << bolvar2;

   return 0;
   }
```

The output of the above program is

```
bolvar1 has a value of 0
bolvar2 has a value of 1
```

Note that the output is 0 and 1, not false and true. Next we describe the repetition or loop structure used in structured programming.

REPETITIONS OR LOOPS

The repetition structure involves the execution of either a single program statement or a block of program statements many times. In such cases, loop constructs such as `for`, `while`, or `do` are used.

The **for** Loop

When you want to repeatedly execute a block of statements a fixed number of times (that is, when you know how many times you want that block executed repeatedly), you will find the for loop convenient. Usually, the for loop consists of (i) an initialization expression, (ii) a test expression, (iii) an increment or decrement expression that usually involves a loop index, and (iv) the body of the loop which is executed whenever the test expression is true (Fig. 3.3).

When there are multiple statements within a loop, enclose them with curly brackets. Note that the initialization expression is executed at the beginning of the loop, the test expression is evaluated at every pass of the loop, and if it results in false the program control goes to the statement after the body of the loop. The increment or decrement expression is also executed at each time. Suppose we want to print the numbers 0 to 2 (inclusive) each on a separate line. We can do it in the following way.

```cpp
//Filename: forloop.cpp
//Demonstration of for loop

#include <iostream.h>

int main()
    {
    int i;                   //Loop index or loop variable
    for (i=0; i<3; i++)      //Loop from 0 to 2 and exit when i=3.
                             //Note no semicolon at the end.
       cout << i << "\n";    //End of for loop; the body of the
                             //loop here is a single statement
    return 0;
    } //End of main
```

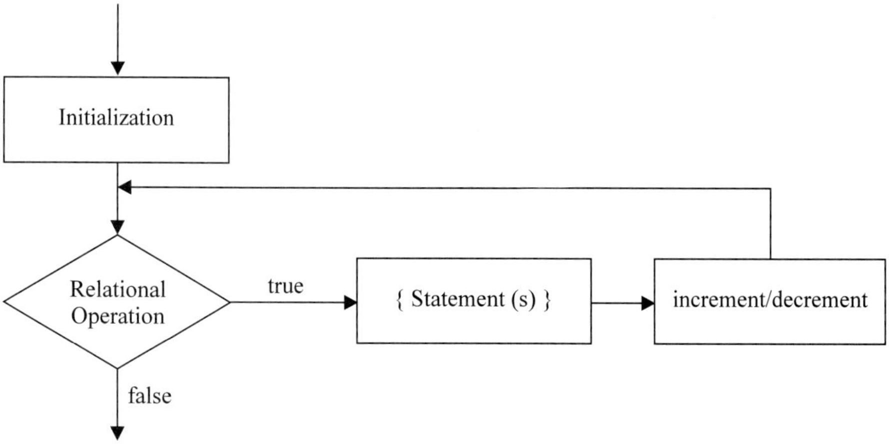

FIGURE 3.3
A common for loop structure.

Common **for-***loop syntax:*
for
(initialization; test;
increment or
decrement){
...
}

The output is

```
0
1
2
```

Another example using a `for` loop:

```cpp
//Filename: for2.cpp
//Demonstration of for loop
#include <iostream.h>

int main()
    {
    //The following for loop prints from z to a
    for (char character = 'z'; character >= 'a'; character--)
        {
        char dummy;
        cout << character;
        cout << " ";
        } //End of for loop. { } enclose the body of the loop.
    return 0;
    }    //End of main
```

Follow a consistent
style when using the
for loop. For ex-
ample, do not
increment or decre-
ment the loop index
within the body of
the
for loop.

In the above program, `character` is defined within the `for` statement. Variables defined in such a manner are visible (or available for use) from the point of definition to the end of the program. However, note that if a variable is defined within the loop in a block of statements (e.g., `char dummy` in the above program) then it is visible only within the block and outside the block it cannot be accessed. Lastly, note in both examples how indentation was used to clearly mark the block of statements within a loop. There are many possible styles for indentation and blocking curly brackets. Use a consistent style throughout your programs.

Note that the three expressions in the `for` loop are optional. If the second expression is omitted, C++ assumes that the test condition is true. If we provide an initial value for the control variable elsewhere in the program, the first expression may be omitted. If no increment is needed, or we increment the control variable with a separate statement inside the loop, the third expression may be omitted.

Nested loops

When there is another loop within a loop we call them nested loops. We need such a structure in many instances, such as when operating on matrices. We will say more about matrices later when studying arrays. The following is a simple example of nested `for` loops.

```cpp
//Filename: nestfor.cpp
//Demonstration of nested for loop

#include <iostream.h>
#include <iomanip.h>
```

```
int main()
    {
    cout << setw(9) << "outer" << setw(9) << "inner" << "\n";

    for (int outer=1; outer <=3; outer++)    //Loop variable
                                             //outer goes
                                             //from 1 to 3.
      {
      for (int inner=0; inner < 3; inner++) //Loop variable
                                             //inner goes
                                             //from 0 to 2
          {
          cout << setw(9) << outer << setw(9) << inner;
          cout << "\n";
          }                                  //End of inner loop
      }                                      //End of outer loop
    return 0;
    }                                        //End of main
```

The output of the above program is

outer	inner
1	0
1	1
1	2
2	0
2	1
2	2
3	0
3	1
3	2

Blocks using braces must be checked in diversions and loops. Incorrect blocking is a common error in these structures.

Try to run this program with the debugging features available in your compiler and watch the different variables as the loop proceeds.

What do you think would happen if we had a `for` loop such as:

```
for (int i=0;i<=2; i)
    { }
```

Watch out for `for` loops that do not terminate (called an infinite loop)! When the program is executing an infinite loop, the computer may be unresponsive to your normal key strokes. Note that the increment expression can be any legal arithmetic expression such as i += 2; also, the loop variable can be of any type such as `float`, `double`, etc. Avoid using `float` or `double` variables in relational expressions (especially involving equality) because of errors that can creep in due to the imprecise manner in which these variables are stored in computers. Do the following to understand this problem. Write a loop where you increment a variable by 0.001 a thousand times starting from zero. At the end of the loop, if you print the variable you most likely will see a number which is slightly different from 1.000. If you used a test condition to stop the loop when the variable equals 1.000, the results may be somewhat unexpected.

The `while` Loop

When you do not know beforehand how many times a block of statements needs to be executed you may think of using a `while` or `do` loop. The following example illustrates the use of the `while` loop. The repetition structure presented in Fig. 3.1(c) corresponds to the `while` loop.

```
//Filename: whilloop.cpp
//Demonstration of while loop

#include <iostream.h>

int main()
    {
    int i = 0;                  //Initialize the loop variable

    while ( i < 3 )             //Loop until the expression (i < 3)
                                //is false.  Note no semicolon at the end


        {
        cout << i << "\n";
        i++;                    //Increment the loop variable
        }                       //End of while loop
      return 0;
    }                           //End of main
```

Forgetting to increment or decrement the loop index (variable) is the common reason for infinite loops.

Note that the output of this program is identical to the program named `forloop.cpp` above. The `while` loop tests an expression and if the expression is true it executes a body of statements. We used this example just to compare the `for` loop with the `while` loop. The more useful place for this loop is when there is a user interaction and we repeatedly execute something when the user inputs correct values, or else, skip the loop. This is illustrated in the following example.

```
//Filename: while2.cpp
//Second demonstration of while loop
//with user interactions.

#include <iostream.h>
#include <math.h>

int main()
    {
    double sqrtop;

    cout << "Enter a positive number for which "
         << "you want to know the square root.\n"
         << "Type a negative number to stop the program.\n";

    cin >> sqrtop;
```

To avoid infinite loops make sure that the relational operation will result in false in a finite number of repetitions.

```
    while ( sqrtop >= 0)                  //Loop until the expression
                                          //(sqrtop >= 0) is false.
        {
        cout << "Square root of "<< sqrtop
             << " is " << sqrt(sqrtop) << "\n";
        cin >> sqrtop;
        }                                 //End of while loop
        return 0;
    }                                     //End of main
```

Note in the above program the placement of cin statements both outside and inside of the loop. These statements can be loosely compared to the initialization and incremental expressions in the for loop. Do not forget to place the curly brackets around the body of statements you want to repeatedly execute. Try to see (compile and execute) what happens when you forget them!!

The do Loop

The following example demonstrates the use of a do loop for the same problem as above.

```
//Filename: doloop.cpp
//Demonstration of do loop with user interactions.

#include <iostream.h>
#include <math.h>

int main()
    {
    double sqrtop;
    cout << "Enter a positive number for which "
         << "you want to know the square root.\n"
         << "Type a negative number to stop the program.\n";
    cin >> sqrtop;
    do
       {
       if (sqrtop >= 0)
          cout << "Square root of  " << sqrtop
               << " is " << sqrt(sqrtop) << "\n";
       cin >> sqrtop;
       }
    while ( sqrtop >= 0);   //Loop until the expression
                            //sqrtop >= 0)
                            //is false
                            //Note the semicolon at the
                            // end of while!!
    return 0;
    }                       //End of main
```

The program `doloop.cpp` behaves exactly like `while2.cpp` except for one drawback. An additional `if` statement is used to avoid abnormal termination. The `while` loop and `do` loop have one major difference. The `do` loop is used when the loop must or can be executed at least once whereas the `while` loop may not be executed at all if the test expression is false. This is because the termination condition in a `while` loop is tested at the beginning of the loop but in the `do` loop it is tested at the end of the loop. Just as in the case of `for` loops, we can have nested loops using `while` and `do` loops.

In summary, the `for` loop is used when you know beforehand the number of times a block of statements has to be repeated; you use the `do` loop when you want the block to be executed at least once and the `while` loop when you want it executed only if a certain condition is satisfied. However, from the examples you have seen above, it is possible to interchange one with another and it is really a matter of style. You will soon learn that for many engineering calculations (for example, vectors and matrices), it is often more convenient to use the `for` loop than the others.

LOGICAL OPERATORS

Suppose you want to take a decision depending upon two different relational operations. For example, it is going to snow if the temperature is below zero *and* it is cloudy. You are joining two relational operations, namely, (temperature < 0) and (cloudy), to get the decision that it is going to snow. When both relational expressions are true, the and operation results in a true value. The results for the binary logical operators and and or, which require two relational operations, and for the unary operator not, which requires only one relational operation, are given in Tables 3.2, 3.3 and 3.4.

TABLE 3.2
Truth table for and (&&)

Logical operation	Result	Example	Result
true and true	true	`(1<=2)&&('a'<='b')`	1
true and false	false	`(2)&&('x'>'y')`	0
false and true	false	`(0)&&('y'>'x')`	0
false and false	false	`(1>3)&&('a'=='b')`	0

TABLE 3.3
Truth table for or (||)

Logical operation	Result	Example	Result
true or true	true	`(1==1)||(egg==egg)`	1
true or false	true	`(bird==bird)||(1>2)`	1
false or true	true	`('x'>'y')||(2)`	1
false or false	false	`(1==0)||('a'=='b')`	0

TABLE 3.4
Truth table for not (!)

Operation	Result	Example	Result
NOT true	false	!(1<2)	0
NOT false	true	!(0)	1

A few things to note are as follows. The parentheses in the above example are optional; however, you are encouraged to use them as they make the program clearer. Secondly, you can use the logical operators to combine more than two relational operations as in

```
if ((1==1) || (2 > 3) && ('x' < 'y'))...
```

&&
||
!
are the three logical operators.

However, be frugal and avoid using more than two relational operations in one `if` statement because it is hard to notice any logic errors while debugging. In C++, the logical operations are done efficiently in the sense that, in the above operation, as soon as the first relational operation (`1==1`) is compared, further comparisons are ***not*** done because of the first logical operator being an or (`||`) operator. Note the operator (`||`) results in true if either one of the operands it is combining is true (see Table 3.3). Because of this, and to increase clarity, avoid using assignment operations in an `if` statement!

MISCELLANEOUS

A few other reserved words that are useful in specific situations are: (i) `break` and (ii) `continue`. We have seen `break` before in combination with the `switch` statement, but it can also be used to break out of a loop. Note that if you have nested loops, a single `break` statement gets you out of only one loop, namely the loop in which it is embedded. Also, if there is a `switch` statement within a loop and a `break` is used within the switch, it will only take you out of the switch. The `continue` statement is the opposite of the break. If the program is executing inside a loop and you want to go back to the top of the loop to start a new iteration, use the `continue` statement.

A useful function is `exit`, which exits the entire program when encountered. Since `exit` is a function, it has to be written in function format, namely, `exit(0)` (or any integer) where the value 0 is similar to the value 0 in the `return(0)` statement mentioned in the last chapter.

A ternary operator `?:` is an operator that operates on three operands and can be used instead of an `if...else` statement. For example,

```
x = (x >= 0) ? x : -x;
```

is equivalent to $x = \text{abs}(x)$. The first operand is the test condition, the second operand after the ? is executed if the test condition is true and the last operand after the : is executed if it is false.

CASE STUDY (SELECTIONS AND REPETITIONS)

Reservoir System Simulator

A Reservoir System Simulator can be used to study the behavior of reservoir systems and lakes. For simplicity, we will consider the simulation of a single reservoir (Fig. 3.4) in discrete time.

Assume you have the storage, inflow, and demand values, as well as the lower and upper bounds for the storage, namely, min_storage and max_storage. The objective is to find the outflow, spill, and storage at the end of the period whose dynamics in discrete time is given by the following if statements.

Case 1:   If $min\_storage \leq storage + inflow - demand \leq max\_storage$
$$outflow = demand$$
$$spill = 0$$
$$storage = storage + inflow - demand$$

Case 2:   If $min\_storage > storage + inflow - demand$
$$outflow = storage + inflow - min\_storage$$
$$spill = 0$$
$$storage = min\_storage$$

Case 3:   If $max\_storage < storage + inflow - demand$
$$outflow = demand$$
$$spill = storage + inflow - demand - max\_storage$$
$$storage = max\_storage$$

The reservoir storage is also called the state variable, whose value at the end of each time period is determined as above. Demands and inflows during all periods are assumed to be non-negative and are given. Outflow is supposed to be equal to the demand whenever possible.

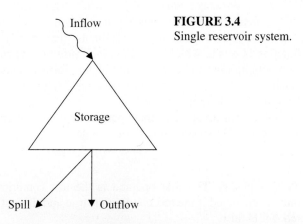

Inflow

Storage

Spill   Outflow

FIGURE 3.4
Single reservoir system.

Simulate the reservoir for the following data. Inflow(time = 1 to 3) = {10, 20, 30}, demand(time = 1 to 3) = {10, 40, 0}; max_storage = {20}, min_storage = {0}; initial storage in the reservoir = {10}. Note that "simulate" here means calculate and output the outflow, spill, and the end of period storage in each period of interest. The user can be asked to input the values (inflow and demand) for each period.

1. Problem analysis

A single reservoir system is to be simulated using data on the system characteristics such as maximum and minimum storage and initial storage. The simulation is to be done for all periods for which data for demand and inflow are input by the user. The required results such as outflow, spill, and storage are calculated for each period. The results are output at each period.

Problem statement: Simulate a single reservoir system with user-supplied input.

Input/output analysis: The inputs required are: maximum storage, minimum storage, initial storage, and inflow and demand for each period.

The outputs are: outflow, spill, and final storage in each period. It might be necessary to output the user-supplied data for convenience.

2. Design

We will use process-based decomposition to solve the problem. You may remember that this technique is also called divide and conquer or the top-down design process. Start with the overall (hard) problem and divide it into easier and easier subproblems. The hardest problems are at the top and the easiest at the bottom. Another trick is to keep levels 0 and 1 basically the same for all problems, as shown in Fig. 3.5.

There! You are on the way to solving the problem. That was not too hard, was it? We will worry about details later. Let us now deal with the process box (Fig. 3.6). We are going to introduce the *Jackson notation* for structured programming. The asterisk in the corner of the box indicates that this box is to be executed repeatedly in a loop. This is a convenient way to represent loops within our decomposition diagrams. In the reservoir problem the processing of certain data is done repeatedly for each period until the user decides to stop.

Another Jackson notation: The box "calculate" corresponds to the calculation of storage + inflow − demand, which we will call temporary storage, and the

An asterisk in the corner of the box indicates a repetition and a small circle indicates selection.

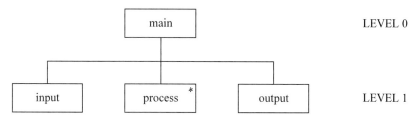

FIGURE 3.5
Level 0 (top) and Level 1 (bottom) of the top-down design.

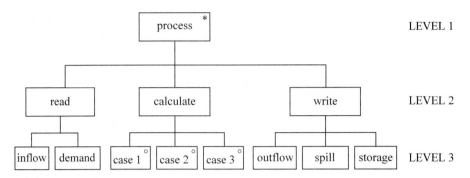

FIGURE 3.6
Levels 1, 2, and 3 of the top-down design.

calculation of the reservoir storage dynamics with the three "if" conditions in the problem statement. In order to indicate that, at any one period, *only one* of the boxes is executed depending upon the value of temporary storage, a small circle is drawn in the top right corner of the box, as shown in Fig. 3.6. If necessary, you can add three more boxes under each of the cases to indicate the assignment statements under each case. If you are wondering about the details under the input and output boxes in Level 1 of the decomposition in Fig. 3.5, they correspond to the data read at the beginning of the simulation, namely, maximum, minimum and initial storage, and the printing of these values to help the user. See the printed output provided later if this is still unclear.

Hand example. Let us use the given data to work out the details of the calculations by hand. We will use a table for convenience (Table 3.5). The calculation in each row corresponds to the calculate box shown above. This is also one of the lowest boxes in the decomposed problem structure. You may remember from Chapter 1 that if the problem is too hard to solve by hand, we have to decompose it further until it is easy enough to solve by hand.

Level 1 input box:
maximum storage = 20   minimum storage = 0   initial storage = 10

Process box:
storage = initial storage

Calculate box:
temp storage = storage + inflow − demand

TABLE 3.5

Inflow	Demand	Temp storage (case)	Outflow	Spill	Final storage
10	10	10 (1)	10	0	10
20	40	−10 (2)	30	0	0
30	0	30 (3)	0	10	20

In the first period, the initial storage is 10, inflow is 10, demand is 10 and hence the temp storage = $10 + 10 - 10 = 10$. Because this value is between the maximum and minimum storages, case 1 is selected (indicated in brackets) and the corresponding outflow is 10, spill is 0, and the final storage is now 10 which is the initial storage for the next period. You can do the calculations for the next two periods similarly in order to understand the values in the table.

Algorithm design. The above calculations can be easily converted into an algorithm. We use both the decomposition diagram and the hand example to help us with the algorithm which will be written in pseudocode (that is, almost like C++ but not quite!). When writing the algorithm, it may be easier to reverse the top-down design process. That is, start from the bottom and go up to the top. This is easier because we know that the easiest problems are at the bottom. As a first step, we will write the algorithm for the box "calculate" with the "if" conditions (boxes for the three cases). Secondly, although testing is done as a separate step, it also can be used during the algorithm design stage to make sure the algorithm will work. Use the hand example to check. Correct your algorithm or refine it as you go along. This multiple testing and refinement will be seldom shown in the book. However, you can rest assured that the authors had to do a few revisions before getting the algorithms in the book right. Unfortunately, to save space, this very important process is not shown in most textbooks and we will show it only sparingly.

First attempt:

```
temp_storage = storage + inflow − demand
if (max_storage <= temp_storage <= min_storage)
    outflow = demand
    spill = 0
    storage = temp_storage   //Final storage in the table
else if (min_storage > temp_storage)
    outflow = storage + inflow − min_storage
    spill = 0
    storage = min_storage   //Final storage in the table
else if (max_storage < temp_storage)
    outflow = demand
    spill = storage + inflow − demand − max_storage
    storage = max_storage   //Final storage in the table
```

Design from the top. Code or write the algorithm from the bottom!

Testing. If we use numerical values for the first period, the temp_storage = $10 + 10 - 10 = 10$ which is between the maximum and minimum storages of 20 and 0, respectively. According to the problem definition, it should fall within case 1. Immediately we notice that we got the first "if" condition wrong as the test condition results in false instead of true. The minimum and maximum storages are switched around. Therefore we will correct it as

if (min_storage <= temp_storage <= max_storage)

Similarly, continue and verify that the algorithm gets the same result as we did by hand in the hand example. It is fortunate that the authors have chosen data such that all the "if" conditions are tested at least once in the hand example. However, in large problems choosing such test data, although essential, is very hard due to the numerous branches that are possible. One of the measures for program complexity, developed by McCabe and called the McCabe complexity number, is based on counting the number of paths in a program, each of which needs to be tested. See Appendix E for further details.

Let us continue by building the loop corresponding to the process box containing the asterisk. Note that this subproblem corresponds to reading the data for the simulation of each period from the user, calculating the storage, and producing the output for each period. Also, we will use to our advantage the non-negativity restrictions (that is, $>= 0$) on the inflow and demand. Negative inflow or demand will be used to signal the end of the simulation period.

The three D's of problem solving using computers are: Discipline, Design and Documentation.

Second attempt:

```
storage = initial storage
read inflow, demand
while (inflow >= 0 and demand >= 0 )
    temp_storage = storage + inflow − demand
    if (min_storage <= temp_storage <= max_storage)
        outflow = demand
        spill = 0
        storage = temp_storage
    else if (min_storage > temp_storage)
        outflow = storage + inflow − min_storage
        spill = 0
        storage = min_storage
    else if (max_storage < temp_storage)
        outflow = demand
        spill = storage + inflow − demand − max_storage
        storage = max_storage
    write inflow, demand, outflow, spill, storage
    read inflow, demand    //End while loop
```

3. Coding and debugging

The corresponding C++ code that solves the simulator problem (1resbug.cpp) is given on the accompanying diskette. The following program contains some syntax and logic errors (bugs). Debug this program first by hand and then in your computer lab. Debugging a program is sometimes easier on paper than at the computer, and this process is called code inspection. Sometimes, when you cannot find a bug, you should try to explain your program to a colleague; often this helps you to find the bug. The (debugged) working C++ program (1ressim.cpp) is also on the accompanying diskette. Do not look at the corrected program until you have completed the debugging exercise to your satisfaction. Note that you can use your hand example to debug.

```
//WARNING: "Program contains errors (bugs)!"
//Program 1resbug.cpp
//Program will simulate a single reservoir system for a given
//demand and inflow series input by the user one by one
```

```
#include <iostream.h>
#include <iomanip.h>

int main()


   //
   cout << "Welcome to the Reservoir Simulator\n";
   cout << "Please input reservoir maximum, minimum "
        << "storages (>= 0) and \n"
        << "the initial storage falling between "
        << "the maximum and minimum\n";

   float max_storage, min_storage, init_storage;
   cin >> max_storage >> min_storage >> init_storage;

   //Check for potential error condition

   while ( ( init_storage >= max_storage ) &&
           ( init_storage <= min_storage ) ||
             ( max_storage < 0 ) && ( min_storage < 0 ) ) {
      cout << "Please input reservoir maximum,"
           << "minimum storages (>= 0) and \n"
           << "the initial storage falling BETWEEN"
           << "the maximum and minimum\n";
      cin >> max_storage >> min_storage >> init_storage;
   }     //End of while loop for input error check

   cout << "Please input current period's inflow and demand\n";
   cout << "-1 -1 (any one negative number) to end simulation\n";

   float inflow, demand;
   cin >> inflow >> demand;

   float storage, outflow, spill;

   storage = init_storage; //Initial condition of the reservoir
   cout << "MAX. STOR. = " << max_storage
        << "   MIN. STOR. = " << min_storage
        << "    INITIAL STORAGE = " << init_storage << "\n\n";


   while ( (inflow > 0 ) || ( demand > 0 ) ) {


      float temp_storage
      temp_storage = storage - inflow + demand;
```

```
            if ( ( min_storage <= temp_storage ) &&
               (temp_storage <= max_storage) ) {
               outflow = demand;
               spill = 0.;
               storage = temp_storage;
            }
            else if (min_storage > temp_storage) {
               outflow = storage + inflow - min_storage;
               spill = 0.;
               storage = min_storage;
            }
            else; { //This corresponds to max_storage < temp_storage
               outflow = demand;
               spill = storage + inflow - demand - max_storage;
               storage = max_storage;
            }
            //End of the three cases

            //Print out results

            cout << setw(12) << "Inflow" << setw(12)
                  << "Demand" //<< setw(12) << "Temp_sto"
                  << setw(12) << "Outflow"
                  << setw(12) << "Spill" << setw(12) << "Fin.Stor." << endl;
            cout << setw(12) << inflow
                  << setw(12) << demand //<< setw(12) << temp_storage
                  << setw(12) << outflow << setw(12)
                  << spill << setw(12) << storage << endl;

            cout << "Please input current period's inflow and demand\n";
            cout << "-1 -1 (any one negative number) to end simulation\n";
            cin >> inflow >> demand;

         }   //End of while loop for different periods

      cout << "\nSimulation ended";
      return 0;

   } //End of main program for reservoir simulation
```

A computer output of the above problem corresponding to the *corrected* version is given below for the hand example:

```
Welcome to the Reservoir Simulator

Please input reservoir maximum, minimum storages (>= 0) and
the initial storage falling between the maximum and minimum,
and maximum > minimum.
```

20 0 10   *User Input*

```
Please input current period's inflow and demand
-1 -1 (any one negative number) to end simulation.
```

10 10   *User Input*

```
MAX. STOR. = 20   MIN. STOR. = 0   INITIAL STORAGE = 10

      Inflow       Demand      Outflow       Spill    Fin.Stor.
          10           10           10           0           10
```

```
Please input current period's inflow and demand
-1 -1 (any one negative number) to end simulation.
```

20 40   *User Input*

```
      Inflow       Demand      Outflow       Spill    Fin.Stor.
          20           40           30           0            0
```

```
Please input current period's inflow and demand
-1 -1 (any one negative number) to end simulation.
```

30 0   *User Input*

```
      Inflow       Demand      Outflow       Spill    Fin.Stor.
          30            0            0          10           20
```

```
Please input current period's inflow and demand
-1 -1 (any one negative number) to end simulation.
```

-1 -1   *User Input*

```
Simulation Ended!
```

4. Integration

Because this program was all in a single function, there was no need for any integration step. However, we developed the program box by box incrementally, first breadth-first with the Level 1 input and output boxes and then depth-first for the middle leg of the hierarchy in the following order.

    main
    input
    output
    process

read
write
calculate

In addition we made sure that not only does each box work well, but together all the boxes work to solve the problem. We will show more of this approach in the next chapter.

5. Testing

We have tested the program only with the data provided for the hand example. Now consider various test cases and inspect the results to decide whether they are correct. Present the results in tabular fashion as shown in Table 3.6, where the results correspond to the corrected program. This is the verification process. The validation process is making sure that the results we get answer the questions stated in the problem.

Note that when you have many "if" conditions (prevalent in almost all programs), it is desirable to use data that will test the bounds of the "if" conditions, called the boundary cases. For example, in this case, use test data that will test all the equality and inequality relational operations in the three "if" conditions. The test cases which fall within the boundary plus the boundary cases are the valid test cases

TABLE 3.6
Test cases and program results (1ressim.cpp)

Test case type	Initial storage	Inflow	Demand	Test results
Valid				
Boundary (max)	10	10	0	Pass
Boundary (min)	10	10	20	Pass
Normal	10	10	10	Pass
Special				
Above max_storage	10	30	0	Pass
Below min_storage	10	20	40	Pass
Boundary (inflow = 0 and demand = 0)	10	0	0	Pass
Stopping criteria	10	−1	−1	Pass
Stopping criteria	10	−10	−15	Pass
Stopping criteria	10	−10	15	Pass
Stopping criteria	10	10	−15	Pass
Stopping criteria	10	0	−1	Pass
Stopping criteria	10	−1	0	Pass
Invalid				
For initial storage	−10			Pass
When max_storage < min_storage				Pass
When init_storage > max_storage				Pass
When init_storage < min_storage				Pass

that the program can expect to face normally. The special cases are valid but unusual and require special care in handling. For example, consider the stopping criteria, that is, the two negative numbers asked of the user, and test if the program really works for various possibilities. Will it stop if the numbers are $-10, -15$, or if one of them is positive and the other is negative, or if one or both of them are zero, etc. The last test case, where both are zero, is a boundary case for valid inflows and is an invalid case for the stopping criterion. An example of an invalid case is the user inputting a negative value for initial storage. You can verify that the program `1ressim.cpp` handles it gracefully. Typically we will need a few iterations before we can be satisfied that the program works well. The results shown in Table 3.6 present details for these various cases. Even for a small problem the test cases become quite large. For this reason, there are many commercial software packages available for automating this process.

SUMMARY

Relational operators compare two values and result in true (1) or false (0). Program diversion can be done using decision statements such as `if` and `if..else` statements. The `switch` statement may be a convenient alternative to nested `if..else` statements. The `for` loop is used when the number of times the loop body needs to be executed is known before the start of the loop. The `while` loop and `do` loop are used when a relational operation is true, with the relational operation being at the beginning of the `while` loop and at the end of the `do` loop. Nested loops are possible in all loop types. Variables defined within the body of a loop are visible only within the loop body. Logical operators help to combine two or more relational operations and result in either true or false.

REVIEW QUESTIONS

1. What are the three basic structures in structured programming?

2. Relational operators _____ two values and result in either _____ or _____.

3. A true condition is equivalent to the integer value _____.
   A false condition is equivalent to the integer value _____.

4. Any nonzero value results in a true condition. True or false?

5. Is (-1) true or false?

6. Fill in the relational operators

   greater than _____
   greater than or equal to _____
   equal to _____

less than _____
less than or equal to _____
not equal to _____

7. Is $(1 = 5)$ a valid relational operation? Explain.

8. After the statement x = ·2==1; is executed, what is the value in x?

9. When would you use (i) a `while` loop, (ii) a `do` loop and (iii) a `for` loop?

10. Can the loop index be changed inside of the body of the `for` loop?

11. Which reserved word causes execution (i) to exit the loop and (ii) to go the top of the loop?

12. What do you think will happen if we have a `for` loop such as:

```
for (int i=5; i>0; ++i)
    {  }
```

13. Write three kinds of loop to write numbers from 1 to 10.

14. Write a loop that will print out x versus sin(x), x = −pi to pi with a step size of 0.6. Is there any problem?

15. Identify the errors (syntax/logic):

```
(i)  while (c=5) {
            cout << c << endl
         ++C;
```

```
(ii) if (age >= "21") {
         cout << "adult\n";
      else;
         cout << "child\n;
     }
```

16. True or false: A default case is required in the `switch...break` combination.

17. Is there a `goto` in C++? Explore.

18. Write C++ statement(s) that will print "It will snow" if the temperature is less than −2 and it is cloudy.

19. What does `enum day_of_the_week (sun,mon,tue,wed,thu,fri,sat);` do?

20. What are the three types of test cases?

EXERCISES

1. Remove one or more of the braces from a loop body, compile, and see if you can understand the error messages. Use any example from the chapter.

2. Write a program that will print either a rectangle or a diamond made up of asterisks. The width and height may be specified by the user, but you will guide the user as to the maximum values possible.

3. Write a program that reads 10 numbers and prints the average of the numbers read.

4. Write a program that reads and prints the average of the numbers input by the user. You do not know beforehand how many numbers will be entered.

5. The real value solutions of a quadratic equation $ax^2 + bx + c = 0$ exist if and only if $b^2 - 4ac \geq 0$. Write a program that will print the real value solutions if they exist. Note that if $b^2 - 4ac = 0$ then there is a single real root at $x = -b/2a$ else if $b^2 - 4ac > 0$ then there are real value solutions at $x = (-b \pm \sqrt{b^2 - 4ac})/2a$. $p54$

6. The resistance of a cylindrical conductor made either from copper, aluminum, or manganese is given by $R = \rho l/A$ in Ω meter where the resistivity ρ of the conductor for the different material is given as 1.8e−10, 2.5e−10, and 1.5e−06, respectively. The length l is in meters and area A is in square meters. The user will input the material, area, and the required resistance of the conductor and your program will output the length of the conductor.

7. The variation of a mass of a particle, according to Einstein's theory of relativity, is given by $m = m_0/\sqrt{1 - (v/c)^2}$ where m_0 is the mass of the particle at velocity $v = 0$ and c is speed of light. Output a table of values for m/m_0 for values of v/c ranging from 0.2 to 0.9.

8. Tabulate the rational function $y = (x^3 + 2x^2 - 7x - 10)/(x^2 - x - 2)$ for x ranging from −3 to 3 in steps of 0.25. Hint: When denominator is close to zero print y as undefined.

9. Write a program that will print a chess board (8×8 square; a black square in the left-hand corner) using nested loops. Each black square can be a 3×3 square of asterisks or any other appropriate character from the ASCII table in your book. The white square can be simply left as blank.

10. A real number x and an integer number n are to be input by the user. Compute the following sum, which is an approximation of the mathematical expression $e^x (e = 2.718281828459...; n! = 1 \times 2 \times 3 ... \times n - 1 \times n)$ given by

$$1 + x + \frac{x^2}{2!} + \frac{x^3}{3!} + ... + \frac{x^k}{k!}$$

Print the results after $k = 1, k = 2, k = 3, ..., k = n$ terms and compare your results with the results of the library function `exp()`. Use a tabular form of output. (Hint: Can you pull out a common factor from the terms following the 1 and not use the `pow()` function?)

11. Write a program that accepts individual digits from 0 to 9. These should be read in with a `while` loop and assembled into a positive number of type `int`. Note that the integer type `int` can hold at least up to 32,767 (and more on some platforms). The input should be terminated on any non-digit character. Print out the number using `cout`.

12. Write a program that evaluates $\sin^2 X$ using a series expansion $\sin^2 X = X^2 - (2^3 X^4)/4! + (2^5 X^6)/6! - \cdots$. Evaluate the series for any user input X, printing the results after 2, 4, 6, 8, ..., 12 terms and comparing the results to the true solution calculated using the library `sin()` function. You are not allowed to build a function to calculate the factorials. (Hint: Can you pull out a common factor from the polynomial?)

13. You have a contract to write software for Airport Authorities of Canada (AAC). AAC wants you to write a program that will read temperature data in Fahrenheit and humidity in percent from three different points in the airport. When the temperature of any one point falls below 2°C (Celsius) and the relative humidity of that point is above 90%, the program will issue a warning that de-icing of airplanes may be needed. Follow the five-step process and test your program with the following data sets.

First set

34.0	95.0
33.0	90.0
32.0	92.0

Second set

-40.0	85.0
-32.0	82.0
-35.0	89.0

Hint: You can convert the temperature using the formula

$$\text{temperature in Celsius} = (\text{temperature in Fahrenheit} - 32) * (5/9)$$

14. Write a C++ program that can simulate the movement of a vehicle at a signal. The condition of the car (whether stopped or in motion) will be input by the user. Your program will generate a random number between 0 and 1. If the random value is between 0 and 0.5 the light is green; if it is above 0.5 but below 0.6, the light is orange, and anything else it is red. Your output should indicate the current state of the vehicle input by the user, the light color, and an appropriate action like stop, start, and prepare to stop. Present the five-step design process. (Hint: The `rand()` function declared in `<stdlib.h>` returns a random number between 0 and RAND_MAX.)

CHAPTER 4

Functions to Aid Modularity

In Chapter 1, we mentioned that functions (procedures, subprograms, and subroutines are other commonly used names) were the first major development in high-level programming languages that reduced the program size and increased clarity. In structured programming a large problem was divided into a number of subproblems. Each of these subproblems is solved using a function. Each function generally had one purpose and had a clearly defined interface to other functions. This chapter describes some simple functions and also how functions are declared, invoked or called, and defined. To understand the interface between functions we explain how variables (or values) are passed to functions, the different ways it can be done, and how functions return results to the calling functions. Although functions aid modularity, they increase program complexity due to the need to pass data. This point is explained in the case study.

SIMPLE FUNCTIONS

A function is a module designed to perform a task that may be used at many points in a program. It will normally return a value, called the *return value*. A program can invoke a function with a *function call*. Information needed by the function to perform its task can be passed with the help of *function arguments and parameters*. Arguments are the actual values passed to a function and parameters are the variables specified in function headers to hold the values passed. The function may be allowed to modify these parameters, and hence function parameters can be used as a means to return output from the function.

Arguments are the actual values passed to a function and parameters are the variables specified in function headers to hold the values passed.

In the next program `simplfun.cpp`, the program `main()` invokes the function `simplefun()`, using the following syntax:

```
simplefun()
```

where `simplefun()` is a function that prints the message "C++ is an Object Oriented Language".

Functions have to be declared before they can be used. A function declaration is also called the function prototype. If the function declaration is omitted before the function call, the compiler considers it a fatal mistake. Notice the declaration for the function `simplefun()`:

```
void simplefun();
```

According to this declaration the function does not return a value (indicated by the type `void`), and it does not require any input or output parameters. If it did, the parameters (at least their types, as explained later) would be listed within the parentheses. The compiler uses the function declaration or prototype to check that calls to the function contain the correct number and type of parameters, and the correct type for the return value. Note that function names are identifiers and follow the same convention as variable names. When a function is declared, defined, or invoked, the function name is followed by parentheses. By convention, in the text, we refer to a function by its name and the trailing parentheses to differentiate it from a variable.

A function definition is where the body of the function is defined. In the example below, the function is defined in the lines:

```
void simplefun()

    {
    cout << "\nC++ is an Object-Oriented Programming Language";
    }               //End of simplefun()
```

The complete program is shown below:

```
//Filename simplfun.cpp
```

*Function
definition
syntax:*

```
#include <iostream.h>

void simplefun();      //Function declaration or function prototype
```

*type
name (parameters)*

```
int main()
    {
    simplefun();    //Invoking or calling the function simplefun()
    return 0;
    }               //End of main
```

{
...
}

```
//Function definition for simplefun()
//

void simplefun()
    {
    cout << "\nC++ is an Object-Oriented Programming Language";
    }               //End of simplefun()
```

The above is the preferred style for defining functions. In the example the function was declared before it was invoked, and then it was fully defined. We can also fully define the function before the function is called, as the following example shows:

```
//Filename simplfn2.cpp

#include <iostream.h>

//Function definition for simplefun().
//Note that the function is defined before the
//main function thus eliminating the need for declaration.

void simplefun()
        {
        cout << "\nC++ is an Object-Oriented Programming Language";
        }                //End of simplefun()

int main()
        {
        simplefun();    //Calling the function simplefun()
        return 0;
        }                //End of main
```

The latter style is less flexible because you must remember the order in which the functions are called and define them in advance. In complicated programs, finding this type of ordering may not even be possible. Therefore, we will not use the second style. In the main() function above, the function call is the only program statement. The function simplefun() is invoked or called just by using its name followed by parentheses.

PASSING ARGUMENTS AND RETURNING VALUES

The simplefun() function is totally self-contained, that is, it requires no data to be passed from the calling function and it returns no results. However, most functions require input data and return results to the calling function. In the following example, the function hypotenuse() calculates the hypotenuse of a triangle, returning this value to the calling program. The function declaration or prototype is:

```
float hypotenuse(float, float);
```

The function returns a value of type float as indicated by its type. It has two parameters of type float.

The value returned from a function must be of a certain type. You may remember that when a function returns no result its type is void. The type of the returned value is the type of the function. In this example, the returned value type is float and is specified in front of the function name hypotenuse(). If the type of the function is not specified, type int is assumed.

Notice that the function `hypotenuse()` invokes the C/C++ library function `sqrt(x)`. This function, like any other function, must be declared before it can be used in a program. The declaration for this function is contained in the header file `math.h` included at the beginning of the program.

Passing Arguments

We use arguments to pass to the function the data it needs to perform its task. Recall that in the function definition we use parameters to hold and manipulate the passed data. The function may be allowed to modify these parameters, and thus, return some output in them. The function parameters are listed in the function declaration (or function prototype) and in the function definition. The type of the parameter is specified in front of its name. However, in a function prototype you have the choice of not specifying the names of the parameters. In this case, both the arguments `base` and `side` are of type `float` and hence the function *declaration* is `float hypotenuse (float, float)`. Of course, you can choose to provide names for parameters in the function prototype as it makes it easier to understand the working of the function. The function *definition* should have the same type and number of parameters as specified in the function declaration. Hence, it is `float hypotenuse (float bas, float sid)`. Arguments can be passed to a function using one of many methods. In this chapter we will consider two: (1) by value and (2) by reference.

Passing arguments by value

When an argument is passed by value, a copy of the actual value of the argument in the calling program is made and this copy is used by the function (see Fig. 4.1). Thus changes to the value of the argument made by the function do not affect the value of the argument in the calling program. This is how arguments are passed in C++ by default, except for the case of array arguments (arrays are explained in Chapter 5). When arguments are passed by value, we are sure that the function will not inadvertently modify the value of the argument in the calling program.

```
int main()
  {
  ...
float base, side, hypot;
  ...
  }
float hypotenuse (float bas, float sid)
  {
  float hypo = sqrt (bas*bas + sid*sid);
  return hypo;
  }
```

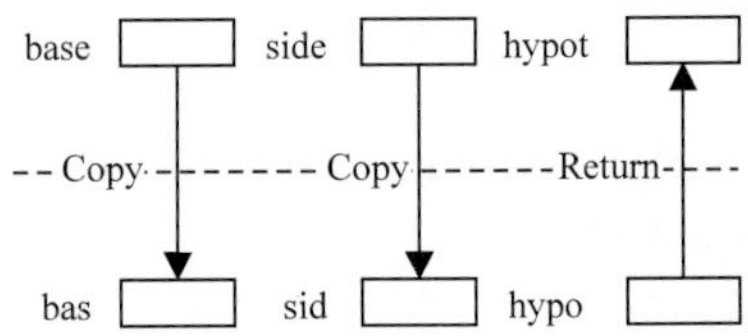

FIGURE 4.1
Passing arguments by value.

In the following program, arguments `base` and `side` are passed to function `hypotenuse()` by value.

```cpp
//Filename hypofun.cpp
//Calculates the hypotenuse of right-angled triangle

#include <iostream.h>
#include <math.h>

float hypotenuse(float, float);    //Function declaration or
                                   //function prototype. There
                                   //are 2 parameters of float type
                                   //and the function returns a
                                   //float type

int main()
    {
    float base,side,hypot;

    cout << "\nPlease enter the base and side of"
         << " the right-angled triangle to calculate"
         << " the hypotenuse\n";
    cin >> base >> side;

    hypot = hypotenuse(base, side);  //Calling the
                                     //function hypotenuse()

    cout << "\nThe hypotenuse of a triangle with base= "
         << base << " and side= " << side << " is= "
         << hypot << "\n";

    return 0;
    }                //End of main

//Function definition for hypotenuse()
float hypotenuse(float bas, float sid) //Different variables used to
                                       //show that they are different
                                       //from the variables base and
                                       //side in main function.

    {

    float hypo = sqrt(bas*bas + sid*sid);  //Calculates hypotenuse
                                           //and stores the result
                                           //in a new variable
                                           //hypo

    return hypo;     //This is the result returned in the name
                     //of the function hypotenuse in the
                     //main program

    }                //End of function hypotenuse()
```

Passing arguments by value is a safe method that leaves the original data in the calling function unchanged.

In Fig. 4.1, the top three boxes correspond to memory allocated for the variables in the main() function. The bottom three boxes correspond to the three variables that are accessible only in the hypotenuse() function. The dashed line symbolically indicates the division between the two groups of variables, where the variables bas, sid and hypo are called local variables because they are only locally accessible, that is, within the function hypotenuse(). We will learn about the scope of variables (local or global) later in this chapter.

As noted in Fig. 4.1, when the value of the variable in the calling function (in the present example it is main()) is copied into the variable of the called function (hypotenuse() here), the argument is being passed by value. Note that the hypotenuse() function has no access to the original variables in the main() function. You can use the hypotenuse() function just like the library functions sqrt(), sin(), etc.

The function definition starts with the type of the function, and the function name has the right number and type of parameters. Make a note that the order of the parameters in the definition of the function and in the function declaration, and the order of the arguments in the function call, all should match exactly. Why?

Argument and parameter mismatching could lead to disastrous results!

The computer (compiler) does not understand that it has to match the variables base and side in the main() function with bas and sid in the hypotenuse() function. For copying corresponding variables, the programmer must make sure the parameters and arguments are matched both in number and type. Compilers may give warning messages if the types do not match.

The value that needs to be returned is returned by the last statement return hypo, and in this case, because of the assignment statement in the main() function, that value is copied into the variable hypot in the main function. If we want to return more than one value to the calling function, we have to find a way of doing so. It will be done, for the time being, using arguments passed by reference, as will be seen next.

Passing arguments by reference

When an argument is passed by reference, a handle to its memory location (address) is passed to the function. The function can access the value of the parameter in the calling program, and change its value. We pass a variable by reference when the same variable is to be used in the calling function and in the function called. A function cannot return more than one value. If more than one result is to be returned then the variables have to be passed by reference. Note that passing by copy is done in only one direction, that is, from the calling function to the called function, and hence cannot be used for returning more than one result.

The following program calls a function that obtains the area and perimeter of a circle based on the value of the radius of the circle. We can see that there are two kinds of data passed between the two functions main() and circle_area_peri(), namely, input (radius) and output (area and perimeter). Because there are two results to return, we need to pass the variables to hold the results by reference as shown below.

```
//Filename circarpe.cpp
//Demonstration of passing by reference

#include <iostream.h>
#include <math.h>

void circle_area_peri(float radius, float& area, float& perimeter);
                              //Function declaration or
                              //function prototype. There are 3
                              //parameters of float type and
                              //two of them are passed by reference

int main()
     {
     float radius, area, perimeter;

     cout << "\nPlease enter the radius of the circle\n";
     cin >> radius;

     circle_area_peri(radius, area, perimeter); //Calling
                                             //the function
                                             //circle_area_peri()

     cout << "\nThe area of the circle is = "
         << area << " and the perimeter is = " << perimeter
         << "\n";
     return 0;
     }              //End of main

//Function definition for circle_area_peri()
//

void circle_area_peri(float rad, float& ar, float& peri) //Different
                              //variable names used; the
                              //last two variables refer
                              //to variables area
                              //and perimeter of
                              //the main function. They
                              //refer to contents of
                              //the same memory locations.

     {
     ar = M_PI*rad*rad;                //Calculates the area
     peri = 2.0*M_PI*rad;              //and the perimeter
     }              //End of function circle_area_peri()
```

Note that in the above function `circle_area_peri()` there is no return statement. This is because the variables `ar` and `peri` in the function refer to the same variables as `area` and `perimeter` in the function, so there is no need to return those values. As they are calculated the values are stored in the memory space of the variables `area` and `perimeter`, respectively, in the `main()` function. Because

```
    ...
int main()
    {
    float radius, area, perimeter;
    ...
    return 0;
    }
void circle_area_
    peri(float rad, float & ar,
        float & peri)
    {
    ...
    }
```

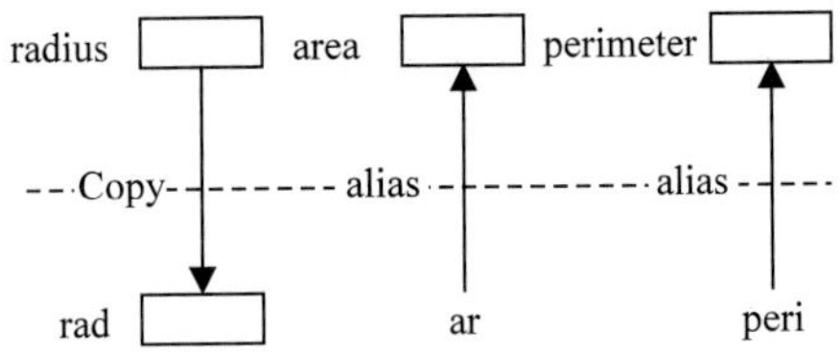

FIGURE 4.2
Passing arguments by reference.

of this property the variable names `ar` and `peri` are simply aliases for `area` and `perimeter`. C programmers should not confuse the ampersand (&) sign to mean the *address of*. We will talk about the meaning of the operator *address of* in Chapter 9 which deals with pointers. You can see that passing by reference also may save memory because functions access data stored in the same memory locations as in Fig. 4.2.

CONSTANT REFERENCE

In the above program, the variable `radius` was passed by value. It required two memory locations, one relating to `main()` and another relating to `circle_area_peri()`. However, we could pass the input parameter `radius` by `const` reference as in

Passing data by const reference is safe and memory efficient.

```
    ...
void circle_area_peri(const float& radius, float& area, float&);
    ...
void circle_area_peri(const float& rad, float& ar, float& peri)
    {
    ...
    }
```

This results in saving one memory space, as well as making sure that the value of `radius` is not modified intentionally or unintentionally in the `circle_area_peri()` function. The compiler will flag an error if any attempt is made to modify `rad` in the `circle_area_peri()` function.

OVERLOADED FUNCTIONS

The same name can be used to define many functions. Such functions are said to be overloaded. An overloaded function works differently depending upon the type and number of arguments passed to it. The following example uses different types of arguments and will clarify the idea of an overloaded function:

```
//Filename overload.cpp
//Demonstration of carrying out absolute value
//function using the overload capability

#include <iostream.h>
#include <math.h>

int my_abs(int i)
    {
    if (i < 0)
      return -i;     // If negative change sign
    else
      return i;
    }  //End of my_abs function for integer values

float my_abs(float x)
    {
    if (x < 0)
      return -x;  // If negative change sign
    else
      return x;
    }  //End of abs function for floating values

int main()
    {
    float temperature = -33.5;
    int difference = -10;

//Print the absolute value of temperature
    cout << "\nmy_abs(temperature) = " << my_abs(temperature);

//Print the absolute value of difference
    cout << "\nmy_abs(difference) = " << my_abs(difference);
    return 0;
    }  //End of main
```

The C++ compiler accepts overloading of functions if the parameter lists are distinct.

Both functions are called my_abs(), but the parameter types are different. In one case it is integer and in the other it is float. In the main() function, depending upon the type of the argument, the appropriate function is called by the compiler. Because of this feature the function my_abs() is called an overloaded function. You may have discovered that, in C++, it was necessary to use iabs() for integer values and fabs() for floating point values.

DEFAULT ARGUMENTS

In C++ it is possible to call a function without specifying all its arguments. Study the following example which calculates the hypotenuse of a triangle even if values for base and side are not supplied when calling the function. Note that the default values for the function arguments must have been declared in the function prototype.

```
//Filename defarg.cpp
//Calculates the hypotenuse of right-angled triangle

#include <iostream.h>
#include <math.h>

float hypotenuse(float base=3, float side=4); //Function declaration
                                  //or function prototype. There are
                                  //2 parameters of float type and
                                  //the function returns a float type
//float hypotenuse(float =3, float =4); //Will also work!

int main()
      {
      float base,side,hypot;
      hypot = hypotenuse(); //Calling the
                              //function hypotenuse()
                              //with default values from the
                              //declaration
      cout << "\nThe hypotenuse of a triangle with base = 3"
           << " and side = 4 " << " is= "
           << hypot << "\n";
      cout << "\nPlease enter the base of"
           << " the right-angled triangle to calculate"
           << " the hypotenuse\n";
      cin >> base;
      hypot = hypotenuse(base); //A single argument is passed!
      cout << "\nThe hypotenuse of a triangle with base= "
           << base << " and side= 4 " <<  " is= "
           << hypot << "\n";
      return 0;
      }               //End of main

//function definition for hypotenuse()
float hypotenuse(float bas, float sid) //Different variables used to
                                  //show that they are different
                                  //from the variables base and
                                  //side in main function.

      {

      float hypo = sqrt(bas*bas + sid*sid);   //Calculates
                                          //hypotenuse
                                          //and stores
                                          //the result
                                          //in a new variable
                                          //hypo.
```

```
    return hypo;       //This is the result returned in the name
                       //of the function hypotenuse in the
                       //main program
    }                  //End of function hypotenuse()
```

In the above program, the first call to the `hypotenuse` does not have input arguments. However, because we had specified default values for these arguments in the function declaration, those values are used for calculating the hypotenuse. In the second call, we pass on only one argument, for the base. The other value is automatically the default value. Note that the missing arguments are assumed to be the variables at the end of the argument list.

INLINE FUNCTIONS

If you have functions that are used often, and are very short (less than 2–3 lines), then you can consider defining them as inline functions. When you *define* the function *before* the function call and declare it as *inline,* the compiler simply inserts the function code wherever the function is called. This saves the overhead involved in calling the function many times. Using inline functions may reduce execution time but may increase the size of the executable program. The syntax is

> `inline` *type function_name (parameter list)*
>   { *body of the function* }

Note that sometimes the compiler might ignore your inline instruction because it has decided that the function is too large to be an inline function.

SCOPE OF IDENTIFIERS AND STORAGE CLASSES

In the previous chapter we referred to the scope of a variable. Recall that identifiers are simply the names of variables, functions, classes, etc. Now that we have introduced functions we need to extend this concept. One of the attributes of an identifier is its storage class. The storage class defines both the visibility boundary of the identifier (scope) and its lifetime. The three storage class specifiers that we need to know are (i) automatic, (ii) static, and (iii) external or global. Automatic variables are created when the block in which they are defined is entered, they exist while this block is active, and they are destroyed when the end of the block is reached. Local variables are by default automatic.

Variables in an argument list have local (function) scope.

    The keyword used to specify the automatic storage class is `auto`. The keywords `extern` and `static` are used to declare variables and functions of the static storage class. These identifiers exist from the beginning of the program and retain their values until the program ends. Global variables and function names default to the

A variable can be declared many times in a program with the extern *specifier but must be defined only once in a program!*

storage class specifier `extern`. The keyword `extern` may be needed when a program is composed of multiple files. It makes an identifier defined in file available to other files. Global variables are declared by placing their declaration outside any function definition. Local variables can be defined as belonging to the static storage class using the keyword `static`.

The visibility of a variable is defined by its scope. An identifier declared outside any function is visible to all functions from the point where it was declared until the end of the file. Examples of these are global variables, function definitions, and function prototypes declared outside any function. An identifier declared within a block is visible only from the point where it was declared until the end of the block. Consider the following example.

```cpp
//Filename storclas.cpp
//Demonstrates the storage classes

const float PI=3.141592;   //A global constant PI. Available
                           //all through the program storclas.cpp
                           //(You can use M_PI instead of pi. This
                           // example is only for illustrating global
                           // constants!!)

void func();              //Function declaration

int main()
    {
    long student_number = 930101; //Automatic variable
    func();           //Call to function
    func();           //Another call to function
    return 0;
    }
//Function definition

void func()
    {
    int local_number;            //Automatic variable
    local_number = 25;           //Whatever is stored in this
                                 //variable gets lost when
                                 //function completes execution
                                 //because the memory space
                                 //allocated is removed

    static int number_of_calls=0; //Static variable
                                 //remembers the current
                                 //value between function
                                 //calls

    number_of_calls++;
    }
```

Automatic or local variables are not initialized automatically by the compiler.

The compiler does not initialize automatic or local variables by default, and hence should always be initialized in a program. By limiting the visibility and lifetime of variables using functions, we are able to modularize the program, prevent accidental changes to their values, and use memory space efficiently. Static variables have the same scope as automatic or local variables (that is, they are visible only within the block or file in which they are defined), but their lifetime is the program's lifetime. For example, in the above program, the static variable `number_of_calls` is used to keep an account of the number of calls to the function `func()`. A static variable is initialized only once during the program's lifetime. On the other hand, automatic variables are initialized every time the function is called.

Initialization of static variables is done only once by the compiler.

Lastly, external or global variables have the lifetime of the entire program and are visible throughout the entire program following their declaration. Unlike automatic variables, external or global variables are initialized to zero if no initialization statement is written in the program. It is good programming practice to limit the use of global variables to cases where they are really necessary.

CASE STUDY (FUNCTIONS AND DATA PASSING)

Reservoir System Simulator

This is the same problem solved in the case study of the previous chapter. But, for the convenience of the reader we will repeat the problem solving steps. Here, we will show how functions can be represented using structure charts. These diagrams are helpful during implementation.

1. Problem analysis

A single reservoir system is to be simulated using data on the system characteristics such as maximum and minimum storages and initial storage. The simulation is to be done for all periods for which data for demand and inflow are input by the user. The required results such as outflow, spill, and storage are calculated for each period. The results are output at each period.

Problem statement: Simulate a single reservoir system with user-supplied input.

Input/output analysis: The input required is: maximum storage, minimum storage, initial storage; inflow and demand must be given for each period.

The output is: outflow, spill, and final storage in each period.

2. Design

We will use process-based decomposition to solve the problem. Each process is represented by a single function. You may remember that this technique is also called divide and conquer or the top-down design process. Start with the overall (hard) problem and divide it into easier and easier subproblems. The hardest are at the top and the easiest at the bottom. Consider the Level 0 and Level 1 decomposition

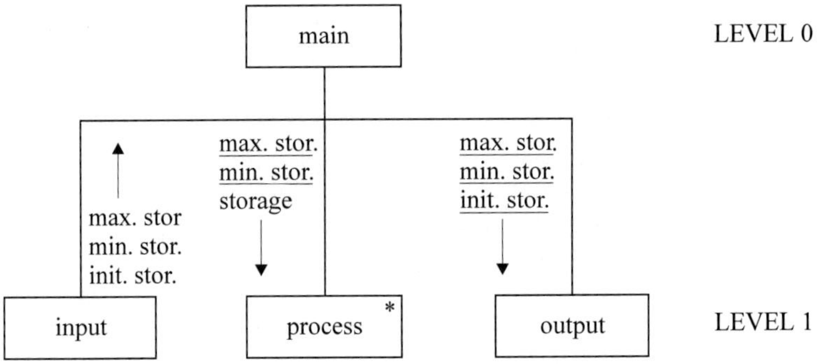

An asterisk in the corner of the box indicates a repetition and a small circle indicates selection.

FIGURE 4.3
Level 0 and Level 1 decomposition structure chart.

shown in Fig. 4.3. The corresponding data flows to the various boxes were filled box by box after drawing the complete decomposition diagram first.

Underlined variables in the structure charts are inputs to functions and should be treated as constants.

Some notational conventions: We use some generic names like main for the main problem, input, process, and output at higher levels to start the problem solving process quickly. However, as we go down the hierarchy, problem-specific names are slowly introduced. In this manner, solutions follow patterns and it is easier to use standard patterns and modify them as the hierarchy deepens than starting from scratch for every problem. In Fig. 4.3, the arrows indicate the flow of data, from tail to head. The variables that are involved in the passing of data are indicated and these will be essentially the parameter list for the respective function. When a variable is underlined, the variable should be protected from any modification in the function to which it is passed. For example, the variable max.stor. (short form for maximum storage), once input by the user, should never be changed and hence remains constant. This is indicated by underlining the variable. When writing the actual function prototype and function header, appropriate types of variables must be specified. There are two possible ways to pass input variables: (i) by value, which requires a local variable in the called function and (ii) by constant reference, which does not require any more additional memory. We will use the second way wherever possible. The third way, passing using pointers, will be discussed in Chapter 9. Note that we are using Jackson notation to indicate loops, that is, an asterisk in the top right-hand corner of the box indicates that the process function will be called many times in the body of the loop.

In Fig. 4.3, the input and output boxes correspond to reading and printing the reservoir system characteristics (like maximum, minimum, and initial storage) as denoted by the appropriate variables. Fig. 4.4 illustrates the details of the second-level decomposition where the read and write boxes correspond to the input data and output for each period, respectively.

The calculate box can be further divided into three boxes as in the previous chapter to indicate the three "if" conditions but because we are focusing on each box as a function, we avoid those additional details here.

We will skip the next two steps, namely, hand example and algorithm design, as they would be exactly the same as in the previous chapter. We will describe the

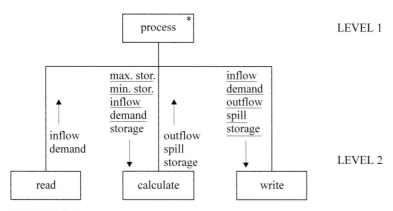

FIGURE 4.4
Level 1 and Level 2 decomposition structure chart.

coding and debugging but now using the concept of developing the individual modules independently.

3. Coding and debugging

Let us first develop the `main()` module. This is necessary because in C++ the `main()` function is where the execution starts. We provide *stubs* which are function declarations and definitions where the definitions may not contain any code except perhaps a simple `cout` statement indicating the execution of the function.

```
//Program 1resfun0.cpp
//Program will simulate a single reservoir system for a given
//demand and inflow series input by the user one by one.
//Uses functions for modularity
//This version has stubs for the first-level functions

#include <iostream.h>
#include <iomanip.h>

//Prototypes for the functions in the first level of decomposition
void system_charac_input(float&, float&, float&);
void system_charac_output(const float&, const float&, const float&);
void process(const float&, const float&, float&);
//Carefully note the correspondence between the above prototypes,
//their parameters, and the diagrams for levels 0 and 1!

int main()
    {

    //
    cout << "Welcome to the Reservoir Simulator\n";

    float max_storage, min_storage, init_storage;
```

```
        //Calls the system_charc_input function

        system_charac_input(max_storage,min_storage,init_storage);

        //Outputs what is read through the system_charc_input function

        system_charac_output(max_storage,min_storage,init_storage);

        float storage = init_storage; //Initial condition of the reservoir

        //Call process to simulate the reservoir

        process(max_storage, min_storage, storage);

        return 0;

        }

void system_charac_input(float& maxsto, float& minsto, float& initsto)
//Precondition: None
//Postcondition: Acceptable max, min, and inital storages available
        {
        }

void system_charac_output(const float& maxsto, const float& minsto,
                          const float& initsto)
//Pre: maxsto, minsto, and initsto should have values
//Post: max, min, and init storages are output
        {
        }

void process(const float& maxsto, const float& minsto, float& storage)
//Pre: maxsto, minsto storage should have been set with
//max > min; max, min >= 0 and
//storage should be set to init. storage >=0.
//Post: outflow, spill, and storage will be calculated for each user
//input for each period.
        {
        }
```

The above program 1resfun0.cpp is a working program but does nothing profound. Before we actually develop any module in detail, what we have done is
to create a working program that reflects Fig. 4.3 showing Levels 0 and 1 of the
decomposition. The prototypes of functions and the current function definitions are
simply stubs that can now be independently developed. If this was a large project
you could send teams of programmers to develop each of the modules (synonymous with functions here) independently. In order to smooth the integration step, we
make sure that each team is aware of the requirements of the other groups by providing them with function stubs as well as, most importantly, the preconditions and

postconditions for each function. The definitions for pre- and postconditions of functions follow next.

- Preconditions: These are conditions that are asserted to be true *before* this function is executed and corresponds to the input data. For example, before the `system_charac_output()` function can be called, the variables `maxsto`, `minsto`, and `initsto` should be set. Before `process()` can be called the preconditions insist on more restricted conditions. For example, `maxsto` should be greater than `minsto` and both should be non-negative. These conditions can be derived from problem analysis and design steps.
- Postconditions: These are conditions that are asserted to be true *after* the function has executed correctly. These conditions could reflect the values of the output variables or the state of the program, including any printed output. In essence, the pre- and postconditions are a contractual agreement between the function user (called a *client*) and the function (called the *server*) and have to be explicit. For example, in the above program, the `process()` function guarantees that, if you satisfy its preconditions, it will calculate correctly the storage, outflow, and spill for each period for the data input by the user.

In addition to the above, you may also see other specifications such as what the function *returns,* what the function *uses,* and how the function can be *trigger*ed. The major advantage of explicitly describing these conditions and their strict enforcement is increased program reliability.

Further coding. We are going to add features to our code to consider also the next level. At this time, we are interested only in function stubs. Add to the function prototypes the following for the Level 2 decomposition.

```
void read_a_period(float&, float&);
void write_a_period(const float&, const float&, const float&,
                   const float&, const float&);
void calc_a_period(const float&, const float&, const float&,
                   const float&, float&, float&, float&);
```

It is clear from Fig. 4.4 that the read box reads two variables (in this case they are of type `float`) which should be available for the level above. We pass these variables by reference. The write box requires many variables but because it is not allowed to modify any of them we pass all of them using `const` reference. The calculate box data requirement includes variables that cannot be modified, as well as variables that are calculated or modified. We pass the latter by reference and the others by `const` reference. The function definitions that need to be added to the above program are:

```
void read_a_period(float& inflow, float& demand)
//Pre: None
//Post: inflow and demand are read from the user
   {
   }
```

```
void write_a_period(const float& inflow, const float& demand,
                    const float& outflow, const float& spill,
                    const float& storage)
//Pre: outflow, spill, and storage are set
//Post: outflow, spill, and storage are output to the monitor
  {
  }


void calc_a_period(const float& max_storage, const float&
                   min_storage, const float& inflow,
                   const float& demand, float& storage,
                   float& outflow, float& spill)
//Pre: storage,inflow and demand have non-negative values
//Post:outflow, spill, and new storage will be calculated
  {
  }
```

However, according to our design in Fig. 4.4, the above functions are called only by the process function. Hence we will modify the process function as follows:

```
void process(const float& maxsto, const float& minsto,
             float& storage)
//Pre: maxsto, minsto storage should have been set with
//max > min; max, min >= 0 and
//storage should be set to init. storage >=0. Note that these
//are checked in the system_charac_input() function and are not
//shown above.
//Post: outflow, spill, and storage should be calculated for
//each user-input for each period.
  {
  float inflow, demand, outflow, spill;

  //Read user data for each period in a loop

  read_a_period(inflow, demand);

  calc_a_period(maxsto, minsto, inflow, demand, storage,
                outflow, spill);

  //Write output for each period

  write_a_period(inflow, demand, outflow, spill, storage);

  }
```

The details regarding the loop can be worked out when developing the process module. Once we have completed the addition of the above stubs, the resulting program is complete in the sense of our problem decomposition described earlier. In other words, the high-level design is complete. The program is now ready for detailed module development. We will show the development of only one module, `calc_a_period()`, because the detailed code of each function would be similar to the code we wrote in the last chapter. The complete program is supplied on the diskette as `1resfuin.cpp`.

   Coding and debugging of calculate module. This module requires maximum storage, minimum storage, demand, and inflow and will calculate the storage, outflow, and spill according to the system dynamics given by the three "if" conditions. The implementation is

```
      void calc_a_period(const float& max_storage, const float&
                         min_storage,const float& inflow,
                         const float& demand, float& storage,
                         float& outflow, float& spill)
   //Pre: storage,inflow, and demand have non-negative values
   //Post:outflow, spill, and new storage will be calculated
      {
      float temp_storage; //Used in selecting the case
      temp_storage = storage + inflow - demand;

      if ( ( min_storage <= temp_storage ) &&
           (temp_storage <= max_storage) ) {
         outflow = demand;
         spill = 0.;
         storage = temp_storage;
      }
      else if (min_storage > temp_storage) {
         outflow = storage + inflow - min_storage;
         spill = 0.;
         storage = min_storage;
      }
      else { //This corresponds to max_storage < temp_storage
         outflow = demand;
         spill = storage + inflow - demand - max_storage;
         storage = max_storage;
      }
      }
```

However, in order to call this function and debug we need to modify the `process()` function as follows:

```
   void process(const float& maxsto, const float& minsto,
                float& storage)
   //Pre: maxsto, minsto storage should have been set with
   //max > min; max, min >= 0 and
   //storage should be set to init. storage =0.
   //Post: outflow, spill, and storage would be calculated for each user
   //input for each period.
      {
      float inflow, demand, outflow, spill;
```

```
      //The following are for development purposes of
      //calc_a_period() only!
      inflow = 10; demand = 10;
 //   inflow = 20; demand = 40;
 //   inflow = 30; demand = 0;
      storage = 10; //Corresponds to the initial storage
                    //at first period.
 //   storage = 0;  //At third period

      calc_a_period(20, 0, inflow, demand, storage,
                       outflow, spill); //maxsto and minsto
                                        //are hard coded!

   //Output to check that calc_a_period() works!
   cout << "inflow, demand, storage " << inflow << " "
        << demand << " " << storage;
   }
```

The following is the output you get when you run the program `1rescalc.cpp` on the diskette, which corresponds to the development of the `calc_a_period()` module, for each of the input data taken from the hand example.

```
      Welcome to the Reservoir Simulator
      Initial Storage = 10
      inflow, demand, outflow, spill, storage 10 10 10 0 10

      Welcome to the Reservoir Simulator
      Initial Storage = 10
      inflow, demand, outflow, spill, storage 20 40 30 0 0

      Welcome to the Reservoir Simulator
      Initial Storage = 0
      inflow, demand, outflow, spill, storage 30 0 0 10 20
```

From inspecting the output and the results from the hand example, it looks like the `calc_a_period()` function seems to be doing its work! It is now possible to develop each module independently, in the same way as above. In fact, the team that developed the `calc_a_period()` function has almost solved the problem of the `process()` module development team!

4. Integration

There are two basic kinds of integration, depth first and breadth first. Secondly, integration could be carried out top-down or bottom-up through the different levels of modules. In many cases it is a mixture of any of the above. We actually developed the code breadth first and then changed to depth first along one of the integration paths that concerned the process module.

5. Testing and validation

See the discussion in the previous chapter which also applies to this program. Testing during and after integration is also necessary because it is possible that some modules do not adhere to their pre- and postconditions.

Although we solved the same problem in the previous chapter, the major advantage of modularization for solving complex problems is the delegation of work to different teams and the development of modules in parallel. We used the high-level decomposition diagrams to develop stubs for each of the required functions. The program developed here has the structure of Solution 2 discussed in Chapter 1. The program developed in the previous chapter solved the entire problem in a single module or function, which was the structure of Solution 1 in Chapter 1. The advantage of Solution 1 was its simplicity (compare `1ressim.cpp` with `1resfuin.cpp`) and the major disadvantage was the impracticality of solving a large or complex problem in that manner. On the other hand, the major disadvantage of Solution 2 developed here (whose design adhered to the principles of structured programming and modularization) is the increased data passing (for example, the calculate function requires seven data arguments to be passed) between various functions. Because of this, the coupling and hence the program complexity increase. Recall that a good design should minimize coupling. We hope to show that, using object-oriented design and programming (as in Solution 3 in Chapter 1), this major disadvantage is quite easily overcome through encapsulation of data and functions into objects. This will be described later in Chapter 7.

Modularization and the use of functions are good for solving complex problems. However, functions increase program complexity due to the need for data passing resulting in coupling.

SUMMARY

The major reason for functions in structured programming languages and in OOP languages is to help organize the program. Functions allow large problems to be divided into many small subproblems. Typically, a function is created for a single purpose, which is to solve one small subproblem. To solve the entire problem using many small functions, it is necessary to pass information to functions, as well as get results back from functions. This is done by passing arguments and returning values, resulting in module coupling.

The simplest functions neither take arguments nor pass results back to the calling functions. All functions have to be declared or prototyped before they can be called. In addition, the functions have to be defined somewhere in the program. The alternative method of defining the function before calling it is less flexible (and not always possible). Arguments to functions can be passed by value, where the function works with the copy of the value sent. Often, a function returns a single result of a given type. To return more than one result, arguments can be passed by reference. When arguments are passed by reference the function has access to the value of the corresponding variable in the calling program, so it can change its value. Passing arguments by reference is helpful for saving memory space, and for returning more than one result from the function.

Overloaded functions have the same name but do things differently depending upon the type and number of arguments. An inline function is a function whose body is inserted into appropriate places (that is, whenever the function is called) by the compiler and hence has to be defined before the call. If functions are declared with values for their arguments, then those functions can be invoked without arguments. The default values are the values from the declaration.

The scope of a variable defines the boundaries of variables and storage class defines both the scope and the lifetime of a variable. Automatic variables are local variables which are available in the block or the function in which they are defined and their lifetime is the same as that of the function block. The values stored in automatic or local variables are lost when the function block is exited. Static variables have the same visibility as automatic variables but their lifetime equals the program's lifetime. External or global variables are visible throughout the program from the point of declaration and their lifetime also equals the program's lifetime. Global variables should rarely be used due to the possibility of accidental corruption.

REVIEW QUESTIONS

1. The purpose of a function is to ＿＿＿＿＿ programs in structured programming languages.

2. A function, like a variable, cannot be used unless it has been ＿＿＿＿.

3. The function declaration syntax is ＿＿＿＿ ＿＿＿＿ (＿＿＿＿).

4. The parameter list in a function declaration need not have names. True or false?

5. A function is invoked by using its name and passing the appropriate arguments. True or false?

6. There are three ways to pass arguments to functions. They are ＿＿＿, ＿＿＿, and ＿＿＿.

7. A function result is returned and it can be assigned to another variable whose type is the same as the result, as in: `double x = sin(y);`. True or false?

8. The function definition contains the program statements that indicate the work the function has to do. True or false?

9. Write a function `foo()` that will take three integer arguments, each of which is passed by value, by reference, and by constant reference, respectively. It will also return the sum of the three integers.

10. Header files may contain function ＿＿＿＿＿s.

11. Overloaded functions are functions with the same ＿＿＿ but different sets of ＿＿＿(s).

12. If function declarations have initialized parameters, they will always be used. True or false?

13. Passing arguments by default can be done for only one argument in the list. True or false?

14. If there are three default arguments in the function declaration and if the function call has two, then the _____ argument will be considered as the default argument.

15. Inline functions speed up / slow down execution. Experiment and discuss.

16. What is a precondition?

17. Write a table where the rows indicate storage classes and the columns indicate lifetime, visibility, initialized to zero or not, and use.

18. What is a postcondition?

19. The extent of module coupling may be indicated by the number of parameters in the function header. True or false?

20. Why should preconditions and postconditions be specified for every function?

21. Discuss: modularity using functions, complex problems, program complexity.

EXERCISES

1. Write a function that will round up a float variable to an integer and return an integer result.

2. Do the same as in Exercise 1 except the input is double and the return type is long. Use function overloading and test it with a `main()` function.

3. Write a function `sort5(int &a1, int &a2, int &a3, int &a4, int &a5)` that will produce the result $a1 \leq a2 \leq a3 \leq a4 \leq a5$.

4. Write a recursive function to calculate gcd(a,b), the greatest common divisor (gcd) of the integers a and b where at least one of them is nonzero and both are non-negative integers. Euclid's algorithm for this problem is

gcd(a,b) = a, if b = 0
else
gcd(a,b) = gcd(b, a % b)

     A recursive function is a function that can call itself. Note that for at least one input condition the function should terminate the process of calling itself, as in the first condition of Euclid's algorithm.

5. Write a C++ program to find the root of a nonlinear equation using the Newton method. Suppose we want to solve $f(x) = 0$, that is, find the value of x, called the root, that satisfies the equation. The Newton method is described below:

Step 1:   start with an initial guess x
Step 2:   while abs(f(x)) > epsilon (for example, 0.0001)
            x = x − [f(x)/f'(x)]
            where f'(x) is the first derivative of f(x) with respect to x.

Use the five-step design process to develop a C++ program that can be used to solve for $f(x) = x^2 - 2$. Show a detailed test of your program starting with the initial guess of $x = 1.1$ for three iterations.

6. Mechanical engineers have defined rotational inertias for different bodies as shown in Table 4.1, where M is the total mass of the body.

TABLE 4.1

Name	Rotational inertia	Parameters
Hoop about cylinder axis	$I = MR^2$	R – radius
Annular cylinder about cylinder axis	$I = \dfrac{M}{2}(R_1^2 + R_2^2)$	R_1 – inner radius R_2 – outer radius
Solid cylinder about central cylinder	$I = \dfrac{MR^2}{4} + \dfrac{Ml^2}{12}$	R – radius l – length

Write a program that will ask users which of the above three types they want to choose. After getting that information, the program will choose the correct function and get from the user the appropriate input to provide the required output.

7. Electrical engineers have classified radio waves according to their frequencies and a partial list is presented in Table 4.2. Your program will ask the user for the frequency value and will print the name of the frequency. Use as many functions as possible.

TABLE 4.2

Range of frequencies	Wave name
0	INVALID
(0–300]	Extra Low Frequency
(300–3000]	Voice Frequency
(3000–30000]	Low Frequency

8. Write a C++ program that can perform arithmetic operations on fractions. It takes in two integer numbers that represent a fraction, that is, fraction 4/13 is entered as two integers: 4 and 13. The program can add, subtract, multiply, or divide. The resulting fraction should also be printed using two integers. Show the five-step design process.

9. The Fibonacci series is given by f(i) = f(i − 1) + f(i − 2), i = 2,3,4, ... where the first few terms are 1,1,2,3,5,8, ... Develop two C++ functions, one of which uses recursion. Run each of them a large number of times in a loop and discuss the merits and problems of using recursion from the point of view of program clarity and program performance.

10. (a) Write a C++ function that will print an ∗ at any given column in a line of 60 characters.

(b) Write a C++ function that will print a horizontal line up to a maximum of 60 characters (and the line cannot go beyond the 60th column) starting at any given column, 1 to 60, in the line. Use the function developed in part (a).

Graph of Angle versus Sine (Angle)

Angle	Sine (Angle)
0	* 0.000e+00
15	* 2.588e-01
30	* 5.000e-01
45	* 7.071e-01
60	* 8.660e-01
75	* 9.659e-01
90	* 1.000e+00

FIGURE 4.5
A sample output.

11. Write a function to print a triangle of any given height or width (as close as possible to an equilateral triangle) using the functions from Exercise 10.

12. Write a program to calculate and graph the sine of an angle, from 0 to a value specified by the user, up to a maximum of 720 degrees. The graph should look as shown in Fig. 4.5.

Show the five-step design process. The program should include as many functions as convenient, for example: a function to round (takes two inputs, namely, the value to be rounded and the number of decimal places to be rounded); a function to output the title; a function to set the x-axis label (maximum five characters); a function to set the y-axis label; a function to draw the part of the axis; and lastly a function to plot the asterisk.

Use the functions developed in Exercise 10 to print the * and the line.

CHAPTER 5

Arrays for Grouping Data of Same Type

An array is a group of items of the same type under one variable name. An individual item in an array is accessed by an array *index*. The grouped data items can be of simple types such as int, float, char, or can be structures and objects which are described in the next two chapters, respectively. The following program introduces a simple array and some array operations. The common array operations we will consider are scanning (that is, going through every element of the array, sometimes called traversing), sorting, and vector and matrix algebra (additions, inner or dot products, multiplications). A practical introduction to algorithms and their complexity is also given. First, the C++ mechanisms for arrays are introduced, followed by some selected problems and the required algorithms. Reading data from and writing to files is also introduced.

An array is an ordered set of elements of same type where the array index indicates the position of the element within the array.

ONE-DIMENSIONAL ARRAY

An array is an ordered set of elements where each element is of the same type. As shown in Fig. 5.1, a float array is a set of float variables with the array index (the integer value in the square brackets) indicating the order in which the element is stored. The following example uses a pair of one-dimensional arrays of types float and integer, respectively, and obtains the average of all the elements in the float array. We need to scan the array in order to access each of its elements.

```
//Filename: Arraver.cpp
//Calculates the average of an array of numbers

#include <iostream.h>

const int MAX = 5;  //Size of array
```

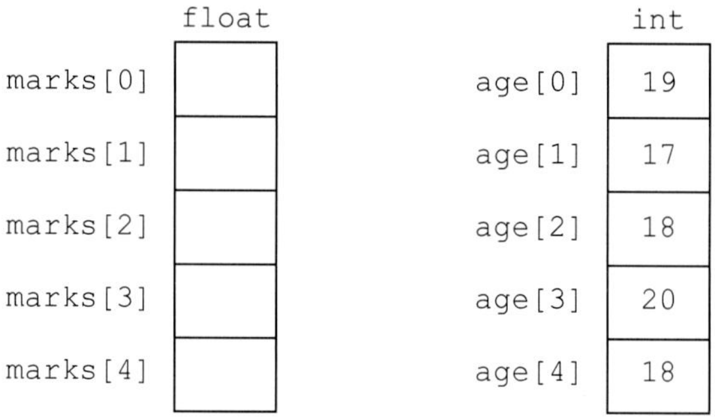

FIGURE 5.1

Allocated memory and its contents for the two arrays `marks[]` and `age[]` just before the second `for` loop.

```
int main()
  {
  int age[] = {19,17,18,20,18};  //Initialization of an array

  for (int i=0; i<MAX; i++)
    cout << "\nElement ["<< i  //Outputs all the array elements
        << "] = " << age[i];    //of age[] with its array index

  float marks[MAX];  //Define array of five elements
  float sum = 0.0;
  for (int j=0; j<MAX; j++)
    {
    cout << "\nEnter Mark " << (j+1) << ", please: ";
    cin  >> marks[j];
    sum += marks[j];        // Sums the marks
    }
  float average = sum/MAX;

  cout << "\nThe average of the marks is = " << average;
  return 0;
  }
```

Notice that the starting value of the array index is 0 and the end value is MAX − 1

A partial output of the program is

```
Enter Mark 1, please: 79
```
                                User enters the marks one by one
```
Enter Mark 2, please: 77

Enter Mark 3, please: 78

Enter Mark 4, please: 80

Enter Mark 5, please: 78

The average of the marks is = 78.4
```

To define the one-dimensional array `marks` in the above program, the number of elements in the array (or size of the array) MAX is written within square brackets following the array name marks[] of type float. But you can also initialize an array, as we have done with the array age[]. In this case you do not need to specify the size. The important thing to note is that the array elements are referenced using array indices *starting from 0 to the size of array minus 1* (refer to Fig. 5.1 which shows the memory allocated just before the execution of the second for loop in the program). Notice that in most other programming languages array indices start from 1. In C and C++ array indices start from 0, so when we refer to marks[2] we are referring to the third element in the array. An array element is accessed using the syntax *array name[array index]*.

MULTIDIMENSIONAL ARRAYS

In C++, arrays can be of any dimension. A table or a matrix can be a two-dimensional array and an array of tables can be a three-dimensional array. In the next program we present two-dimensional array examples.

```
//Filename: matintro.cpp
//Introduction to 2-dimensional arrays (matrices)

#include <iostream.h>

const int ROWS = 2, COLS = 3;

int main()
    {
    int mat1[ROWS][COLS]; //Defining a matrix of size 2 × 3
    int mat2[][COLS] = { {1,2,3},
                         {4,5,6} }; //Initialization of a matrix

    for (int i=0; i<ROWS; ++i)
        {
        cout << "\n";                    //Start a new line for each row
        for(int j=0; j<COLS; ++j)
            {
            mat1[i][j] = mat2[i][j];  //Assigning values to mat1 matrix
            cout << " " << mat1[i][j];
            }
        }
    return 0;
    }                                    //End of main
```

In C++ there is no limit to the number of dimensions possible.

Notice how the new matrix gets its values through assignment statements in a nested for loop. In the above program, we cannot use mat1 = mat2. To do that you need to define matrices as objects as described in Chapter 7. Once again, the indices of the matrices go *from 0 to size of the array minus 1* of the corresponding dimension! Matrices also can be thought of as arrays of arrays. Note that the first dimension of a multidimensional array need not be specified at initialization nor in function prototypes and definitions.

ARRAYS AS FUNCTION ARGUMENTS

Either of the following two statements can be used to prototype a function with a matrix as an argument.

```
void show_matrix( int [ROWS][COLS]);    or
void show_matrix( int [][COL]);
```

The following is the function call where mat1 is a matrix passed as an argument.

```
show_matrix(mat1);
```

Arrays are by default passed by reference. In fact, the array name mat1 represents the *memory address* where the array starts, a concept that will become clear when we study pointers in Chapter 9. For now, however, you can consider the above call as equivalent to passing by reference, as in the case of variables. That is, the same array is used both in the calling function and in the called function. But in the case of the function show_matrix() you could use a different name for the matrix mat1 as shown below in the function definition, as we saw in passing by reference for variables. But, note that no & is used in the parameter list. The function definition starts with

```
void show_matrix( int matrixx[ROWS][COLS])
```

where we assume that ROWS and COLS are global constants, and that matrixx in the show_matrix() function is an alias for mat1 in the main() function.

NO ARRAY BOUNDS CHECK

In C and C++, if you inadvertently access array elements beyond the maximum you have specified, neither at compile time nor at the execution time will you get any error message. Sometimes, the program will even work according to what you expect. However, there is no guarantee that it will always do so and most often the data beyond the bounds could be written anywhere in memory, causing the program to crash. So watch out! The alternative is to use a C++ array class from a class library provided by either the compiler vendor or other third-party class library vendors.

ARRAY OF CHARACTERS (A.K.A. STRINGS)

Arrays of characters are used to store and manipulate strings as shown in the program below.

```
//Filename string.cpp
//Demonstration of strings

#include <iostream.h>
#include <string.h>
```

```
const int MAX = 9;      //Size of the string array

int main()
    {
    char str1[MAX];     //Defining a string str1[].
    char str2[] = "Learning is not a Spectator Sport"; //A string
                                                        //constant
```

char

str1[0]	W
	.
	.
	.
str1[7]	o
str1[8]	\0

```
    cout << "\n" << str2 << "\n";
    for (int i=0; i<strlen(str2); ++i) //Function to find
        cout << str2[i];               //string length
    cout << "\nPlease Enter A String\n";
    cin >> str1;  //Enter Waterloo (8 characters long)
    cout << "\nYou Entered: " << str1;
    for (i=0; i<MAX; i++)
        cout << "\nIndex i = " << i << " " << str1[i];
    return 0;
    }   //End of main
```

Character arrays are very similar to other arrays (see figure where a null character is used as the last character to indicate end of string), and just as in other arrays, exceeding the array bound can cause unpleasant results! For example, if the user were to input something longer than eight characters in the above program, parts of memory *not allocated for str1* could be overwritten (depends on the compiler), with unpredictable (and possibly disastrous) consequences. For this reason, it is a *bad idea* to use cin>> to input strings. Instead, use the following syntax:

```
    cin.getline(str1, MAX);      //Second parameter indicates
                                 //the length of our array.
```

The getline() function will only accept the first (MAX-1) characters of the input. Why only MAX-1 characters and not MAX? The usable space in the character array has to be reduced by one character because a null character is stored at the end of each string to indicate its end. Therefore, when manipulating strings, you have to remember to add a null character ('\0') at the end of the string. However, before writing a function for manipulating strings, check to see if one exists already. The standard library has many such functions—for example, the function strncpy(str2,str1,n) can be used to copy string str1 to string str2. The variable n indicates the length of the str2 array. Note that you cannot use str2=str1, unless they have been declared as objects allowing the assignment operation. You could use a statement similar to the following to output a string if the last character of the string is the null character:

```
        cout << string_name;
```

READING DATA FROM A FILE

Data files are used when there is a large amount of data to be input or output. Such files may contain data in various formats. Text (or ASCII) and the binary format are most common. The following example illustrates how data can be read from a file containing data in text format.

```
//Filename: readfile.cpp
//Reads data from file

//Calculates the average of numbers read.

#include <iostream.h>
#include <fstream.h> //For file input and output

const int MAX = 5;    //Size of array

int main()
    {
    ifstream infile("marks.dat");  //Opens input file marks.dat
                                   //for read only by default!
    float marks[MAX];              //Defining array of five elements
    float average;
    float sum = 0.0;

    if (!infile)  //Checks to see if file opened;
        cout << "ERROR! FILE DID NOT OPEN!!\n";
    else
        {
        for (int j=0; j<MAX; j++)
            {
            infile >> marks[j];    //Reads just like cin!
            sum += marks[j];       //Sums the total marks
            }
        }


    average = sum/MAX;

    cout << "\nThe average mark is = " << average << endl;

    infile.close(); //Closes the file

    return 0;
    }
```

Some other commands for reading data (as available with `cin`) are: `infile.get()`, `infile.getline()`, among others. Consult your compiler manual for help on these commands and other related facilities.

WRITING TO A FILE

The following example shows how data can be written to a file. Note that formatting commands such as setprecision(), setw(), etc. can also be used when writing to files. If you want to store a large amount of data, you should check the compiler manual for commands that help you write binary files, which are stored more efficiently. The disadvantage is that binary files cannot be easily viewed using normal text editors.

```
//Filename: writefil.cpp
//Writes data to a file

#include <iostream.h>
#include <fstream.h> //For file input and output

int main()
    {
    ofstream outfile("out.dat");    //Opens output file marks.dat
                                    //for write by default!

    outfile << "This is an output test\n" << endl;


    return 0;
    }
```

Next we discuss some common problems solved using arrays and their corresponding algorithms.

ALGORITHMS

For processing large amounts of data we often use arrays. Some common processing done with arrays is searching, sorting, and vector–matrix algebra. There are many well-known algorithms for these common problems. Recall that algorithms are steps used to solve a given problem with the key quality that it takes a finite amount of time to complete. Often, there are many possible ways to solve a problem and it is necessary to choose an appropriate algorithm. Algorithms can be compared using their time complexity, as explained below. But different situations may warrant different algorithms; for example, when there is a need for speed you may choose a fast algorithm, when the need is to minimize memory resources you may choose another, if you need simplicity you may choose yet another, and so on. However, the common trade-offs involved in choosing an algorithm are speed, memory requirement, and simplicity.

Evaluating the Efficiency of an Algorithm

It is likely that there are many possible algorithms to choose from. How do we determine which one is more efficient? The efficiency of an algorithm may be measured in terms of how much more effort is needed with respect to an increase in the size of the problem. The effort exerted by an algorithm may relate to the CPU time which, in turn, is related to the number of operations or the amount of memory required to solve the problem, or both. Here we will limit ourselves to the effort required in terms of the number of operations, as memory is seldom a limiting factor these days. For the algorithms we will be considering, the size of a problem is indicated by the number of elements in an array.

The main trade-offs to consider in choosing an algorithm are CPU time, memory requirement, and simplicity.

The big O notation

Suppose the number of elements in an array is N and the time taken to solve a given problem is 1.1N. That is, assume that each element takes 1.1 CPU seconds to process. Because we have N elements it takes a total of 1.1N seconds to solve the problem. If we double the original size of the problem then the time to solve the new problem is simply 2.2N (1.1 * 2N). This information can be displayed in a graphical form and the two data points (the original problem and the larger problem) are joined by a straight line, that is, a linear function as shown by the solid line in Fig. 5.2. Note that, irrespective of the size, there is an initial setup time which we assume as constant for all sizes. Similarly, if a problem takes 2 seconds for every element we will get a relation (the dashed line in the figure) as shown in Fig. 5.2.

The time complexity of the above problem is proportional to N. In mathematical notation this is written as time ~ O(N). [This is somewhat a simplification but sufficient for now.] For large problem sizes, compared to the constant of proportionality (in our examples 1.1 and 2), the time is dominated more by the term within the brackets following the big O. The big O simply reads *order of*. This becomes clearer for problems whose solution increases nonlinearly with respect to the size N as shown in Fig. 5.3 for selected cases. A linear function is also plotted for comparison. It is clear from the figure that we prefer to have algorithms that have a lower

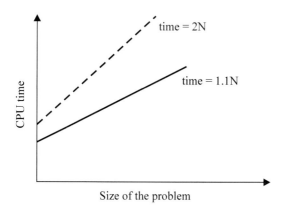

FIGURE 5.2
Algorithms with linear time complexities.

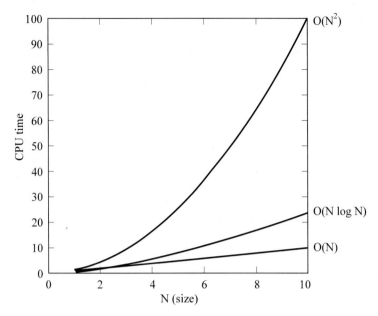

FIGURE 5.3
A comparison of algorithms with linear and nonlinear time complexities.

order of complexity; for example, O(N) is better than O(N log N) which is vastly superior to $O(N^2)$.

Although efficiency is important in selecting algorithms, ease of implementation is no less important. Unless speed or memory is critical, we are better off choosing algorithms that are easier to code, debug, and maintain.

NEED FOR ARRAYS

Arrays are used when a large number of elements of the same type need to be stored in memory (RAM). As a counter-example, in the problem solved by the program readfile.cpp, there was no real need to store all the marks in memory. We could have read each mark, added it to the variable sum, and discarded the mark read because the work of calculating the average does not require the mark any further. The program was used to illustrate reading the file. But, in most operations concerning vector–matrix algebra of arrays, it is customary to keep all the elements of the problem in memory and hence there is a real need for arrays. Similarly, sorting arrays is another common example where arrays are needed. Array operations occurring in these two application areas are illustrated in the next two sections. Because we will be concentrating on array manipulations and on well-known algorithms, we will not follow the five-step design process for these examples.

Vector–Matrix Algebra

A vector is an ordered set of elements (that is, each element has a unique position in the array; it does not necessarily mean that the elements are ordered in any order, ascending or descending) and hence one-dimensional arrays are used to store and manipulate them. A matrix is a rectangular array of elements or array of arrays and hence two-dimensional arrays are used. Each element has an associated unique row and column index. Common operations for vectors that will be described are assignment, addition, scalar multiplication, and dot (or inner) product. Matrix addition and matrix multiplication will also be explained along with the corresponding time complexities.

Examples of vectors and matrices

Examples of vectors and matrices are given below.

$$v1 = [1\ 3\ 5\ 7\ 11], \quad v2 = \begin{bmatrix} 2 \\ 6 \\ 10 \\ 14 \\ 22 \end{bmatrix}, \quad m1 = \begin{bmatrix} 1 & 2 \\ 3 & 4 \\ 5 & 6 \end{bmatrix}, \quad m2 = \begin{bmatrix} 1 & -1 \\ 3 & 4 \end{bmatrix}$$

In the above examples, $v1$ is called a row vector and $v2$ is called a column vector, and they are both stored using one-dimensional arrays in C++. In the computer there is no difference in terms of storage or access between row vectors and column vectors. But, matrices are stored in memory by rows. The memory allocation for matrix m1 is shown in Fig. 5.4; the memory addresses (the unique identification of each cell of memory, see Chapter 2) increase contiguously from top to bottom, that is, in the order m1[0][0] to m1[2][1]. Notice that these indices have 1 less value than in a normal mathematical convention.

Note also that this storage scheme is different from languages like Fortran where the matrices are stored by columns. For most problems these differences are of no consequence; however, if performance is critical then you may have to select your algorithms to suit the style of storage schemes in each programming language.

	int
m1[0][0]	1
m1[0][1]	2
m1[1][0]	3
m1[1][1]	4
m1[2][0]	5
m1[2][1]	6

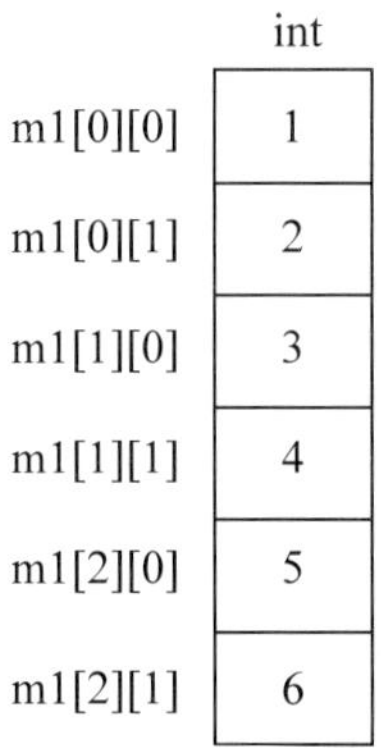

FIGURE 5.4
Memory allocation
for matrix m1.

C++ stores matrices by rows unlike Fortran which stores by columns.

Examples of vector operations

Scalar multiplication of a vector is defined as the multiplication of each element of the vector by a given scalar. In the above example, $2 * v1 = [2\ 6\ 10\ 14\ 22]$. A vector addition is defined as the addition of corresponding elements of two vectors of equal sizes (the same number of elements); using the above example: $v1 + v1 = [2\ 6\ 10\ 14\ 22]$. A dot product of two vectors is defined as the scalar sum of the multiplication of corresponding elements of two vectors of equal sizes. For example,

$$v1 \cdot v2 = 1 * 2 + 3 * 6 + 5 * 10 + 7 * 14 + 11 * 22 = 410$$

We present below the C++ code segment for vector assignment, scalar multiplication of a vector, a vector addition, and a dot product. Our example corresponds to the above numerical examples.

```
//CODE SEGMENTS

//Reading in a vector
for (int i=0; i<MAX; ++i)
    cin >> v1[i];  //Initialization
...
//Assignment of a vector
for (int i=0; i<MAX; ++i)
    v2[i] = v1[i];  //Assignment
...
//Scalar multiplication
for (int i=0; i<MAX; ++i)
    v2[i] *= 2; //Scalar multiplication
...
//Vector addition
for (int i=0; i<MAX; ++i)
    v2[i] = v1[i] + v1[i]; //Addition and assignment
...
//Dot (Inner) product of two vectors
int dotprod = 0;       //Initialization of dotprod to zero
                       //which is used to accumulate the
                       //element by element multiplication
for (int i=0; i<MAX; ++i)
    dotprod += v1[i]*v2[i]; //Dot product
```

Time complexity. The time complexities of the above four problems are $O(N)$ because the time increases only linearly with increasing problem size, which is given by the maximum value of the loop index.

Examples of matrix operations

A matrix addition of two matrices is defined only if both matrices are of the same size. An example is

$$m1 + m1 = \begin{bmatrix} 1 & 2 \\ 3 & 4 \\ 5 & 6 \end{bmatrix} + \begin{bmatrix} 1 & 2 \\ 3 & 4 \\ 5 & 6 \end{bmatrix} = \begin{bmatrix} 2 & 4 \\ 6 & 8 \\ 10 & 12 \end{bmatrix}$$

The resulting matrix has elements obtained by summing the corresponding elements of the operands in the matrix operation. A matrix multiplication of two matrices m1*m2 is possible only if the number of columns of m1 is equal to the number of rows of m2. An example is:

$$m1 \times m2 = \begin{bmatrix} 1 & 2 \\ 3 & 4 \\ 5 & 6 \end{bmatrix} \times \begin{bmatrix} 1 & -1 \\ 3 & 4 \end{bmatrix} = \begin{bmatrix} 1*1+2*3 & 1*-1+2*4 \\ 3*1+4*3 & 3*-1+4*4 \\ 5*1+6*3 & 5*-1+6*4 \end{bmatrix} = \begin{bmatrix} 7 & 7 \\ 15 & 13 \\ 23 & 19 \end{bmatrix}$$

Note that each element of the resulting matrix is obtained by a dot product of a row from matrix m1 with a column from matrix m2. We present below the C++ code segment for matrix multiplication. It corresponds to the above numerical example. Consider the number of rows in m1 as M, its columns as N, and similarly N and K, respectively, for m2. That is, m1 is of size M $\times$ N and m2 is of size N $\times$ K. As you can see, the matrix multiplication is possible because of the match of the inner dimensions.

```
//CODE SEGMENTS

//MATRIX MULTIPLICATION OF MATRICES m1 and m2
//m1 is M by N and m2 is N by K and the result
//is in m3 which is an M by K matrix.
for(int r=0; r<M; ++r) {
    for (int s=0; j<K; ++s) {
      m3[r][s] = 0;
      for (int t=0; t<N; ++t)
        m3[r][s] += m1[r][t]*m2[t][s]; //Dot product
    } // For each column of m3 (fills up a single row)
} //For each row of m3 (fills up all rows)
```

Time complexity. We will assume that both m1 and m2 are square matrices of size N $\times$ N. It is easier to understand the time complexity of matrix multiplication if the matrices are square. Then, from the above example, we know that for each element of the resulting matrix we need one dot product whose time complexity is O(N) (see also the vector example above) which corresponds to the innermost loop. There are N^2 such elements in the resulting matrix. Therefore, the total time complexity is $N^2 \times O(N) = O(N^3)$. As you can imagine, this is a fairly time-consuming work!

Sorting

Ordering an array according to some criterion is a common problem in computing. For example, to print student names and grades we might use an alphabetical order for the names whereas the original data may be stored according to some other criterion such as student number. There are many sorting algorithms and we need to be able to compare their efficiency and choose the one that is most efficient and appropriate for our problem. The section on Evaluating the Efficiency of an Algorithm explains some basic concepts of algorithm complexity. To keep it simple we choose just one easy-to-implement sorting algorithm. In the exercises you will find others. As before, we also show how you can use the code (or pseudocode) to analyze the time complexity. This method is easy to understand but not mathematically rigorous because it depends on your implementation of the algorithm.

Selection sort

The problem is to arrange an array of integers into ascending order. We will assume that we are not short of memory and we will fill a new array which will be the ordered array as desired. The selection sort algorithm is simple: Scan the entire array, find the smallest element in the original array and store it as the first element of the ordered array. Start again and find the next smallest element and copy it as the second element of the ordered array. Continue until the ordered array is complete. This process is shown in Fig. 5.5. Each scanning of the array is called a pass. At the end of each pass, the copied element in the old array is marked so that it does not get chosen again.

First refinement: Let us assume there are N elements in the array.

Selection sort: for pass = 1 to N
                              find the smallest element in the original array
                              copy it to the pass position in the ordered array
                              destroy the copied element in the original array
                          end

Second refinement:

Selection sort: for pass = 0 to N − 1
                              //Find the smallest in the original array
                              small = original_array [0]
                              index = 0

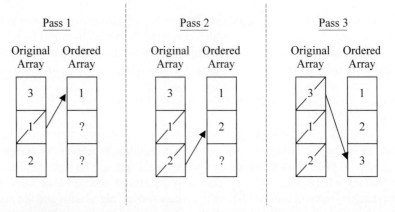

FIGURE 5.5
Selection sort using a new array.

```
for i = 1 to N − 1
    if original_array[i] < small
        small = original_array[i]
        index = i
    end if
end for
//Copy it to the ordered array
ordered_array[pass] = small
//Destroy the copied element in the original array
//That is, make sure it won't be chosen again
original_array [index] = infinity
end for
```

The time complexity in the selection sort used in our example can be evaluated as follows: Always estimate the time taken for the innermost loop first. It is approximately O(N). Why? The loop index goes from 1 to N − 1. The comparison will be done every time. The assignment within the loop is something that can happen a maximum of N − 1 times the first pass, N − 2 times the second pass (because, for sure, at least one of the comparisons will fail due to the destroyed element). The sure thing is the comparison and we will use it for estimating the complexity of the inner loop. Although it is really N − 1, for convenience we will call it O(N). There are N passes and hence the time complexity of the algorithm is $O(N^2)$. There are much better sorting algorithms than this in terms of time complexity; for example, heapsort has an O(N log N) complexity and we know, by using the graph we studied earlier (Fig. 5.3), that it is much faster than the selection sort's $O(N^2)$. Notice that, unlike the examples of vector–matrix algebra we saw before where the time complexity did not depend on the actual values of the array, in sorting problems the time complexity depends also on the actual values. Because of this problem mathematicians often talk of worst-case complexity versus average complexity. These concepts are outside the scope of the book and the time complexity we normally talk about here is the worst-case complexity. In the next section we discuss common errors that arise when using arrays.

COMMON ERRORS WHEN USING ARRAYS

You may find that when using arrays you seem to be getting more bugs than before and this is not unusual. We will identify some of the common errors; whenever you have a problem consider this list first.

(i) The off-by-one error. Exceeding or not reaching the maximum (or minimum if you are decrementing the loop index) is a common error. Most often we use integers for loop indices that we increment by one (or decrement by one). Hence the name off-by-one error.

(ii) The off-by-one error in storage access. Note that a C++ index starts at 0 and goes to the maximum number of elements minus one.

(iii) Incorrect access because no array bound check is made. For example, your loop index is in the invalid range and you are accessing an array during initialization or assignment.

(iv) When using while or do loops forgetting to increment or decrement the loop index. When using the while or do-while loops make sure that the loop index is changed once every iteration and check whether it should be done at the beginning of the loop or at the end of the loop.

(v) In strings, not remembering that the last element is the null character. This is a special off-by-one error.

(vi) Confusing loop indices and assuming that the computer "understands" the rows and columns of a matrix are some other common errors.

SUMMARY

Arrays are used to put together many items of the same type under one variable name. The individual elements are accessed using array indices. Arrays can be of simple types, or structures, or objects. Multidimensional arrays are possible with a matrix defined as an array of arrays. Passing arrays as arguments is done by its address, and hence, no copies of arrays are stored. Normally, C++ does not do any array bound checks and hence bounds must be checked by the program to avoid any disastrous results. Character arrays are used to store strings; a null character is stored as the last character of the string, to indicate the end. Many string functions exist for the convenient handling of strings.

REVIEW QUESTIONS

1. Define an array rain that can hold 10 values of rainfall available in real numbers.

2. Write a statement that will print the first and last value in the above array.

3. Write a statement that will print the entire array.

4. Define an array to store rain that has fallen for each day of the week in each hour.

5. Write the program statements necessary to read the data in Question 4.

6. C++ stores a table by columns. True or false?

7. Write C++ statements to read your first name and last name and print (i) both names on the same line and (ii) each name on different lines. Hint: cin.get (name,10) reads up to 10 characters in name or up to the newline character, whichever is first.

8. Write the statements necessary to read 10 integer data from a file.

9. Write the statements necessary to write 5 strings to a file.

10. Arrays are passed to functions by reference. Discuss.

11. Can we change the size of the array while the program is executing?

12. What is an algorithm?

13. The complexity of an algorithm is measured by the effort (time and memory) required as a function of the problem size. True or false?

14. An algorithm with $O(\sqrt{N})$ is faster than $O(N)$. True or false?

15. Draw a graph of N versus 2^N and compare it with $O(N^2)$. Discuss.

16. Why can we not use the best sorting algorithm always? Why do we need to know many algorithms?

17. What is the time complexity of a vector–matrix multiplication? That is, in $A \times B$, A is a matrix and B is a vector.

18. Operations common in spreadsheets can be done in C++ using arrays. Discuss.

19. Strings are arrays of characters with a null character as the last character to indicate the end of the string. True or false?

20. Find out what the following string functions do: (i) `strncpy(out, in, MAX)` and (ii) `strncat(orig, add)`.

EXERCISES

1. Write a program with *functions* for (i) vector addition, (ii) inner product (dot product) of two vectors, (iii) matrix addition, and (iv) matrix multiplication. The size and element values of vectors and matrices will be input by the user. Your program will also display the input and output appropriately. Note that arrays you define can be a fixed maximum size which the user cannot exceed.

2. Modify the selection sort algorithm in the text such that only a single array is used. You can use the swapping of two elements to achieve the sorting order.

3. Write a function called `bubblesort(n,x)` which will sort the n elements in array x into an ascending order using the Bubblesort algorithm.

Bubblesort algorithm: The principle of the algorithm is to move the heaviest (largest) to the bottom of the array in a single pass. In order to do that, pairs of elements from top to bottom are compared and exchanged if they are out of order. Therefore, Bubblesort is an exchange sort. Start at the top and compare the two elements of the array (that is, positions 0 and 1) and exchange if necessary. Then do the same with the next two elements starting with index 1, and so on until the end of the array. This is the first pass and at the end of it the largest element will be at the bottom. Start with the second pass similarly and go up to the last element but 1. (Why?) Continue until the array is sorted.

4. Write a function that will read a list of real numbers and calculate the mean and median. Hint: You may need the sorting algorithm for finding the median.

5. Write a function which will take a string from a file and a character as its input and returns an integer which indicates the number of times the character occurred in the given string. Test for many strings.

6. Write a program that can be used to decide who won the election or if there are any ties. The input data file may contain a large list of integers indicating the voters' choice (assume that there are four candidates and hence the values are 1 to 4).

7. Write a program that will read a string of characters and print whether the string read is a palindrome. A palindrome reads the same whether you read it from left to right or right to left, for example `stats`.

8. Write a program that will merge into a new array the contents of two other arrays, each of which is already sorted. The two arrays may have different lengths but the new array length will equal the sum of the other two arrays. Generate at least three test cases: the first array gets exhausted first; the second gets exhausted first; both get exhausted at the same time. An example of the second type is given below. Show that the algorithm used has a linear time complexity (that is, O(N)).

Example: {1 15 26 29} merge with {3 16 24} to get {1 3 15 16 24 26 29}

CHAPTER 6

Structures to Group Data

So far we have seen data of types `int`, `char`, and `float`. These are built-in data types. We used arrays to group data of the same type. What if we have information (or data) that requires us to store details under one variable name but consisting of different types of data? For example, a student record may contain a student number (an integer type), gender information like 'F' for female and 'M ' for male (a character type), and the Grade Point Average (GPA) in the range 0 to 4 (a real number). In Pascal we can use the record type to store these varied types of information under one type called the student_record. Similarly, in C++, we use a structure type which can be a collection of many variable types.

STRUCTURE DECLARATION

In order to specify how the structure is organized the following syntax is used in C++.

```
struct student_record
    {
    long student_number;
    char gender;
    float gpa;
    };
```

Structure syntax:
struct name
{
...
};

Note the keyword `struct` comes first and then the structure name or tag; in the example above it is `student_record`. Within the structure specification we specify the different variables (their names and types) that we want to group under one name. The specifications are enclosed within braces with a semicolon after the end brace. We have just declared what kind of structure we want.

With the declaration the computer is simply asked to note that a new type of variable may be defined, which is yet to be done. For this reason memory space is not yet allocated for this structure type. Memory gets allocated when we define a variable of this structure type as explained next.

STRUCTURE DEFINITION

Let us look at an example program where the structure type as specified above can be used.

```cpp
//Filename: studenre.cpp
//A program demonstrating the use of structure variables.

#include <iostream.h>

struct student_record       //Simply declares the structure
   {
   long student_number;     //There are three data members
   char gender;             //in this structure type
   float gpa;
   };

int main()
   {
   student_record mark_godd;  //Defines a structure variable
                              //similar to defining built-in types


   /*Structure members are accessed using the dot operator*/

   mark_godd.student_number = 93010101;  //Assigns a value to
                                         //the student_number member
   mark_godd.gender = 'M';               //Value for the gender data

   mark_godd.gpa = 3.5;                  //Value for the gpa data

   cout << "\nStudent Number " << mark_godd.student_number;
   cout << "\nGender " << mark_godd.gender;
   cout << "\ngpa " << mark_godd.gpa;
   return 0;
   }
```

An individual data member of a structure variable is accessed using the dot operator

The output of the program is

```
Student Number 93010101
Gender M
gpa 3.5
```

Note that the structure declaration came before the `main()` function. Using structures we are extending the capability of C++ by creating a new data type called the `student_record`. This new data type is available for the entire program. A data member is accessed using the name of the structure variable, `mark_godd`, the dot operator, and the name of the data member, for example a `student_number` as in `mark_godd.student_number = 93010101.`

Just as we can initialize other variables, we can also initialize a structure variable with a single statement:

```
student_record mark_godd = { 93010101, 'M', 3.5 };
```

This single statement can replace the three assignment statements in the first program `studenre.cpp`. Suppose we had defined another structure variable `jane_doe`. Then we can use assignment to assign the data in `mark_godd` to this new variable as shown below:

```
    ...
    ...
      student_record jane_doe;
    ...
    ...
      jane_doe = mark_godd;
```

However, you cannot do arithmetic operations or comparisons with structure variables. At least not yet! We will need the concept of operator overloading in Chapter 7 for such operations.

NESTED STRUCTURES

Suppose one of our desired data members in the student record is the birth date. This is stored as date, month, and year—all separately, using integer numbers. Then we can define a new structure variable as

```
struct birth_date        //Simply specifies the structure birth_date
  {
  int date;              //There are three members
  int month;             //to this structure
  int year;              //Of course, we could have done
                         //this in one line
  };
```

The following program uses the above structure within the original structure.

```
//Filename: neststr.cpp
//A program demonstrating the use of structure variables.

#include <iostream.h>

struct birth_date        //Simply specifies the structure birth_date
  {
  int date;              //There are three members
  int month;             //to this structure. Of course,
  int year;              //we could have done this in one line!
  };
```

```
struct student_record
  {
  long student_number;    //There are now four data members
  char gender;            //to this structure
  float gpa;
  birth_date bdate;       //Structure within structure
  };

int main()
  {
  student_record mark_godd;      //Defines a structure variable

  /*Structure members are accessed using the dot operator*/

  mark_godd.student_number = 93010101;  //Assigns a value to
                                        //the student_number member
  mark_godd.gender = 'M';               //Value for the
                                        //gender member data

  mark_godd.gpa = 3.5;                  //Value for the gpa member

  mark_godd.bdate.date = 28;            //Defines the date of birth
                                        //with date,
  mark_godd.bdate.month = 5;            //month (Do not write 05!)
  mark_godd.bdate.year = 1975;          //and year

  cout << "\nStudent Number " << mark_godd.student_number;
  cout << "\nGender " << mark_godd.gender;
  cout << "\ngpa " << mark_godd.gpa;
  cout << "\nThe birth date is year " << mark_godd.bdate.year
       << " month " << mark_godd.bdate.month
       << " date "  << mark_godd.bdate.date;
  return 0;
  }
```

The output of the program is

```
Student Number 93010101
Gender M
gpa 3.5
The birth date is year 1975 month 5 date 28
```

Note how the dot operator is used twice when accessing structures within structures as in `mark_godd.bdate.date = 28`. The depth of nesting can be many structures, but for clarity it may only be a few. The initialization of the data can be done in a single statement as

```
student_record = { 93010101, 'M', 3.5, { 28,5,1975 } };
```

Note the order of members in this line!

ARRAYS OF STRUCTURES

Arrays containing data items of type structure can be defined and used in the following manner.

```
//Filename: arraystr.cpp
//A program demonstrating the use of arrays of structures.

#include <iostream.h>

const int NSTUDENTS = 4;

struct student_record      //Simply specifies the structure
  {
  long student_number;    //There are three data members
  char gender;            //to this structure
  float gpa;
  };

int main()
  {
  student_record stdrec[NSTUDENTS];   //Defines an array
                                      //of student_records.

  /*Structure members are accessed using the dot operator*/
  for(int i=0; i<NSTUDENTS; ++i)
     {
     cin >> stdrec[i].student_number;
     cin >> stdrec[i].gender;
     cin >> stdrec[i].gpa;
     }
   return 0;
  }   //End of main
```

The above example shows how to access arrays of structures using both the array index and the dot operator.

SUMMARY

Structures allow you to define new data types that are not built into C++. Structures within structures are allowed, and a dot operator is used to access the members of structures. An array of structures can be easily defined. We will rarely use structure variables because objects, defined in the next chapter, can do everything structures can do.

REVIEW QUESTIONS

1. A structure can be used to create a new data type. True or false?

2. A structure can group data items of the same or different types. True or false?

3. A structure declaration starts with the keyword _____ followed by the name of the _____ and followed by a set of braces within which the _____s of the structure are defined.

4. The closing brace of the structure declaration followed by a _____.

5. A structure declaration allocates memory space. True or false?

6. A structure definition allocates memory space. True or false?

7. Individual structure members are accessed with the _____ _____.

8. Write a structure declaration that stores as its members three integers corresponding to hour, minute, and second.

9. Initialize each of the members in Question 8 for noon.

10. Write an array of structures whose elements belong to the structure type in Question 8.

11. Initialize the first element of the structure array in Question 10 with 8:30:45.

12. Write the declaration for a structure whose data members are feet held as an integer and inches held as a real number.

13. Declare an array of structures in Question 12 and initialize the first one with 10 feet and 3.5 inches.

EXERCISES

1. Create a structure to store time in hours, minutes, and seconds. Design an algorithm for adding two variables `time_1` and `time_2` of type `time`, and store the result in the variable `time_3`.

2. Create a function called `sum_times` whose input arguments are two structures of the type `time` as in Exercise 1. The function should return a value that is the sum of the two input arguments.

3. Modify the function in Exercise 2 to get a new function called `sum_diff_times` such that the function returns both the sum and the difference of the two input arguments.

   Note: You need to follow the five-step design process for the following problem.

4. This problem will help you understand user-defined data types using `struct` and arrays in C++. You have to read the enclosed (on the diskette) copy of a structure (called a record in Pascal) of type `daily_river_flow` containing the river ID and station number (first 8 characters), year number (only 3 characters, for example, 951 for year 1951), month number (2 characters), and the card number. The last integer in the first card indicates the number of days in that month. If no data is necessary, for example when there is no 29 Feb in Year 1951, then the data is given as −1111. Any non-available data is given as −9999. Each of the daily flow takes up 5 characters and there are a maximum of 10 days in a row. Design a program that will store the entire data of a year of a single station in one structure. The program should be able to read and display the entire record as well as print the maximum daily flow for each record. You do not need a sorting routine.

Q02GA015951011	3.74	4.73	11.6	63.4	30.0	21.2	13.6	11.6	9.91	8.50	31
Q02GA015951012	7.16	6.34	5.80	5.38	5.01	4.67	4.81	4.93	5.10	5.21	
Q02GA015951013	13.4	12.3	10.1	8.33	6.82	5.66	4.67	4.42	4.16	3.91	3.68
Q02GA015951021	3.45	3.31	3.14	4.53	5.58	5.21	3.62	4.93	5.01	5.89	28
Q02GA015951022	5.58	5.21	7.79	8.95	8.33	7.79	7.08	7.33	6.60	7.79	
Q02GA015951023	9.63	10.6	12.5	12.7	12.1	14.2	24.3	18.8	−1111	−1111	−1111

CHAPTER 7

Encapsulation of Data
and Functions in Classes

Classes unite data and functions and provide encapsulation.

From previous chapters we have learned to use simple data types such as integers, real numbers, and characters. Arrays helped us handle multiple data items of the same kind. We have learned to define new data types using structures (if you have skipped Chapter 6 on structures, don't worry!). We have seen functions which help organize programs in a modular fashion. In this chapter, we will learn how to define and use classes which encapsulate the concepts of data and functions. Encapsulation protects the user from dealing with unnecessary implementation details when using new data types.

Classes also allow for creation of new data types.

Objects are instances of classes just like an integer variable is an instance of an integer data type. The concept of data hiding is used to protect data and functions of objects from unauthorized use. However, functions are usually provided by the class to allow us to interface with objects of that class. Data hiding and encapsulation are some of the fundamental principles on which object-oriented programming and design are based. The objects we can design with classes can closely resemble real-world objects. These "software objects" can "simulate" in the computer the real-world object's appearance and activities. This is a good time to read Chapter 1 again where we presented the description and merits of object-oriented programming.

A SIMPLE CLASS

Classes encapsulate data and functions together as in Fig. 7.1. The three most important pieces of information about a class are: its *name or identity,* its *data or state* and its *services or behavior* as defined by its *member functions or methods.*

In a class, by default, data members and functions are private to restrict access by nonmembers of the class. Data and functions declared as public are accessible

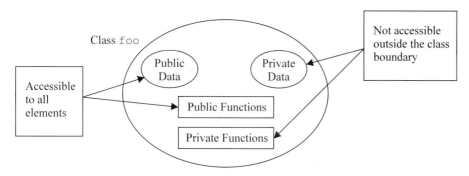

FIGURE 7.1
Encapsulation of data and functions in a class called `foo`.

from outside and inside the class boundary. Once a class is specified, any number of objects of that class type can be defined using the following syntax:

```
foo fooObject1, fooObject2, fooObject3;
```

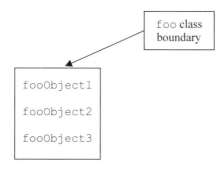

The objects `fooObject1`, `fooObject2`, and `fooObject3` are of `foo` class type. The syntax is similar to declaring integer variables `number1` and `number2` as in

```
int number1, number2;
```

Objects are instances of classes.

A VECTOR CLASS

The following example shows the syntax for specifying a two-dimensional vector class `vector`; the concepts of member functions, privileges of member functions, how to use a class, and data hiding are also discussed. A two-dimensional vector has a pair of coordinates (x, y), where x and y are some real numbers. The addition of two vectors $v1 = (x1, y1)$ and $v2 = (x2, y2)$ is defined as $v1 + v2 = (x1 + x2, y1 + y2) = v3$, a new vector. For example, if $v1 = (1.5, 2.5)$ and $v2 = (3.5, 4.5)$, then $v3 = v1 + v2 = (5, 7)$. The following program shows how to define vector classes and objects respectively. It also shows how to set the coordinate values of the vector objects and how to display these values.

```
//Filename: vectclas.cpp
//Demonstrates a simple vector class and object

#include <iostream.h>

class vector          //Declares the class
   {
   public:
     void setdata(float x, float y)  //Member function to
                                     //set data
     //Pre:  None.
     //Post: Vector coordinates are defined.
          { xCo=x; yCo=y; }

     void showdata()          //Member function for display
     //Pre:  The vector is defined.
     //Post: The vector coordinates are displayed.
          { cout << "\n(X,Y) = " << "(" << xCo << ","
                 << yCo << ")"; }
   private:
     float xCo, yCo;   //Class data hidden from all except
                       //member functions
   };                  //End of specification (note semicolon)

int main()
   {
   vector v1, v2;        //Two objects v1&v2 are defined

   v1.setdata(1.5,2.5); //Calls member function to set data
                        //in vector object v1
   v2.setdata(3.5,4.5); //Calls member function to set data
                        //in vector object v2

   v1.showdata();     //Calls member function to display data
                      //in vector object v1
   v2.showdata();     //Calls member function to display data
                      //in vector object v2

// cout << v1.xCo;     //Compiler Error! Main() cannot access
                       //private member! Data hiding works!
   return 0;
   }                   //End of main
```

The output of the program is

```
                         (X,Y) = (1.5,2.5)

                         (X,Y) = (3.5,4.5)
```

Declaration of a Class

A class is declared using the keyword `class`. There are three other relevant keywords for class declarations: `private`, `public`, and `protected`. The keyword `protected` will be explained in Chapter 8 on inheritance. The keyword `private` is used to specify the members of the class that are visible only to other members of the same class. Data members of a class should almost always be defined as `private`. In our vector example, xCo and yCo are private data members.

The set of all public methods declared in a class with their names, corresponding parameter lists, and return types is known as the class (object)'s interface. The interface also defines the object's type.

The keyword `public` declares members of the class that are visible outside the class. Access to private data members is provided through public member functions. Public functions constitute the interface to an object. In our vector example, functions `setdata()` and `showdata()` provide access to private data members xCo and yCo. The function `setdata()` can be used to set xCo and yCo to a particular value and the function `showdata()` to print the value of xCo and yCo.

Specifying a class is similar to specifying a structure. Structures can also have member functions. If the keyword `struct` is used, all members are considered public unless the `private` keyword is specified. On the other hand, if the keyword `class` is used, all members are considered private unless the `public` keyword is specified. For clarity, we will use the following convention. Although C++ structures can have member functions, we will reserve the use of member functions to classes only. In classes we will clearly separate the private data and public functions using the respective keyword and we will always place `public` members before the `private` members because this shows the interface first and hides the details, as in

```
class foo
   {
   public:    //Public functions go here
     .....
     .....
   private:   //Private data and functions go here
     .....
     .....
   };
```

Data inside the object is directly accessible to functions inside the object (Fig. 7.2). Public functions in the object provide an interface to the object: they are the only way in which nonmembers can access private data in the object. Objects provide a way to encapsulate data and functions as units and protect the user from dealing with unnecessary implementation details. This concept is called *data hiding* and *encapsulation* in OOP. Software objects can closely represent real-life objects because data and functions operating on the data are represented as a unit. This is one of the major advancements on procedural languages which kept data and functions separate.

An object is a generalized module that has data and provides services through its member functions.

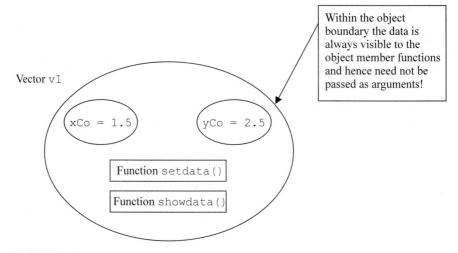

FIGURE 7.2
Object: Vector `v1`.

Using the Vector Class

Let us look at the `main()` function of the example program `vectclas.cpp`. Notice the program statement

```
vector v1, v2;
```

where two objects `v1` and `v2` are defined. These two objects are instances of the class `vector`. Access to the private data of these two vectors is gained using the two object member functions: `setdata()` and `showdata()`.

The dot operator is used to access the individual member function or data of an object.

Notice how the value of the vector can be displayed (Fig. 7.3). This is the notation used to invoke a member function. The function `showdata()` does not need any arguments. It can access the data directly from the object and display it because it is a member function of the object. The function `setdata()` takes two arguments, and uses these values to initialize the vector object.

Function `main()` does not have access to the private data of objects `v1` and `v2` directly. The (commented out) statement

```
cout << v1.xCo;
```

Object name

Member function name

```
v1.showdata();
```

FIGURE 7.3
Calling an object member function.

in the `main()` function would create a compiler error such as: `Private members cannot be accessed`. Thus, the data in the object is hidden from other functions and thus is safe from unauthorized use.

You can see that when we say direct access we mean that visibility already exists (example: object member functions can directly access object data). When we say access, we mean the data is visible if passed as arguments (example: any object passed to a member function of another object of the same class) as shown with an example later. When we say no access we mean that there is no visibility unless public member functions exist to provide access (example: object data for program elements that do not belong to the same class as the object).

When a class is declared no memory is allocated, because the class declaration is considered to be only a type declaration. Memory is only allocated when an object ("instance") of a class is defined ("instantiated").

In some other OOP languages such as Smalltalk, member functions are called *methods*. A call to a member function or method is a *message* sent to the object to perform a particular service on the object's data. The data in an object is also called attributes or characteristics of the object.

CONSTRUCTORS AND DESTRUCTORS

Constructors are special member functions that are automatically invoked when an object is created. For example, when this declaration is encountered during execution, a constructor function is called:

```
vector v1; // Create object v1, an instance of Class vector.
```

A constructor function may perform memory allocation and initialize data members of the object. When the object is no longer needed, a destructor function is called. The destructor can be used to free memory allocated by the constructor. You will need to write constructor and destructor functions if you need to do special processing each time the object is created or destroyed. If you do not explicitly code these functions, the compiler will use default constructors and destructors.

Specifying a constructor

The name of the constructor function is the same as the class. For the vector class in the previous example, the constructor function is defined as:

```
public:
    vector();      // Constructor function.
```

Constructors do not return any values and do not have any type specification. There can be more than one constructor defined for the same class. In the example below we have:

```
public:
    vector(); //Constructor used when vector is
                  //declared without initial values, e.g., vector v1
    vector(float x, float y); //Constructor used when initial
                                  //values are provided in
                                  //declaration, e.g., vector v1(3.0,5.0)
```

Specifying a destructor

The name of the destructor is the name of the class with ~ (tilde) as its prefix. For the vector class in the previous example, the destructor function is defined as:

```
Public:
    ~vector();
```

Destructors do not take any arguments, do not return any values and do not have any return type specification.

Constructors provide convenient means of object initialization.

In the previous example program (`vectclas.cpp`), the function `setdata()` was used to initialize the objects. Alternatively, constructors can take over the work of initialization. A destructor can be used to free any memory used by the object. In general, both constructors and destructors are defined as public. Here is the `vectclas.cpp` program, rewritten using constructors and destructors.

```
//Filename: consdest.cpp
//Demonstrates a simple class and object using constructors
//and destructors

#include <iostream.h>

class vector          //Declares the class
   {
   public:
     vector()          //No-argument constructor
                         //Same name as class
     { cout << "vector constructor called\n";}
```

A good programming practice would be to validate input values within a constructor.

```
     vector(float x, float y)    //Two-argument constructor
                                 //to initialize vector with data
     //Pre:  None.
     //Post: Vector coordinates are defined.
         { xCo=x; yCo=y; }
     void setdata()  //Set coordinates supplied by the user
     //Pre:  None.
     //Post: User-input vector coordinates are set.
         { cout << "Enter X-Coord.= "; cin >> xCo;
           cout << "Enter Y-Coord.= "; cin >> yCo;
         }
```

```
      void showdata()                   //Member function for displaying
      //Pre:  The vector is defined.
      //Post: The vector coordinates are displayed.
           { cout << "(X,Y) = "    //data
                << "(" << xCo << ","
                << yCo << ")\n";
           }
      ~vector()                          //Destructor name is
           { cout <<                     //same as class but with
            "vector Destructor called\n";  //a tilde as a prefix.
           }
   private:
     float xCo, yCo;    //Class data hidden from all except
                        //member functions
   };                          //end of class declaration


vector v0;             //Global object defined just for demonstration.

int main()
   {
   cout << "\nThe main program starts here\n";
   vector v1;            //Object v1 is defined
   vector v2(3.5,4.5); //Object v2 is initialized

   v1.setdata(); //Calls member function to get
                 //data from the user.

   v1.showdata();    //Calls member function to display data
   v2.showdata();

   cout << "Main Program Ends Here!" << endl;
   return 0;
   }                    //End of main
```

The output of the program is

```
vector constructor called              Corresponds to object v0

The main program starts here
vector constructor called              Corresponds to object v1
Enter X-Coord.= 1.5
Enter Y-Coord.= 2.5                     User enters the input 1.5 and 2.5
(X,Y) = (1.5,2.5)
(X,Y) = (3.5,4.5)
Main Program Ends Here!
vector Destructor called               Corresponds to object v2
vector Destructor called               Corresponds to object v1
vector Destructor called               Corresponds to object v0
```

Constructors and destructors are called automatically. If global objects exist, such as vector v0 above, the constructors of such objects are called before `main()` is invoked. Note the first two lines in the output above. If the objects are of the same storage class, the destructors are called in the reverse order of constructor calls.

Note that there are two function definitions for the constructor `vector()` in the above program. Depending on the arguments used when declaring the object, different constructors are called. This is possible due to the ability to overload functions in C++. In the above example, the destructor is activated when the function `main()` ceases to operate. That is, destructors are activated when the code blocks (such as functions) where the objects are created complete execution. This is because objects defined within a function are like local variables and can be accessed only within the function where they are defined. See Chapter 4 on functions for a definition of local variables. The main purpose of destructors is to deallocate memory, and hence they are necessary for efficient memory management. In order to do that we need to know how to use pointers, which are discussed in Chapter 9. Until then our destructors are merely ornamental.

OBJECTS USED AS FUNCTION ARGUMENTS AND RETURN VALUES

The following example program `vector0.cpp` shows how objects can be passed as arguments to functions and how member functions can be defined outside a class using a scope resolution operator (`::`).

```
//Filename: vector0.cpp
//Demonstrates a simple class and object using constructors
//and destructors and how objects are passed as function arguments.

#include <iostream.h>

class vector                       //Specifies the class
   {
   public:
     vector() { }                  //No-argument constructor
                                   //Same name as class
     vector(float x, float y)  //Two-argument constructor
                                   //to initialize with data
          { xCo=x; yCo=y; }

     //Get coordinates from the user
     void getdata();

     //Member function for display
     void showdata();

     // Add two vectors.
     void add_vect(vector, vector);
```

```
    ~vector() {}      //Destructor. Same name as class
                      //but with tilde as a prefix.
    private:
      float xCo, yCo;  //Class data hidden from all except
                       //member functions
    };                //End of specification (note semicolon)

//Get coordinates from the user
void vector::getdata()
//Pre:  None.
//Post: Vector coordinates are defined.
    { cout << "\nEnter X-Coord.= "; cin >> xCo;
      cout << "\nEnter Y-Coord.= "; cin >> yCo;
    }

//Member function for display
void vector::showdata()
//Pre:  The vector is defined.
//Post: The vector coordinates are displayed.
    { cout << "\n(X,Y) = " << "(" << xCo << ","
         << yCo << ")";
    }
// Add two vectors.
void vector::add_vect(vector u, vector v)
//Pre:  The coordinates of the two input vectors are defined.
//Post: Addition of the two input vectors is stored in
//the calling vector.
    {
    xCo = u.xCo + v.xCo;   //Adding the x-coord.
    yCo = u.yCo + v.yCo;   //Adding the y-coord.
    }

int main()
    {
    vector v1, v3;      //Objects v1 and v3 are defined
    vector v2(3.5,4.5); //Object v2 is initialized

    v1.getdata(); //Calls member function to get
                  //data from the user.
    v3.add_vect(v1,v2);

    v1.showdata();   //Calls member function to display data
    v2.showdata();
    cout << "\nThe addition of the above two vectors is = ";
    v3.showdata();

    return 0;
    }                 //End of main
```

The output of the above program is

```
Enter X-Coord.= 1.5
Enter Y-Coord.= 2.5
(X,Y) = (1.5,2.5)
(X,Y) = (3.5,4.5)
The addition of the above two vectors is =
(X,Y) = (5,7)
```

In the `main()` function of the above program notice the line

$$v3.add\_vect(v1,v2);$$

Function `add_vect()` is called to add `v1` and `v2`. The result is stored in `v3`. When objects are passed as arguments, they are passed by value. That is, a copy of the argument is made, so if function `add_vect()` modifies the data in `v1` or `v2` the invoking function (`main()` here) would not be aware of these changes. In Fig. 7.4, you can see that `v1` and `u` are stored in separate memory locations. A change to `u` will not affect `v1`.

Visibility of Data

Once again we will study visibility using an example. Consider the program statement

$$v3.add\_vect(v1, v2);$$

When the function `add_vect()` is invoked for object `v3`, the function has *direct access* to the data in `v3`. We do not need to pass `v3` as an argument. The same function has access to copies of `v1` and `v2` because they are passed as arguments and their data members are accessible because `v1`, `v2`, and `v3` belong to the same vector class.

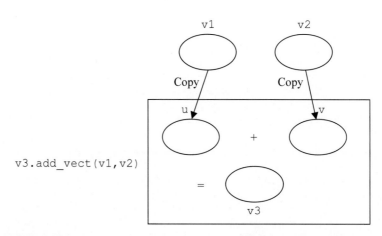

FIGURE 7.4
Member function `v3.add_vect()` adds two vectors (`v1` and `v2`) into vector `v3`.

Scope Resolution Operator (::)

The member function add_vect() is defined outside the class. However, to indicate that this function is really a member function of the class vector we use the scope resolution operator (::), as in the statement

```
void vector::add_vect(vector u, vector v)
              {...} //Function body
```

The scope resolution operator helps to present classes clearly by allowing us to postpone the presentation of details of its member functions until later. Besides, any method defined inside the class declaration is considered inline which may not be appropriate.

There is more than one way to add vectors, as shown in the next example. The example also demonstrates how to return objects from functions.

The scope resolution operator :: is used to identify or access a particular function or data of a class. It is also used to access global and class variables and functions (see Chapters 8 and 10)

```
//Filename: vector.cpp
//Demonstrates how functions can return objects as return values.

#include <iostream.h>

class vector            //Declares the class
   {
   public:
     vector() { }           //No-argument constructor
                            //Same name as class
     vector(float x, float y)    //Two-argument constructor
                            //to initialize with data
         { xCo=x; yCo=y; }

     void setdata()   //Get coordinates from the user
     //Pre:  None.
     //Post: Vector coordinates are defined.
         { cout << "\nEnter X-Coord.= "; cin >> xCo;
           cout << "\nEnter Y-Coord.= "; cin >> yCo;
         }
     void showdata()        //Member function for display
     //Pre:  The vector is defined.
     //Post: The vector coordinates are displayed.
         { cout << "\n(X,Y) = " << "(" << xCo << ","
               << yCo << ")"; }
     vector add_vect(vector);  //Declaration of member
                            //function which returns
                            //value of type vector
     ~vector() {}  //Destructor. Same name as class
                   //but with tilde as a prefix.
   private:
     float xCo, yCo; //Class data hidden from all except
                     //member functions
   };                     //End of specification (note semicolon)
```

*Good programming practice dictates that all implementation of class functions be done outside the class declaration using the scope resolution operator. This separates class **interface** from class **implementation**. A class interface is a permanent measure but its implementation is not and can often be changed as necessary. Users of the class interact through only the interface and need not be burdened with details.*

```
vector vector::add_vect(vector v) //Function definition
//Pre:     Input vector data is defined, calling
//vector's data is defined.
//Post:    None.
//Returns: Result of addition: input vector + calling vector.
   {
   vector temp;            //Temporary vector type variable
   temp.xCo = xCo + v.xCo;   //Adding the x-coord.
   temp.yCo = yCo + v.yCo;   //Adding the y-coord.

   return temp;
   }

int main()
   {
   vector v1, v3;        //Objects v1 and v3 are defined
   vector v2(3.5,4.5); //Object v2 is initialized. This is
                       //more convenient than a setdata() function.

   v1.setdata(); //Calls member function to get
                 //data from the user.
   v3 = v1.add_vect(v2);   //v3 = v1 + v2
                           //Note an object is assigned to
                           //another of the same type!!

   v1.showdata();   //Calls member function to display data
   v2.showdata();
   cout << "\nThe addition of the above two vectors is = ";
   v3.showdata();
   return 0;
   }                 //End of main
```

The output of program vector.cpp is the same as the output of program vector0.cpp and hence is not repeated. The add_vect() function from the program vector.cpp is presented in Fig. 7.5.

In the main() function, the add_vect() member function of object v1 is invoked and the object v2 is passed as an argument. The object v is a copy of object v2. Like structures, objects can be copied into other objects of the same type. This operation of copying an object to a new object is done by a *copy constructor*; if no copy constructor has been defined, as here, then a *default copy constructor* provided by the compiler is used which simply does a bit-wise copy of the object, sometimes called a *shallow* copy (see Chapter 10 on writing copy constructors that can make a proper copy or *deep* copy). The add_vect() function adds two vectors v1 and v2 and stores the result in a local vector called temp; the object temp is returned and the value is assigned to vector v3. When an object is assigned to an already existing object as in the main() function, an assignment operator is invoked. If no assignment operator has been defined, as here, then a *default assignment operator* provided by the compiler is used. Later, in Chapter 10, we will see how to build our

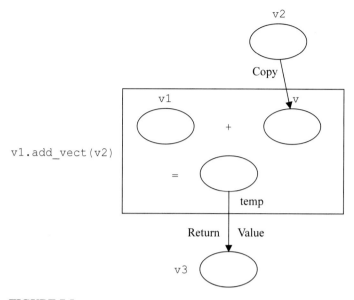

FIGURE 7.5
Member function `v1.add_vect()` adds two vectors (`v1` and `v2`) and
returns a vector (`temp`).

own overloaded assignment operators that are necessary when using pointers as data
members of classes.

Copy constructors can be invoked to simplify functions which return objects,
by eliminating the need for defining a local temporary object. Here is the above
`add_vect()` member function rewritten using this technique:

```
vector vector::add_vect(vector v)
{
    return vector(xCo + v.xCo, yCo + v.yCo);
}
```

This version creates and returns a local (unnamed) temporary vector by invoking the
two-argument constructor of the vector class.

Is it possible to avoid local objects `u` and `v` in program `vector0.cpp`?
Is it possible to pass objects by reference? Moreover, is it possible to pass objects by reference and at the same time protect the object from being changed in
the member function? All these can be done if we pass the arguments as `const`
`object_name&`. Do the exercises (Problem 2) for answers to these questions in
detail.

*Call by constant ref-
erence is a safe and
memory-efficient
way to pass objects
to functions.*

Finally, what we would like to have is simply a statement like

```
v3 = v1 + v2;
```

for adding two vectors (`v1` and `v2`) and storing the result in the new vector `v3`. This
can be done using operator overloading, described later in the chapter in the section
on Operator Overloading.

ARRAYS AS CLASS MEMBER DATA AND ARRAYS OF OBJECTS

The following simple example is used to illustrate how arrays can be used as class member data and how arrays of objects can be defined.

```cpp
//Filename arrayobj.cpp
//Array of objects with an array as class member data

#include <iostream.h>

const int MAX = 4;

class vector          //Declares the class
   {
   public:
     vector() { }   //No-argument constructor

     void setdata(float x[])   //Initializes array
         { coord[0]=x[0]; coord[1]=x[1]; }

     void showdata()          //Member function for display
        { cout << "\n(" << coord[0] << ","
              << coord[1] << ")\n";    }
   private:
     float coord[2]; //Class data hidden from all except
                     //member functions. Coord is an array of
                     //2 elements.
   };                     //End of specification (note semicolon)

void main()
   {
   vector v[MAX];    //An array of MAX objects is defined
   float temp[2];

   for (int i=0; i<MAX; ++i)
      {
      cout << "Input data for vector #" << i << ":" << endl;
      cin >> temp[0] >> temp[1];
      v[i].setdata(temp); //Array temp is the input argument
      }

   cout << "\nThe coordinates entered are:";

   for (i=0; i<MAX; ++i)
      v[i].showdata();

   }                      //End of main
```

The output of the program, depending on what you enter as input, may look like this:

```
Input data for vector #0:
1 2
Input data for vector #1:
3 4
Input data for vector #2:
5 6
Input data for vector #3:
7 8


The coordinates entered are:
(1,2)

(3,4)

(5,6)

(7,8)
```

The class vector now has an array coord[] which holds the two coordinates. It is important to note that, because the input data is an array, function arguments may have to contain an array as an argument; see function setdata() for an example. Secondly, the array of objects is defined in the main() function with MAX being the maximum number of objects in that array. Once again, v[0] corresponds to the first object, v[1] corresponds to the second object, and so on, with v[size of the array-1] corresponding to the last, that is, the MAXth object. Study carefully how the input data is passed to the ith object v[i] within the for loop in the main program using an array temp, the dot operator, and the function setdata():

```
for (int i=0; i<MAX; ++i)
      {
    cin >> temp[0] >> temp[1];
    v[i].setdata(temp); //Array temp is the input argument
      }
```

MEMORY ALLOCATION

Although we have enclosed data and functions and considered them as a single unit, for efficient use of memory, the functions are really created and stored only once in memory and are shared by class member objects. The data of each object is kept separately, of course (see Fig. 7.6). This is something a programmer generally does not worry about because, for all practical purposes, we can consider data and functions to be contained in every object created.

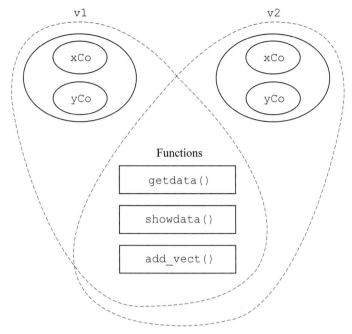

FIGURE 7.6
Objects of the same class share the functions.

Static Class Data and Static Functions

In the examples above, the storage class of the data xCo and yCo is automatic. This means that a separate copy of the data is created for each instance of the vector object. If a single copy of the object data is needed (common to all instances of the class), the object can be declared using the static storage class. If a function is declared as static, the function can be invoked without referencing any object, using the syntax:

class_name::function_name()

instead of

object_name.function_name()

In the following example, the data member total_objects is used to count the total number of objects of this class that have been created. We need to keep a single copy of total_objects and increment it each time an object is created. Function show_total() is an example of a static function.

```
///Filename:statdafu.cpp
//Demonstrates the use of static data and static functions

#include <iostream.h>
```

```
class anyclass {


public:
  anyclass()
      {                    //No-argument constructor
    total_objects++;         //Adds when object is created
    id_object = total_objects; //Current total is the object id
      }

  // Function to show total number of objects.
  static void show_total() {    //Static function to
                                //show the total_objects
  //Pre:  Data for "anyclass" is defined.
  //Post: The total number of objects in the class is displayed.
    cout << "\nThe total number of objects is = " << total_objects;
    }

  //A non-static function to show the ID of each object
  void show_id() {
  //Pre:  Data for "anyclass" is defined.
  //Post: Displays ID data.
    cout << "\nThe ID number of this object is OBJECT"
        << id_object;
    }
private:
static int total_objects;  //Total number of objects of this class
int id_object;             //Each object's identification number

};    //End of class specification

int anyclass::total_objects = 0;

int main() {

  anyclass a1;

  anyclass::show_total();

  anyclass a2, a3, a4;

  anyclass::show_total();

  a1.show_id();
  a2.show_id();
  a3.show_id();
  a4.show_id();

  return 0;
} //End of main program
```

The output from the above program is

```
The total number of objects = 1
The total number of objects = 4
The ID number of this object is OBJECT1
The ID number of this object is OBJECT2
The ID number of this object is OBJECT3
The ID number of this object is OBJECT4
```

It is clear that (i) the data `total_objects` needs to be shared by all objects of the same class, and (ii) to print the total number of objects of the class `anyclass`, we need a function that is not attached to any object. Hence, we use static data `total_objects` and a static function `show_total()` which is called as `anyclass::show_total()`. Because class specification is only a declaration and not a definition, no storage is allocated in memory until definition; therefore, the initialization of the static data is done outside the class declaration using the syntax

```
int anyclass::total_objects = 0;
```

OPERATOR OVERLOADING

Earlier, in the program `vector.cpp` two vector objects were added and the result was obtained using the statement: `v3 = v1.add_vect(v2);` a more natural (or mathematical) statement should have been `v3 = v1 + v2;`. To achieve this we need to overload the operator + , that is, we need to define a plus operator of our own for the `vector` class. This operator will understand how to add two vectors.

We define the meaning of the + operator for a class by specifying a function for the class. The function name consists of the keyword `operator` followed by +. Other operators are overloaded in a similar way. The precedence of these operators cannot be changed. The C++ operators that cannot be overloaded are: the scope resolution operator (: :), the dot operator (.), the member access operator (. *), and the ternary conditional operator (? :).

When a class represents a dynamic data structure it is good practice to overload the assignment operator, copy constructor, and destructor. An example of these is given in Chapter 10.

OVERLOADING THE + OPERATOR OF THE SIMPLE VECTOR CLASS

A rather simple modification to the program `vector.cpp` achieves this in the following way. The program also presents the overloading of unary - operator.

```
//Filename: vectopov.cpp
//Demonstrates a simple class and object using constructors
//and destructors. Overloaded unary and binary operators
```

```
#include <iostream.h>

class vector          //Specifies the class
   {
   public:
     vector() { }         //No-argument constructor
                          //Same name as class
     vector(float x, float y)  //Two-argument constructor
                               //to initialize with data
          { xCo=x; yCo=y; }
     void getdata()  //Get coordinates from the user
          { cout << "\nEnter X-Coord.= "; cin >> xCo;
            cout << "\nEnter Y-Coord.= "; cin >> yCo;
          }
     void showdata()        //Member function for display
          { cout << "\n(X,Y) = " << "(" << xCo << ","
                 << yCo << ")" << endl; }
     vector add_vect(const vector&);     //Declaration of member
                                         //function
     vector operator - ();   //Overloaded unary minus operator
     vector operator + (const vector&); //Overloaded plus operator
     ~vector() {cout <<"Destructed\n";} //Destructor.
                                        //Same name as class
                                        //but with tilde as a prefix.
   private:
     float xCo, yCo;  //Class data hidden from all except
                      //member functions

   };               //End of specification (note semicolon)

vector vector::add_vect(const vector& u) //Function definition
   {
   return vector(xCo + u.xCo, yCo + u.yCo);
}

vector vector::operator - () //Function definition for unary -
   {
   return vector(-xCo, -yCo);
   }
vector vector::operator + (const vector& u) //Function definition
   {
   return vector(xCo + u.xCo, yCo + u.yCo);
}

int main()
   {
   vector v1, v3;       //Objects v1 and v3 are defined
   vector v2(3.5,4.5); //Object v2 is initialized
   cout << "Get info from user: \n";
   v1.getdata();        //Calls member function to get
                        //data from the user.
```

Overload the operators such that the meaning is self-evident. For example, in a string class + may mean concatenation but the minus (-) operator is ambiguous so do not overload.

```
//Change the sign and output
cout << "changing the sign of the vector you input\n";
v1 = -v1;
v1.showdata();
cout << "Add two vectors: \n";
v1.showdata();        //calls member function to display data
v2.showdata();
cout << "\nThe addition of the above two vectors is = ";
v3 = v1 + v2;
v3.showdata();
return 0;
}                     //End of main
```

The output of the program is:

```
Get info from user:

Enter X-Coord.= 1

Enter Y-Coord.= 2
changing the sign of the vector you input
Destructed

(X,Y) = (-1,-2)
Add two vectors:

(X,Y) = (-1,-2)

(X,Y)= (3.5,4.5)

The addition of the above two vectors is =
Destructed
Destructed
(X,Y) = (2.5,2.5)
Destructed
Destructed
Destructed
```

This example demonstrates how to overload a unary operator as well as a binary operator. The binary + operator took a single argument and the unary operator took no argument. Carefully count the number of "Destructed" objects and try to understand their origins. Except for the last three "Destructed", all the other "Destructed" correspond to temporary objects created and destroyed. If these objects are very large there could be problems with resources like CPU time and memory.

For example, the first "Destructed" corresponds to the program statement v1 = -v1 and the operator-() function of the minus operator. A temporary object is created and destroyed due to the statement return vector(-xCo, -yCo) in the operator-() function. Similarly, the next two "Destructed" correspond to the statement v3 = v1 + v2 and the function operator+(). The temporary objects are the local object u and the object constructed due to the statement `return vector(xCo + u.xCo, yCo + u.yCo)`. Note that the actual number of temporary objects created may vary from compiler to compiler!

The line `v3 = v1 + v2` is equivalent to `v3 = v1.operator+(v2)`. You can see that `operator+` is a function. Unlike ordinary functions, binary operator functions can have only one or two parameters; at least one of these must be a class.

USING OBJECTS

Vectors and matrices are important objects in linear algebra. In the sample programs above we have seen how a simple vector class can be defined to create vector objects. These objects stored data, such as the coordinates, and also manipulated them to produce useful results, for example vector addition. In the next section we will build and use a simple matrix class. The use of objects will be demonstrated throughout the remainder of the book. So be patient! These examples should also demonstrate the convenience of software or programming objects that closely represent objects that are known to engineers. Note that in previous chapters we have already used matrices using arrays and also have performed operations such as matrix addition, matrix multiplication, etc. In this chapter we will develop a simple matrix class to perform the same set of operations that we are already familiar with, like matrix addition, matrix subtraction, etc.

Object-Oriented Programming for Linear Algebra

In this section we will develop a simple matrix class that will encapsulate necessary data and functions. Public member functions will provide access to the data in the matrix object. To display the data of the matrix the function `display()` will be needed. Any function defined outside the object will not be able to access the private data of the object (the matrix).

The matrix class diagram is shown in Fig. 7.7 where the name of the class is shown in the top part, the data in the middle part, and the functions or services provided in the bottom part. Obviously, the function `Matrix()` is a constructor for the class.

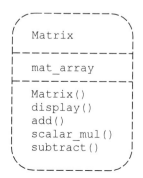

FIGURE 7.7
Class diagram for a simple matrix class.

Using Matrix Objects

We will start with the `main()` function and show how the matrix class is used for the usual matrix operations. We will show the C++ program for the class definition later and explain the various elements.

```
//Filename simmatrx.cpp
//Demonstrates the use of a simple matrix class for use
//in Linear Algebra

const int ROWS = 2, COLS = 2;   //Global definition for the number of
                                //rows and columns

//Main function shown first for demonstration of the matrix class

int main()
   {
   float temp[ROWS][COLS] = {1,2,3,4};   //Elements are stored
                                         //by rows. First row = {1,2},
                                         //second row = {3,4}.
//Initialize a matrix and display. Note that the constructor
//argument has to be a two-dimensional array.
   Matrix matrx1(temp);

   matrx1.display();                  //Display matrx1

   //Define two other matrices
   Matrix matrx2, matrx3;   //Here a no-argument constructor is used

   matrx2 = matrx1;                   //Assignment operation
                                      //with default assignment operator
   matrx2.display();

   //Scalar multiplication of a matrix
   matrx2 = matrx1.scalar_mul(3.0);   //Multiplies matrx1 by 3.0
                                      //and assigns the result to
                                      //matrx2
   matrx2.display();

   //Matrix addition
   matrx3 = matrx1.add(matrx2);       //matrx3 = matrx1 + matrx2
   matrx3.display();                  //Display the resulting matrix

   //Matrix subtraction
   matrx3 = matrx2.subtract(matrx1);  //matrx3 = matrx2-matrx1
   matrx3.display();                  //Display the resulting matrix

   Matrix matrx4 = matrx3;            //Initialization anywhere.
   matrx4.display();
```

```
      return 0;
      }                                    //End of main function
```

One of the advantages of using OOP is syntax simplification. If you are *not* using object-oriented programming techniques, then the addition of two matrices is probably done using the following statement:

```
        matrix_add(matrx1,matrx2,matrx3);
```

In contrast, we have here

```
        matrx3 = matrx1.add(matrx2);
```

The more natural linear algebraic notation used in the comments, for example

```
        matrx3 = matrx1 + matrx2
```

OOP simplifies function calls by reducing the number of arguments passed to the function.

is also possible using operator overloading described earlier. Therefore, with OOP, our program syntax is closer to the algorithm symbolic notation. Because of this feature (i) it becomes easy to translate from algorithms to computer programs, (ii) the translation process becomes less error prone, and (iii) if errors exist they become relatively easy to identify.

Declaration of a Matrix Class

Because we are keeping our matrix class simple, we will assume that the dimensions are fixed by changing the global constant definition at the top of the program. This is a minor irritant that will be overcome with pointers in Chapter 9. For the time being, we will concentrate on building classes and understand how to use objects.

```
//Matrix class definition
class Matrix
   {

   public:
      Matrix();                        //No-argument constructor which
                                       //initializes a matrix to zeros
      Matrix(float [ROWS][COLS]);      //Constructor for initialization
      void display();                  //For displaying the matrix
      Matrix add(Matrix);              //For adding two matrices
                                       //and returning the result
      Matrix scalar_mul(float);        //Multiply by a scalar
                                       //and return the result
      Matrix subtract(Matrix);         //For subtracting 2 matrices
      ~Matrix();                        //A simple destructor
   private:
      float mat_array[ROWS][COLS];     //Matrix of dimension ROWS
                                       //by COLS
   };     //class declaration ends.
```

```
//No-argument constructor
Matrix::Matrix()
//Pre: None
//Post: Initializes all elements of matrix of ROWS by COLS to zero.
   { //Initialize the matrix to zeros
   for(int row=0; row < ROWS; row++)
     {
      for(int col=0; col < COLS; col++)
        {
        mat_array[row][col] = 0.0; //mat_array is directly accessible
        }
     }
   }  //End of constructor

//Constructor for initialization
Matrix::Matrix( float elements[ROWS][COLS])
//Pre: None
//Post: Initializes matrix of ROWS by COLS to what is passed.
   { //Initialize the matrix
   for(int row=0; row < ROWS; row++)
     {
      for(int col=0; col < COLS; col++)
        {
        //mat_array is directly accessible but
        //elements[][] is local.
        mat_array[row][col] = elements[row][col];
        }
     }
   }  //End of constructor

//Function for displaying the matrix
void Matrix::display()
//Pre: Matrix is initialized
//Post: Matrix is displayed
   {
   for(int row=0; row < ROWS; row++)
     {
     cout << endl;  //Start a new line for each row
     for(int col=0; col < COLS; col++)

       cout << mat_array[row][col] << " ";

     }
   cout << "End of Matrix Display" << endl;
                 //After the matrix is printed out
   }  //End of function

//Function for addition of two matrices
Matrix Matrix::add(Matrix mat_local)
//Pre: Two matrices of the same size have been initialized
```

```
//Post: None
//Return: Result of the addition of two matrices (calling and called)
//is returned (as a matrix object).
   {
   Matrix temp;  //Temporary matrix for returning result
   for(int row=0; row < ROWS; row++)
     {
      for(int col=0; col < COLS; col++)
        {
        //mat_array of all matrices directly accessible
        //because of membership privilege.
        temp.mat_array[row][col] = mat_array[row][col] +
                              mat_local.mat_array[row][col];
        }
     }
   return temp;  //Return the result
   }               //End of function

//Function for scalar multiplication of a matrix
Matrix Matrix::scalar_mul(float scale)
//Pre: Matrix is initialized
//Post: None
//Return: A scalar multiplication of a calling matrix is returned.
   {
   Matrix temp;
   for(int row=0; row < ROWS; row++)
     {
      for(int col=0; col < COLS; col++)
        {
        temp.mat_array[row][col] = mat_array[row][col]*scale;
        }
     }
   return temp;
   }

//Function for subtraction of two matrices
Matrix Matrix::subtract(Matrix mat_local)
//Pre: Matrix of same sizes is initialized
//Post: None
//Return: A matrix result of caller-called is returned
   {
   Matrix temp;
    for(int row=0; row < ROWS; row++)
     {
      for(int col=0; col < COLS; col++)
        temp.mat_array[row][col] = mat_array[row][col] -
                              mat_local.mat_array[row][col];
     }
   return temp;  //Return the result
   }               //End of function
```

The definition of the matrix class was very similar to the vector class and hence is self-explanatory. The one thing you may notice from the above program is the creation of a lot of temporaries in the member functions including the `Matrix temp`'s. As you may imagine, the temporaries do take up a lot of computer resources. To understand this, modify the destructor to be as follows:

```
~Matrix()                              //A simple destructor
    {
    cout << "\nDestructed\n";
    }
```

and run the above program. You will get the following output.

`1 2` `3 4  End of Matrix Display`	*Corresponding program statements:* *matrx1.display()*
`1 2` `3 4  End of Matrix Display`	*matrx2.display()*
Scalar multiplication of a matrix Starts	*matrx2 = matrx1.scalar_mul(3.0)*
`Destructed`	
`Destructed`	
`3 6` `9 12  End of Matrix Display`	*matrx2.display()*
Matrix addition Starts	*matrx3 = matrx1.add(matrx2)*
`Destructed`	
`Destructed`	
`Destructed`	
`4 8` `12 16  End of Matrix Display`	*matrx3.display()*
Matrix subtraction Starts	*matrx3 = matrx2.subtract(matrx1)*
`Destructed`	
`Destructed`	
`Destructed`	
`2 4` `6 8  End of Matrix Display`	*matrx3.display()*

```
2  4
6  8  End of Matrix Display                    matrx4.display()
```

End of main() function

```
Destructed

Destructed

Destructed

Destructed
```

The last four "Destructed" correspond to the four matrices created in the main program. The first two "Destructed" correspond to the scalar multiplication and the next two sets of three "Destructed" correspond to the matrix addition and matrix subtraction calls, respectively. The actual number may vary from compiler to compiler. For example, the first set of three "Destructed" corresponds to the three matrices used in the add() function, namely temp, mat_local and a temporary matrix for the object matrx3 that called the function. This is a major disadvantage of object-oriented programming techniques, especially if naively applied. To some extent, these inefficiencies can be overcome by constant references and using a somewhat less intuitive programming style (see Exercises 2 and 3).

MORE ON OBJECT-ORIENTED PROGRAMMING AND DESIGN

A common question that comes to mind is: If objects provide public interfaces, then how can corruption of private data be prevented? How can data hiding work in this case? First, without at least one public member function, interfacing with objects is not possible. Therefore, it is necessary to provide at least minimal services through these public interface functions. Secondly, interfaces provided by public member functions (and constructors) can do safety checks, such as a range check on the input data. For example, if you have a date class the constructor or the setdata() function can check that an integer number between 1 and 31 is input. Similarly, a getdata() function that provides access to data can limit access and supply only what is necessary in an appropriate format. For example, in a student_record class it may provide the student number and marks but not the name of the student, for confidentiality reasons.

Is there a unique way to design a class? There may not be, although there may be bad designs and good designs. In procedural languages the design step may involve an iterative loop connecting all the five steps of the top-down design process (see Chapter 1 for a review). In object-oriented design, additionally, the class design may be redone as many times as necessary until one feels comfortable with the design. The idea of inheritance, discussed in the next chapter, also provides for marginal modifications of classes, allowing the reuse of original classes already designed and coded. This concept is called reusability, which is another fundamental reason for object-oriented programming and design.

The principle advantage of OOP and OOD is that distracting implementation details can be hidden from the user with the provision of easy-to-use interfaces.

On the whole, the idea of classes is to provide users with interface functions where necessary, and hide from them the implementation details and drudgery. This allows for a good level of abstraction. For example, most of us drive cars without actually knowing how the car really works. What we need to know is how to use the steering wheel, brakes, accelerator, and yes, the stereo, among other functions provided by the car manufacturer. We do not generally care how these services are implemented. In this way, manufacturers can keep implementing improvements to the way cars work but we do not need any retraining to use the "improved" cars (objects) because the standard interfaces are retained. That is, data hiding and encapsulation also mean that unnecessary details are encapsulated and hidden from the user who surely will be glad to see friendlier and easy-to-use objects.

Class Invariants

A practical method to define a class is to first identify objects (existing or future) that your program is supposed to model. A class has to be defined such that *no* instance of a class violates the class invariants. Class invariants are class data and their acceptable range plus methods with their pre- and postconditions which all the instances of a class must obey. Suppose we define a student class with the following member data: student number and a year name such as "first year electrical engineering." If you have non-degree students taking courses and they are not attached to any year, then defining a non-degree student as an instance of the class will violate the class invariants. In such cases do one of the following: (i) allow a year name called non-degree, (ii) redefine the class or (iii) do not allow instantiation of non-degree student objects. Another example: Suppose you are defining an adult class and one of the member data is age with the condition age >= 21. Then, when instantiating an object of the adult class make sure that all objects of this class obey the age condition. Otherwise, you will be violating a class invariant. Note that this could be done with an assert() statement as in

```
assert( age >= 21);
//Construction of the object continues
```

Good programming dictates that all class invariants be checked before exiting constructors and member functions!

The class invariants include member data and methods. For example, a bird class has been defined with the method fly(). If you instantiate an object Clark, which is an ostrich, then you are violating a class invariant because ostriches do not fly! Therefore, the set of *all* instances of a class should obey all class invariants. By adhering to this design rule we increase the reliability of our programs.

COMMON ERRORS WHEN USING CLASSES/OBJECTS

Many common errors are identified (directly or indirectly) by the compiler. For example, a non-class member attempting to access a private member of a class will be easily (directly) identified by the compiler. On the other hand, missing a semicolon at the end of a class declaration is only indirectly identified by the compiler by providing you with messages that are hard to connect with this particular error. Beware if you are using the constructor to call setdata functions of the class. Construction and initialization of an object is guaranteed to be complete only when the constructor completes execution. Therefore, if a setdata or other member function of the class is called from a constructor the data members may not be in a usable state. This is a phenomenon that may vary from compiler to compiler due to variability in implementations. Other errors that are easily identified by the compiler include not returning appropriate objects that match with member function prototypes. Design and implementation errors are discussed in the case study under testing.

CASE STUDY (OBJECT-ORIENTED DESIGN AND PROGRAMMING)

Reservoir System Simulator

The problem is described in Chapters 3 and 4. We will use a diagram to show a reservoir object and the corresponding reservoir class. The diagrams are useful during both design and coding and are also very helpful for independent development of modules. So far, modules have been synonymous with functions but from here on they may also mean classes.

1. Problem analysis

A single reservoir system is to be simulated using data on the system characteristics such as maximum and minimum storage and initial storage. The simulation is to be done for all periods for which data on demand and inflow are input by the user. The required results such as outflow and spill are calculated for each period. The results are output at each period.

Problem statement: Simulate a single reservoir system with user-supplied input.

Input/output analysis: The inputs required are: maximum storage, minimum storage, initial storage; inflow and demand must be given for each period.

The outputs are outflow, spill, and final storage in each period. It might be necessary to output the user-supplied data for convenience.

2. Design

We will use object-based decomposition to solve the problem. Encapsulation of data and functions into objects is one of the major paradigms (organizing principles) on which object-oriented design and programming are based. Fig. 7.8 shows the object/class diagram for the reservoir. The name of the class is in the top part, the member data in the middle part and the member functions in the bottom part. We may not write the constructors and destructors explicitly but they are assumed to be available for all classes.

This problem involves only a single object/class. The name of the class, the data members, and the member functions of this class can easily be filled in immediately after the input/output analysis. Notice that in this case, we are also influenced by the process-based analysis carried out in Chapter 3.

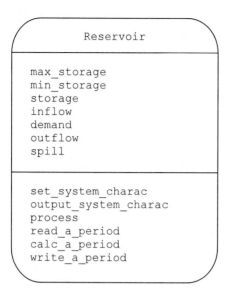

FIGURE 7.8
Reservoir class diagram.

A digression: Many object-oriented purists imply that a class or object can be designed without resorting to any process-based decomposition. However, much of the current work in object-oriented programming involves converting older structured programming to object-oriented programming. If structure charts such as the ones developed in Chapter 4 exist, use them, if convenient, to fill in your new object/class diagrams. Secondly, when you are trying to understand a large or complex problem it may be preferable to consider the problem from as many views as possible. In that case, process-based decomposition may provide you with an additional view. Lastly, if you have many views, for example process-based and object-based, consider using them all to verify that you have not left out any important aspects of the problem. If you are starting from scratch you may use the following approach.

Object-oriented modeling. Natural language provides clues for object-oriented modeling; for example, common names express concepts or classes (e.g., a tiger, a city), proper names indicate objects (e.g., Shircan, Waterloo), adjectives qualify attributes (e.g., ferocious, friendly), verbs indicate processes, actions, services (e.g., roars), prepositions connect objects to show dependency and relationships (e.g., the teeth of Shircan are sharp). Let us follow this process for the reservoir problem. We repeat the problem from Chapter 3. We will identify objects by underlining nouns and pronouns, attributes (data), and methods (verbs) and keep them in a tabular form.

A Reservoir System Simulator can be used to study the behavior of reservoir systems and lakes. For simplicity, we will consider the simulation of a single reservoir in discrete time. Assume you have the storage, inflow and demand values, as well as the lower and upper bounds for the storage, namely, the min_storage and max_storage. The objective is to find the outflow, spill, and storage at end of the period whose dynamics in discrete time is given by the following "if" statements.

Case 1:   If *min_storage* ≤ *storage* + *inflow* + *demand* ≤ *max_storage*

outflow = demand

spill = 0

storage = storage + inflow − demand

Case 2:   If *min_storage* > *storage* + *inflow* − *demand*

outflow = storage + inflow − min_storage

spill = 0

storage = min_storage

Case 3:   If *max_storage* < *storage* + *inflow* − *demand*

outflow = demand

spill = storage + inflow − demand − max_storage

storage = max_storage

The reservoir storage is also called the state variable whose value at the end of each time period is determined as above. Demands and inflows during all the periods are assumed to be non-negative and are given. Outflow is supposed to be equal to the demand whenever possible.

Simulate the reservoir for the following data. Inflow(time = 1 to 3) = {10, 20, 30}, demand(time = 1 to 3) = {10, 40, 0}, max_storage = {20}, min_storage = {0}; initial storage in the reservoir = {10}. Note that simulation here simply means calculate and output the outflows and the storages in each period of interest. The user can be asked to input the values (inflow and demand) for each period.

From the statement of the problem, it is necessary to consider only a single reservoir for now, and ignore nouns such as Reservoir System Simulator, system, etc. Although inflows and outflows are nouns, currently they are considered simply as attributes of the reservoir. Identify nouns, verbs, and adjectives corresponding to the reservoir object, underlined above when they were encountered for the first time, and fill in the following table. Note that non-negative is an adjective. Adjectives may be added to the table when necessary.

Objects	Attributes	Methods
Reservoir	minimum storage, maximum storage, storage, time period, demand, inflow, outflow, spill, initial storage	simulate, calculate, output, input

Looking at the list of methods, we can discard the word simulate, since simulate for our example is the same as calculate and output. Also, initial storage can be simply the initial value of the storage attribute and hence need not be considered in the class diagram. Lastly, to be consistent with our previous solutions for this problem, we have omitted the explicit consideration of the time period (or discrete time) attribute. Because the input and output methods can be further subdivided into methods that are called once per simulation and once per period, we have modified the class diagram accordingly and used appropriate names to provide consistency.

In summary, we can use the problem description to identify necessary objects and their attributes and methods. We can follow an iterative process for designing their respective classes. We will skip the next two steps, namely, hand example and algorithm design, as they will be exactly the same as in the previous chapters.

3. Coding and debugging

We present the full program which was developed in the following manner. First, the class prototype was created based on the class diagram and a `main()` function was written to test the prototype for any syntax errors. The method definitions were then written, one at a time, starting with `set_system_charac()` and `output_system_charac()`. The function `process()` was constructed partially first and used as a starting point to develop `read_a_period()`, `write_a_period()`, and `calc_a_period()`. Then, the development of `process()` was completed. The `main()` function evolved during the development of the individual methods.

```cpp
//Program 1rescla.cpp
//Program will simulate a single reservoir system for a given
//demand and inflow series input by the user one by one.
//Uses Simple Objects!

#include <iostream.h>
#include <iomanip.h>

class Reservoir
{
  public:
      Reservoir(float maxsto=0., float minsto=0., float stor=0.)
      {
            max_storage = maxsto;
            min_storage = minsto;
            storage = stor;

      }
      void set_system_charac ();
      void output_system_charac ();
      void process ();
      ~Reservoir(){cout << "\nReservoir Destructed \n";}
  private:
      float max_storage;
      float min_storage;
      float storage;
      float demand;
      float inflow;
      float outflow;
      float spill;
      void calc_a_period ();
      void read_a_period ();
      void write_a_period ();
}; //End of Reservoir Class Declaration
```

```
void Reservoir::set_system_charac()
//Precondition:   None
//Postcondition: Reads acceptable max, min, and initial storages

{

   //Read inputs and check for potential error condition

   do {
     cout << "Please input reservoir maximum,"
          << " minimum storages (>= 0) and \n"
          << "the initial storage falling BETWEEN"
          << " the maximum and minimum,\n"
          << "maximum storage > minimum storage\n";
     cin >> max_storage >> min_storage >> storage;
   } while ( (max_storage < min_storage ) ||
           ( storage > max_storage ) ||
           ( storage < min_storage ) ||
           ( max_storage < 0 ) || ( min_storage < 0 ) );
     //End of do-while loop for input error check

   output_system_charac(); //Echo (print) of input data

}


void Reservoir::output_system_charac()
//Precondition: max, min, and init storages should have values and
//preferably should be called before process().
//Postcondition: max, min, and initial storages are output

{
   cout << "MAX. STOR. = " << max_storage
        << "   MIN. STOR. = " << min_storage
        << "    INITIAL STORAGE = " << storage << "\n\n";
}


void Reservoir::process()
//Pre: max, min and storage should have been set.
//Max >= min; max, min, storage >= 0;
//Post: outflow, spill, and storage will be calculated for user
//input in each period with outflow and spill >= 0 and
//min_storage <= storage <= max_storage.

{

   //Read user data for each period


   read_a_period();
```

```
            //Calculate outflow, spill and new storage for each period

            while ( (inflow >= 0 ) && ( demand >= 0 ) ) {

               calc_a_period();

               //Write output for each period

               write_a_period();

               read_a_period();


            } //End of while loop

        } //End of function process

        void Reservoir::read_a_period()
        //Pre: None
        //Post: Inflow and demand are read from the user

        {

           cout << "Please input current period's inflow(>=0) \n";
           cout << "-1 -1 (any one negative number) to end simulation\n";
           cin >> inflow >> demand;
        }

        void Reservoir::write_a_period()
        //Pre: Outflow, spill, and storage have been calculated. Call this
        //after calling calc_a_period().
        //Post: Outflow, spill, and storage are output to the monitor

        {
           //Print out results

             cout << setw(12) << "Inflow" << setw(12)
                  << "Demand" //<< setw(12) << "Temp_sto"
                  << setw(12) << "Outflow"
                  << setw(12) << "Spill" << setw(12) << "Fin.Stor." << endl;
             cout << setw(12) << inflow
                  << setw(12) << demand //<< setw(12) << temp_storage
                  << setw(12) << outflow << setw(12)
                  << spill << setw(12) << storage << endl;

        }

        void Reservoir::calc_a_period()
        //Pre: Storage, inflow, and demand have non-negative values
        //Post: Outflow, spill, and new storage will be calculated
```

```
{
    float temp_storage;
      temp_storage = storage + inflow - demand;
      if ( ( min_storage <= temp_storage ) &&
            (temp_storage <= max_storage) ) {
         outflow = demand;
         spill = 0.;
         storage = temp_storage;
      }
      else if (min_storage > temp_storage) {
         outflow = storage + inflow - min_storage;
         spill = 0.;
         storage = min_storage;
      }
      else { //This corresponds to max_storage < temp_storage
         outflow = demand;
         spill = storage + inflow - demand - max_storage;
         storage = max_storage;
      }
      //End of the three cases

}


int main()
{

Reservoir single_res;

single_res.set_system_charac();
single_res.process();

return 0;
}
```

The output of the program is as follows.

```
Please input reservoir maximum, minimum storages (>= 0) and
the initial storage falling BETWEEN the maximum and minimum,
maximum storage > minimum storage
20 0 10
MAX. STOR. = 20   MIN. STOR. = 0   INITIAL STORAGE = 10

Please input current period's inflow and demand
-1 -1 (any one negative number) to end simulation
10 10
      Inflow      Demand      Outflow      Spill   Fin.Stor.
          10          10           10          0          10
Please input current period's inflow and demand
-1 -1 (any one negative number) to end simulation
20 40
```

```
        Inflow      Demand      Outflow       Spill   Fin.Stor.
            20          40           30           0           0
Please input current period's inflow and demand
-1 -1 (any one negative number) to end simulation
30 0
        Inflow      Demand      Outflow       Spill   Fin.Stor.
            30           0            0          10          20
Please input current period's inflow and demand
-1 -1 (any one negative number) to end simulation
-1 -1

Reservoir Destructed
```

4. Integration

Consider the previous sections and note that we have designed just a single class to solve this problem. Therefore, if there is need for integration it is not because of many classes but because of the many services (member functions) in a single class. Hence, the integration steps are similar to those performed in the solution of the case study in Chapter 4 using functions. We develop the class declaration at the highest level (similar to the decomposition in the solution using structured programming), which includes only the set_system_charac(), output_system_charac() and process() methods, first. Because the interface of each one was defined at stub level, independent development of these functions could be done. Similarly, we develop read_a_period(), write_a_period(), and calc_a_period(), independently, all of which correspond to the breadth-first strategy. See Chapter 8 for more details on integration in object-oriented programming.

5. Testing

In addition to errors that can creep in during the implementation of individual methods of objects (they can be tested as before), object-oriented programming produces errors which are unique. For example, violation of class invariants is the major cause of error. In our example, the constructor for the Reservoir class does default initialization with valid object data, which is good programming practice. However, within the constructor, the class invariants (here, they are simply the acceptable data range for reservoir member data) are not verified. For example, the set_system_charac() function, when it takes input from the user, checks all the input for validity. Similarly, the constructor should do validity checks. Therefore, the testing of objects should start with the initialization of the three types of test cases (valid, unusual, and invalid) and iterative improvements to the code and design should be carried out. Continue the same process for all the member functions. It is better to identify test cases while writing the class invariants, preconditions, and postconditions during design and coding. Design and implement such that every constructor and every method establishes and maintains the class invariants, respectively. We could use assert() for that purpose (see Exercise 6). See also Chapter 3 for more details on test cases.

In summary, the programming solution we have here corresponds to Solution 3 in Chapter 1. The program demonstrates one of the major advantages of object-oriented programming, namely, encapsulation of data and functions into a single class. Because of encapsulation there was absolutely no need to pass the member data to member functions, thus reducing coupling, which in turn reduces program complexity when compared with Solution 2. Therefore, in that sense, the program here is as simple as our Solution 1, where, because everything was done in a single function, there was no need for data passing. However, in the above program, using member functions, we were able to "divide and conquer," that is, write many methods, thus maintaining the advantages of functions. When we solve problems with many objects and interactions having a high complexity, the advantages of object-oriented programming and design will become more evident. Some of those advantages can be gleaned from the case study and exercises in Chapter 8.

SUMMARY

Data that is related can be grouped using a structure. A class is similar to a structure in that it allows the grouping of related data, but it also allows the definition of functions needed to manipulate the data. The data and functions in a class are usually defined as private or public or protected (as explained in Chapter 8). Data in the class is usually defined as private so that only the functions in the class have access to the data so defined. This property is called data hiding, an important concept of object-oriented programming.

The functions of the class are called member functions and they have privileged access to the data of that class. Constructors are similar to member functions and are used to initialize objects. Destructors can release the memory allocated for an object. Objects can be passed as arguments to functions as well as returned from functions. A member function can be defined outside the class using the scope resolution operator (: :). Data hiding and encapsulation isolate users from implementation details and provide user-friendly interfaces to objects that can closely model the real-world objects.

REVIEW QUESTIONS

1. Class is used to create new user-defined _____ types.

2. The two important reasons for classes are _____ and _____.

3. What is the class syntax?

4. True or false: There is a unique way to design classes.

5. The keywords in a class specification are _____, _____, and _____.

6. Class members can access _____, _____, and _____ data and member functions of that class.

7. _____ data and functions can be accessed by all program elements, including non-members of the class.

8. An object has the same relation to a _____ as a real variable to _____ data type.

9. An instance of a class is called _____.

10. An object's member function has/does not have direct access to all its data and hence need/need not be passed as arguments.

11. Objects of the same class can access each other's data and functions without restriction. True or false?

12. Write a class declaration for a `time` class with `hrs`, `min`, `sec` as private data members.

13. The dot operator is used to access _____ or _____ of a _____.

14. The scope resolution operator _____ identifies the data or functions of a class with the syntax *class_type class_name* _____ *class_data* or *class_function*.

15. Add to the `time` class in Question 12 a public interface function to set data with hours, minutes, and seconds passed as arguments.

16. Add three public get functions, one each for `hrs`, `min`, and `sec`, to the `time` class of Question 12.

17. Write the statement for instantiating an object `time_of_birth` of the `time` class of Question 12.

18. Instantiate an array of objects of `times` of size `MAX_TIMES` of class `time` of Question 12.

19. Constructors are used to automatically and conveniently ____ objects.

20. A constructor is a special member function with the name of the class it belongs to. True or false?

21. Many different constructors for the same class are possible. True or false? If true, how do we invoke them?

22. Write a no-argument constructor for the `time` class that will initialize all the private data to zero (see Question 12).

23. Add a constructor to the `time` class for initializing data members.

24. Add to the constructor in Question 23 statements that check for the violation of class invariants.

25. After Question 24, is the following statement valid in the `main()` function? `time time_of_birth2(8,15,30);` If valid, what does it do?

26. If you said yes to Question 25, show the memory allocation.

27. Write the statement in `main()` to access the `hrs` data of `time_of_birth2` in Question 25.

28. To define a `display()` function for the `time` class outside the class we use the _____ _____ operator.

29. Add to the `time` class a public interface function that will display the time in the format `hrs:min:sec`.

30. In Question 18, assume `MAX_TIMES` = 2. Show the memory allocation for both data and functions after initializing the objects with arbitrary data.

*31. Add to the `time` class a member function such that two objects of `time` can be added with the syntax `time3.add_time(time1, time2)`.

32. Destructors have the same syntax as the class with a prefix _____.

*33. Add another function to the `time` class such that it returns the result of two objects of `time` added with the syntax `time1.add_time(time2)`.

34. Constructors and destructors are functions with no return type specifiers. True or false?

35. Could a destructor take arguments like the constructors? Why not?

36. Write a destructor for the `time` class with a statement `cout << "\nTime object destroyed\n"`.

37. Static class data is initialized only once for all the objects of the same class. True or false?

38. Calling a static function of a class is done using the dot operator. True or false?

39. Operator overloading makes selected operators polymorphic. Explain.

40. Why is operator overloading needed?

41. Without operator overloading, how might you do the following on matrices A, B, and C?
(i) C = A + B, (ii) C = A − B, (iii) C = A * B, (iv) C = A + B * A − A * A * B

42. When you overload an operator, the precedence of that operator remains the same. True or false?

43. In Question 41, part (iv), how many program statements were needed? Does operator overloading reduce the number of program statements in such problems? Does it make it more intuitive?

44. What will be the preferred operator to overload for matrix inverse as in $x = A^{-1}b$?

45. Discuss why the following operators cannot be overloaded: (i) `.`, (ii) `::`, (iii) `.*`, and (iv) `?:`.

46. In C++, only existing operators can be overloaded. True or false?

47. Data hiding and encapsulation make it easy/hard for the user to use objects and it is easy/hard to corrupt data inadvertently.

EXERCISES

1. Add a member function for matrix multiplication to the matrix class developed in the chapter.

2. Modify the matrix class so that all arguments are passed as constant references. Are there fewer temporary objects created with this modification?

3. Modify the class designed in Exercise 2 to do the following. The two statements are `matrx3 = matrx1; matrx3.add(matrx2);`. The result of the two statements should be equal to `matrx3 = matrx1 + matrx2`. Compare the number of temporary objects created here with the program in the chapter. Note that the same should be attempted at the end of Chapter 9 after learning the `this` pointer. Analyze the results and compare the number of temporaries.

4. Overload the operator `[]` so that it returns the *i*th element of an array `a` when using `a[i-1]`.

5. Add appropriate overloading of operators to the matrix operations program.

6. Add an ample number of `assert()` conditions to the various functions in the Reservoir class in the chapter to check for violation of all class invariants, pre- and postconditions. Test with various cases (see Chapter 3) to see if you can produce a fail-safe (no failures) or safe-fail (safe shutdown or alternatives when there is a failure) Reservoir class!

7. Assume that the following information is necessary to describe your C++ book. The title of the book is C++ for Engineers, the author name is your name, the publication year is this year, the ISBN is some arbitrary number (similar to ISBN numbers you see in books), the subject is programming, and the price is $60.99. The main function contains the following definition:

```
book_record book1;
```

Design a class with only the data and show the memory allocation.

8. Add to the class in Exercise 7 the following: Member functions to set data, display data, and access data for the author name and the ISBN number. Write a program that will use this class and set data (you can use all your textbooks for this purpose!) in an array called `book_shelf`. Which books cost less than $60? Print out all the information in a tabular form.

9. Build a class for the population census of cities with the following data: the city name, city location expressed as longitude and latitude (for simplicity, you can simply use Cartesian *x* and *y* coordinates), population by age groups (have only 3–4 age groups). Add member functions that will allow for inputting data and for getting data so that your program can answer the following question. Which cities have a population over 1000 in the 13–19 age group?

10. Create a new class called `complex` for storing complex numbers. A complex number is expressed as $x + iy$, where x is a real number expressing the real part, y is a real number expressing the imaginary part and $i = \sqrt{-1}$. Note that complex numbers are similar to two-dimensional vectors with some special rules for the arithmetic. Write constructors for inputting data. Write member functions for some or all of the following operations which operate on two complex numbers:

$$(a + ib) + (c + id) = (a + c) + i(b + d)$$
$$(a + ib) - (c + id) = (a - c) + i(b - d)$$
$$(a + ib) * (c + id) = (ac - bd) + i(ad + bc)$$
$$\frac{a + ib}{c + id} = \frac{ac + bd}{c^2 + d^2} + \frac{i(bc - ad)}{c^2 + d^2}$$

11. Add operator overloading to the `complex` class in Exercise 10.

12. Design a class for storing information on food; for example, name of the food, type of the food (meat, vegetable, etc.), calories per serving, and cost of food per serving. By this time you should have noticed that we always need member functions and/or constructors to set the data. We also need functions to get data for at least some of the data items. Write appropriate member functions.

*13. Design a class for the river flow data analysis problem described in Chapter 6, Exercise 4.

*14. Design a class that can be used in the mapping of genes, useful for Genome research. The data may consist of the size of the sequence, name of the sequence, number of related sequences and their names, and the sequence itself, consisting of some letters of the alphabet. For example, DNA molecules consist of sequences containing only A, G, C, and T. Write a function that can compare two sequences and indicate if they are related. We say that two sequences are related if they have the same character in the corresponding positions for at least 75% of the characters.

*15. Define a mesh class with the following information: the number of triangles and a list of triangles. The triangle class should contain an id (an integer number), and the nodes that make up the triangle. The node class should have a node id (an integer number) and 2-D Cartesian coordinates. In addition to the usual member functions (figuring that out for this example should be interesting), write member functions that (i) will calculate the maximum number of nodes for the given mesh object, and (ii) will produce a sparse matrix of size = maximum number of nodes. The matrix will have plus one for all connections and zeros elsewhere. You can use the example in Fig. 7.9 as a test case. Note the diagonal of the matrix has 1's and not zeros. This is a convention because every node is assumed to be connected to itself.

16. Instead of the sparse matrix function in Exercise 15 you can have a function that will print the node number and the number of edges emanating from it. This number will indicate how well connected this node is to the rest of mesh. Additionally, each edge

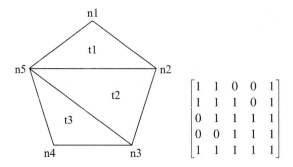

FIGURE 7.9
A sample mesh.

may have a name associated with it. Therefore, add to the mesh class a list of edges that will indicate the connections (node numbers) and a name, for example Edge1 for edge1 which connects node 1 to node 2. Write member functions to set, get, and print appropriate data from the modified mesh class.

17. A tridiagonal matrix is a square matrix which has zeros everywhere except the diagonal, the sub-diagonal above the diagonal and the sub-diagonal below the diagonal. An example is

$$\begin{bmatrix} 2 & 1 & 0 & 0 & 0 \\ 1 & 4 & 1 & 0 & 0 \\ 0 & 1 & 4 & 1 & 0 \\ 0 & 0 & 1 & 4 & 1 \\ 0 & 0 & 0 & 1 & 2 \end{bmatrix}$$

Design a matrix class that will consider the above types of matrices. You should have appropriate constructors, get functions, display functions, and functions for some basic linear algebra operations like add, subtract, scalar multiplication, and multiplication. Consider efficient ways to do the operations because of the large number of operations on zeros that may not be necessary. You can assume that the size of the matrix is known before compilation.

18. Following is a linear system of equations with n equations and n variables.

$$Ax = b$$

Sometimes (when the matrix is diagonally dominant, for example, the absolute value of the diagonal element is larger than the sum of the absolute values of other elements in the same row or column) such a system can be solved iteratively using the following equation for the ith variable.

$$x_i = \frac{1}{a_{ii}}\left(b_i - \left(\sum_{\substack{j=1 \\ j \neq i}}^{n} a_{ij}x_j\right)\right)$$

Note that an initial guess, say $x = 0$, is used to find the new value for x using the above equation and then the new x becomes the guessed x. The iterations continue until the following condition is satisfied:

$$\left(\sum_{j=1}^{n} (x_i^{new} - x_i^{old})^2 \right) < 10^{-5}$$

(a) Write a C++ member function for a standard matrix class to solve such a system. Your function is written in such a way that the main program can have the following statement:

```
vector x = A.GSsolve(b);
```

where A contains the matrix of coefficients and b has the right-hand side of the linear system for solving the linear system.

(b) Overload the \ operator so that we can use the following statement:

```
vector x = A\b;
```

19. When n resistors are connected in series in an electrical circuit, the total resistance is given as $R_{total} = R_1 + R_2 + \ldots + R_n$ and if they are connected in parallel the total resistance is given as $1/R_{total} = 1/R_1 + 1/R_2 + \ldots + 1/R_n$.

   If a series of resistors are connected to a voltage source V, then the current in the circuit is calculated as $I = V/R_{total}$. The individual voltages in the circuit are calculated as $V_i = IR_i$ where the subscript i denotes the ith resistor.

   If the n resistors are connected to a current source I in parallel, then the voltage in the circuit is calculated as $V = IR_{total}$ and the individual currents are calculated as $I_i = V/R_i$.

   Write a C++ program that will take from the user the value of n, the value of resistors, voltage or current source and its value, and outputs the appropriate results. There should be at least four classes, namely, component, resistor, voltage source, current source, and a system class. The system class should have a member function `Solve()` which will actually solve the given system with its input.

   Test Example (1): **Input:** V = 22 volts, Resistors = (2, 5, 1, 3) Ohms. **Results:** Current = 2 Amps and Voltages = (4, 10, 2, 6) volts.
   Test Example (2): **Input:** I = 7 Amps, Resistors = (1/3, 1/5, 1/2, 1/4) Ohms. **Results:** Voltage = 0.5 volt and Currents = (1.5, 2.5, 1, 2) Amps.

*20. Add to the matrix class developed in the chapter a function `solve()` which will solve a system of linear equations using the Gaussian Elimination algorithm. Consider a 3×3 linear system as below.

$$a_{11}x_1 + a_{12}x_2 + a_{13}x_3 = b_1$$
$$a_{21}x_1 + a_{22}x_2 + a_{23}x_3 = b_2$$
$$a_{31}x_1 + a_{32}x_2 + a_{33}x_3 = b_3$$

where a_{ij} means the element in the ith row and jth column. The x_i's are unknown and the rest known. The Gaussian Elimination algorithm (without pivoting) is done in two steps called forward elimination and back substitution. The pseudocode for forward elimination is

```
for i=1 to n-1
  for j=i+1 to n
    multiplier = a[j][i]/a[i][i]
    for k=i+1 to n
      a[j][k] = a[j][k]-a[i][k]*multiplier
    end for
      b[j] = b[j]-b[i]*multiplier
  endfor
endfor
```

The pseudocode for back substitution is

```
for i=n downto 1
  sum = b[i]
  for j=i+1 to n
    sum = sum - multiplier*x[j]
  endfor
  x[i] = sum/a[i][i]
endfor
```

where n is the total number of unknowns, for example 3. You should write the function such that in the main program the following statement should be possible, which will give the solution for x.

```
vector x = matrix_a.solve(vec_b);
```

Note that when you write the C++ program the array element starts from 0.

21. **Dynamic simulation of systems:** Many systems can be simulated using ordinary differential equations as given below (e.g., Spring-Mass Oscillation, RL-Circuits, or predator–prey competition).

$$\frac{dx_1}{dt} = a_{11}x_1 + a_{12}x_2$$

$$\frac{dx_2}{dt} = a_{21}x_1 + a_{22}x_2$$

or in matrix form:

$$\frac{dX}{dt} = AX$$

where X is a vector and A is a matrix of coefficients. X represents the state of the system (for example, x_1 represents the position and x_2 represents the velocity in the spring-mass problem at time t), dx_i/dt represents the instantaneous change in the ith variable, and a_{ij}'s represent the coefficients that model the interactions between the variables. If we know the initial values of x_1 and x_2, we can simulate (that is, determine the values of the system variables) over a time horizon T. Although analytical solutions exist ($X = e^{At}X^0$, X^0 being the initial solution) for problems like the above, we are going to use numerical methods, as they are more generally applicable.

Implicit Euler method for linear dynamic systems: The following is the equation used in solving the above problem.

$$HX^{n+1} = X^n, n = 0, 1, \ldots, \frac{T}{\Delta t}, H = I + A * (-\Delta t),$$

where I is an identity matrix $I = \begin{bmatrix} 1 & 0 \\ 0 & 1 \end{bmatrix}$ and Δt is a small value like 0.1 and T is the horizon length. The accuracy of the solution depends on Δt. A system of linear equations is solved at each n to determine the result. The Gaussian Elimination method (explained in Exercise 20) can be used to solve the linear system.

   You are given programs with classes that implement the Gaussian Elimination method, and the plotting routines needed (available on the accompanying diskette). Let $A = \begin{bmatrix} -1 & -1 \\ 1 & -1 \end{bmatrix}$, $X^0 = \begin{bmatrix} 100 \\ 100 \end{bmatrix}$ and $T = 10$. Solve the above problem and plot the solution as

(i) x_1 versus x_2 (called phase-plane diagram), and
(ii) R versus x_i , $i = 1$ and 2.

   Note that you have to add two overloaded operators, (i) matrix times a scalar and (ii) matrix addition, as well as a constructor `matrix (float mat[ROWS][COLS])` and destructor to the matrix class supplied to you. Give the class/object diagrams. The graphic class you need is given below (and on the accompanying diskette) with an example usage.

```
//Filename: graph.cpp
//Graphic class for simple plotting
#include <iostream.h>
#include <string.h>
#include <iomanip.h>
#include <math.h>

const int ROWS = 26, MAXSTR1 = 20, MAXSTR2 = 6;  //Global

//Vector class declaration
class Vector
{
   public:
      Vector();              //No-argument constructor which
                             //initializes a vector to zeros
      Vector(float [ROWS]);   //Constructor for
                              //initialization
       float get_array(int i);
       float find_max();
       float find_min();
      ~Vector(){}                 //A simple destructor
   private:
      float array[ROWS];
};    //Vector class declaration ends.
```

```
//Graph class
class Graph
{
   public:
        Graph(){}
        void set_title(char_title[MAXSTR1]);
        void set_x_axis_label(char x_axis[MAXSTR2]);
        void set_y_axis_label(char y_axis[MAXSTR2]);
        void graph_it(Vector, Vector);
        ~Graph(){}
   private:
        char title[MAXSTR1];
        char x_axis_label[MAXSTR2];
        char y_axis_label[MAXSTR2];
};


int main()          //Example usage
{
   float temp[ROWS];
   int i=0;
   for (float angle=-1*M_PI; angle<=1*M_PI; angle += .25) {
      temp[i] = angle;
      cout << temp[i] << endl;
      i++;
      }
   int vecsize = i-1;

   Vector X(temp);  //Initialize the x vector

   //Generate the values for a sin curve
   for (i=0; i<vecsize; ++i)
     temp[i] = sin(temp[i]);

   Vector Y(temp); //Initialize the y vector

   Graph plot1;    //Instantiate a graph object

   plot1.set_title("An example of graph");
   plot1.set_x_axis_label("Xaxis");
   plot1.set_y_axis_label("Yaxis");
   plot1.graph_it(X, Y);

   return 0;
}                                        //End of main function
```

22. The discrete Leslie model describes a single age-structured population with discrete age group i. The model used to describe the time series of different age groups is

$$x(t + 1) = Lx(t), t = 0, \ldots, T - 1$$

where x is an n-element vector, L is an $n \times n$ matrix. For example, for an 8 age group problem, the matrix is

$$
L = \begin{bmatrix}
0 & 0 & 0 & 8 & 0 & 0 & 0 & 12 \\
1/3 & 0 & 0 & 0 & 0 & 0 & 0 & 0 \\
0 & 1/2 & 0 & 0 & 0 & 0 & 0 & 0 \\
0 & 0 & 1/2 & 0 & 0 & 0 & 0 & 0 \\
0 & 0 & 0 & 1/2 & 0 & 0 & 0 & 0 \\
0 & 0 & 0 & 0 & 2/3 & 0 & 0 & 0 \\
0 & 0 & 0 & 0 & 0 & 1 & 0 & 0 \\
0 & 0 & 0 & 0 & 0 & 0 & 1 & 0
\end{bmatrix}
$$

   Plot the population of any age group, say 8. Note that the top row represents the birth rate of the age group and the other nonzero elements in matrix (just one subdiagonal) represent the survival of individuals from one group to the next. You have to build a matrix class with operator overloading to implement the Leslie equation.

Inheritance to Aid Reusability

In C++, inheritance is the main reuse mechanism.

Inheritance is to OOP languages as functions are to procedural languages. It adds extensibility, flexibility, and clarity. Inheritance is defined as the ability to build new (derived) classes that inherit data and functions from one or more previously defined (base) classes, with the possibility of redefining or adding new data and functions. That is, inheritance allows the reuse of classes. Our notations are based on those of Coad and Yourdon and will be used in diagrams to show relationships between classes (or objects). The C++ mechanisms (syntax) required to implement inheritance is described with simple programming examples. In order to use inheritance correctly, new modeling rules are described which extend the concept of class invariants, pre- and postconditions. Lastly, a multi-reservoir system case study that builds on the single reservoir case studied in Chapter 7 is presented, using some features of inheritance.

HIERARCHY OF CLASSES

A hierarchy of classes can be created using inheritance. For example, a class of motorized vehicles shares common characteristics such as an engine, a horn, an accelerator, and brakes. Classes such as cars, buses, and trucks can be derived from the motorized vehicle class because they share the common characteristics defined in the base class. Their unique characteristics may be added to the corresponding class. Note that the derived classes inherit *all* the characteristics from the base class. Therefore, it is important to design classes keeping this fact in mind.

Multiple inheritance is possible in C++ although it is not available in many other OOP languages. A minivan can be derived from the car and truck classes; then the minivan class is said to use multiple inheritance. The authors recommend that users of OOP try to avoid multiple inheritance, at least in situations where single inheritance can be easily used. However, multiple inheritance is ideal for situations where classes can be derived from two disjoint base classes. For example, a simulation program where the user interface forms a disjoint class from the classes that implement computational algebra would be a convenient place to use multiple inheritance.

Class Relationships

A mammal *is* a kind of animal. A building *has* floors. A car *uses* lubricants. The elevator *knows* the floor it has stopped on. Each of these four statements describes associations between two separate classes. However, each of the four associations here are distinct and are modeled differently. Similar associations exist between objects which are instances of classes. The last two relationships are relatively weak compared to the first two. The implementation of any of these associations could be language-dependent and may be done the same way for more than one type of relationship. On the other hand there may be more than one way to implement them. The rest of the chapter is mainly concerned with implementing the first type of relationship, namely, the *is-a* relationship. The *has-a* relationship is implemented by defining appropriate data members of a certain class in another class, as explained in the multi-reservoir case study. The *uses-a* and the *knows-a* relationships are not described but can easily be implemented, for example through message passing with appropriate methods (member functions) and arguments, or through pointers as member data (Chapter 9).

SINGLE INHERITANCE

Figure 8.1 illustrates a hierarchy of classes created by single inheritance. Each derived class has only a single parent (base) class. The head of the curved arrow corresponds to the base class from which the class at the tail is derived. The boxes indicate that these are classes (boxes will be used also for objects and it should be clear from the context whether it is an object or a class). The top section of a box indicates the name of the class, the middle section indicates data members, and the bottom section indicates the member functions.

Note that, in this case, the functions of the derived classes have the same names but override the functions of the base classes. The following program illustrates how the base class `resident` is declared along with the derived class `employee`. It also illustrates other features such as accessibility of base class data and functions in derived classes.

```
//Filename inher0.cpp
//Derives employee class from resident class
//No constructors used
#include <iostream.h>

const int MAXSTR = 9;
```

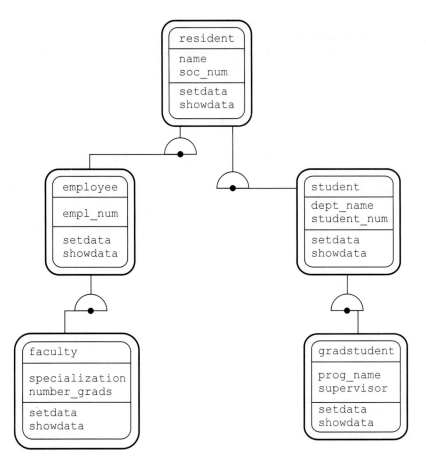

A class diagram is essential to get a good idea of the class interrelationships.

FIGURE 8.1
An example of single inheritance hierarchy.

```
class resident
    {
    public:

        void setdata()
        //Pre: None.
        //Post: Resident data (name and social insurance no.)
        //is defined.
            {
            cout << endl
                << "Enter name with no spaces (8 characters stored): ";
            cin.get(name,MAXSTR);;
            cout << endl
                << "Enter your social insurance number"
                << "(9 digits number): ";
            cin >> soc_num;
            }
```

```
      void showdata()
      //Pre: Resident data is defined.
      //Post: Resident data is displayed: name and social number.
         {
         cout << endl << "Name: " << name;
         cout << endl << "SIN: " << soc_num;
         }
   protected:
      char name[MAXSTR];      //Resident's name
      unsigned long soc_num;  //Resident's social
                              //insurance number
 };

class employee : public resident   //Employee class publicly
                                   //derived from resident
   {
   public:
   void setdata()
      //Pre: None.
      //Post: Employee data (empl_name) is defined.
      {
      resident::setdata();
      cout << "\nEnter employee number (5 digits): ";
      cin >> empl_num;
      }
   void showdata()
      //Pre: Employee data is defined.
      //Post: Employee data is displayed: name, social number
      //and employee number.
      {
      resident::showdata();
      cout << "\nEmployee Number: " << empl_num;
      }
   protected:
   unsigned long empl_num;
};

int main()
   {
   employee e1;

   cout << "Enter the data for employee 1 " ;

   e1.setdata();

   cout << "\nData of employee 1: \n";

   e1.showdata();

   return 0;
   }
```

*Make data mem-
bers protected if you
expect that in fu-
ture the class will be
used as a base class.*

TABLE 8.1
Data access specifiers and inheritance

| | Specification type in base class | | |
Accessibility to base class data	Public	Protected	Private
Base class can access?	Yes	Yes	Yes
Derived class can access?	Yes	Yes	No
Others can access?	Yes	No	No

In the above program, the reserved word `protected` is used instead of private and this difference will be discussed later. The class `resident` is declared first and then the class `employee` is declared using inheritance. That is, the employee class is derived from the resident class. Both classes have functions that set data corresponding to the incremental information necessary at that class. For example, in the employee class the incremental information is the employee number `empl_numb`. However, objects are defined by a single class name, for example `employee e1;`. In the `main()` function, in order to include the information of `name` and `SIN`, the base class function is invoked in the line `resident::setdata()` in the employee class. However, because publicly derived classes have access to any data that is declared under `protected` in the base class, the alternative method is to set the data of the base class in the derived class. This means, replace the line `resident::setdata()` with appropriate statements in the `setdata()` of the employee class. Changing `private` to `protected` is the major change required when declaring classes that may be useful as base classes. If the data is not declared under `protected` or `public` then the derived classes have no direct access to base class member data. Table 8.1 presents the accessibility of base class data under different categories and assumes that classes are publicly derived.

Accessibility can always be increased by providing appropriate member functions declared either as public (accessible to all) or as protected (accessible to the class and derived classes). Note that if the classes are derived as protected then public and protected members of the base class become protected members of the derived class. On the other hand, if the classes are derived as private then the public and protected members of the base class become private members of the derived class. The most common form of derivation is public (suitable for *is-a* relationships) and will be the only one used in this book.

DEPTH OF INHERITANCE

The following program illustrates the derivation of the `gradstudent` class and the `faculty` class whose depth of inheritance is at level 2. It is easy to derive classes of any depth as presented in the program.

```
//Filename level2in.cpp
//Inheritance example with depth of level = 2.
#include <iostream.h>
```

```
const int MAXSTR = 9;

class resident
    {
    public:
        void setdata()
        //Pre: None.
        //Post: Resident data (name and social insurance no.)
        //is defined.
            {
            cout << endl << "Enter name with no spaces"
                << " (8 characters stored): ";
            cin >> name;
            cout << endl << "Enter your social insurance number"
                << " (9 digits number): ";
            cin >> soc_num;
            }

        void showdata()
        //Pre: Resident data is defined.
        //Post: Resident data is displayed: name and social number.
            {
            cout << endl << "Name: " << name;
            cout << endl << "SIN: " << soc_name;
            }
    protected:
        char name[MAXSTR];        //Resident's name
        unsigned long soc_num;    //Resident's social insurance number

};

class student : public resident           //Student class publicly
                                          //derived from resident
    {
    public:
    void setdata()
    //Pre: None.
    //Post: Student data is defined: department name, student number.
        {
        resident::setdata();
        cout << endl << "Enter dept. name with no spaces"
            << " (8 characters stored): ";
        cin >> dept_name;
        cout << "\nEnter student number (6 digits): ";
        cin >> student_num;
        }
    void showdata()
    //Pre: Student data is defined.
    //Post: Student data is displayed.
        {
        resident::showdata();
```

```
                        cout << "\nDepartment: " << dept_name;
                        cout << "\nStudent Number: " << student_num;
                        }
                 protected:
                 char dept_name[MAXSTR];
                 unsigned long student_num;
          };

     class gradstudent : public student           //Gradstudent class publicly
                                                    //derived from student
              {
              public:
              void setdata()
              //Pre: None.
              //Post: Gradstudent data is defined: program name, supervisor.
                   {
                   student::setdata();
                   cout << endl << "Enter prog. name (MASC or PHD): ";
                   cin >> prog_name;
                   cout << "\nEnter Supervisor name (no spaces, 8 char's): ";
                   cin >> supervisor;
                   }
              void showdata()
              //Pre: Gradstudent data is defined.
              //Post: Gradstudent data is displayed.
                   {
                   student::showdata();
                   cout << "\nDegree Program: " << prog_name;
                   cout << "\nSupervisor: " << supervisor;
                   }
              protected:
              char prog_name[MAXSTR];
              char supervisor[MAXSTR];
          };
     class employee : public resident             //Employee class publicly
                                                    //derived from resident
              {
              public:
              void setdata()
              //Pre: None.
              //Post: Employee data is defined: employee number
                   {
                   resident::setdata();
                   cout << "\nEnter employee number (5 digits): ";
                   cin >> empl_num;
                   }
              void showdata()
              //Pre: Employee data is defined.
              //Post: Employee data is displayed.
                   {
                   resident::showdata();
```

```cpp
      cout << "\nEmployee Number: " << empl_num;
      }
   protected:
   unsigned long empl_num;
};

class faculty : public employee      //Faculty class publicly
                                     //derived from employee
   {
   public:
   void setdata()
   //Pre: None.
   //Post: Faculty data is defined: specialization.
      {
      employee::setdata();
      cout << endl << "Enter specialization"
           << " (no spaces, 8 char's) : ";
      cin >> specialization;
      cout << "\nEnter Number of grad. students: ";
      cin >> number_grads;
      }

   void showdata()
   //Pre: Faculty data is defined.
   //Post: Faculty data is displayed.
      {
      employee::showdata();
      cout << "\nSpecialization: " << specialization;
      cout << "\nNumber of graduate students supervised: "
           << number_grads;
      }
   protected:
   char specialization[MAXSTR];
   int number_grads;
};

int main()
   {
   faculty f1;

   cout << "Enter the data for faculty 1 " ;

   f1.setdata();

   cout << "\nData of faculty 1: \n";

   f1.showdata();

   return 0;
   }
```

Note that the derived classes do not explicitly show the level of inheritance. Any good compiler will provide tools that show these levels of inheritance which may be necessary especially for debugging purposes! In the next section we show how constructors are used when using inheritance.

CONSTRUCTORS IN DERIVED CLASSES

The following program presents the use of constructors in derived classes. You may remember that constructors are useful for defining and initializing objects which are instances of classes.

```cpp
//Filename coninher.cpp
//Examples of inheritance using constructors
#include <iostream.h>
#include <string.h>  //For using the strncpy function

const int MAXSTR = 9;

class resident      //Base class
    {
    public:
        resident(){};           //No-argument constructor
        resident(char _name[MAXSTR],
                unsigned long _soc_num) //Two-argument constructor
            {
            strncpy(name, _name, MAXSTR); //Using string copy function
            soc_num = _soc_num;
            }
        void showdata()
        //Pre: Resident data is defined.
        //Post: Resident data is displayed: name and social number.
            {
            cout << endl << "Name: " << name;
            cout << endl << "SIN: " << soc_num;
            }
    protected:
        char name[MAXSTR];      //Resident's name
        unsigned long soc_num;  //Resident's social insurance number
    };

class employee : public resident            //Employee class publicly
                                            //derived from resident
    {
    public:
    employee() : resident() {}              //No-argument constructor
    employee(char _name[MAXSTR], unsigned long _soc_num,
            unsigned long _empl_num)
                                            //Three-argument derived
                                            //class constructor
```

```
                : resident(_name, _soc_num)      //and this for calling
                                                 //the base class
                                                 //constructor
        {
        empl_num = _empl_num;                    //Setting the
                                                 //employee number
        }

    void showdata()
    //Pre: Employee data is defined.
    //Post: Employee data is displayed.
        {
        resident::showdata();
        cout << "\nEmployee Number: " << empl_num;
        }
    protected:
    unsigned long empl_num;
};

int main()
    {
    resident r1;
    employee e1;
    char name[MAXSTR];
    unsigned long number, empl_num;

    cout << "Enter the data for resident 1 " ;
    cout << endl << "Enter name with no spaces"
         << " (8 characters stored): ";
    cin >> name;
    cout << endl << "Enter your social insurance number"
         << " (9 digits number): ";
    cin >> number;
    cout << "\nEnter employee number (5 digits): ";
    cin >> empl_num;

    employee e2(name, number, //Set the data using the
                empl_num);    //three-argument constructor

    cout << "\nData of employee 1: (printing uninitialized object)\n";
    e1.showdata();                          //Garbage will be printed

    cout << endl << "\nData of employee 2: \n";
    e2.showdata();
    e1 = e2;                                //Default copy constructor
    cout << endl
         << "Printing results to show default"
         << " copy constructor works\n";
    e1.showdata();
```

```
    resident r2 = e1;                    //Assigning a derived-class object
                                         //to base class object is allowed!
    cout << endl
        << "Printing results from assigning derived class object"
        << " to base class object\n";

    r2.showdata();

    return 0;
    }
```

The following is a sample session from the execution of the above program.

```
Enter the data for resident 1
Enter name with no spaces (8 characters stored): Ponnu
Enter your social insurance number (9 digits number): 909090909
Enter employee number (5 digits): 55555

Data of employee 1: (printing uninitialized object)

Name:
SIN: 4294910359
Employee Number: 959920772

Data of employee 2:

Name: Ponnu
SIN: 909090909
Employee Number: 55555

Printing results to show default copy constructor works

Name: Ponnu
SIN: 909090909
Employee Number: 55555

Printing results from assigning derived class object to base class
object

Name: Ponnu
SIN: 909090909
```

The constructors of the base class are defined as usual. However, one of the constructors of the derived class employee has a new syntax:

```
employee(char _name[MAXSTR], unsigned long _soc_num, unsigned long
_empl_num)
            : resident(_name, _soc_num)
```

The constructor has three arguments with the first two belonging to base class resident and the last one belonging to the derived class employee. However, instead of the line resident::setdata() as in the program inher0.cpp above, the data is passed to the base class with the statement `resident (_name, _soc_num)` following the colon. It is noted that all the variables in the argument list of the constructor are local to that constructor. Note that `resident r2 = e1;` is used for assigning a derived-class object to a base class object. This is allowed even though the data types don't match because `employee` is a subclass of `resident`.

MULTIPLE INHERITANCE

The following program illustrates how multiple inheritance is used to derive a child class from two of its parent classes, namely the papa class and the mama class! We do this without constructors, just for this example. Note that the parent class data is declared as protected and hence is directly accessible to all the derived classes.

```
//Filename: multinh0.cpp
//Demonstration of multiple inheritance without constructors
#include <iostream.h>

class mama
    {
    public:

    void setdata()
    //Pre: None
    //Post: Mama class data is defined.
        {
        cout << "\nInput mama class data (any integer number): ";
        cin >> x;
        }

    void showdata()
    //Pre: Mama data is defined.
    //Post: Data is displayed.
        {
        cout << "\nThe mama class data is: " << x;
        }
    protected:
    int x;
    };                      //End of mama class declaration

class papa
    {
    public:

    void setdata()
    //Pre: None
    //Post: Papa data is defined.
        {
        cout << "\nInput papa class data (any integer number): ";
        cin >> y;
        }
```

Multiple inheritance is not available in most of the OOP languages and it is considered a hard concept to implement.

```
    void showdata()
    //Pre: Data for papa is defined.
    //Post: Data is displayed.
       {
       cout << "\nThe papa class data is: " << y;
       }
    protected:
    int y;
};                       //End of papa class declaration

class child : public mama, public papa
    {
    public:

    void setdata()
    //Pre: None
    //Post: Child class data is defined.
       {
       mama::setdata();
       papa::setdata();
       cout << "\nInput child class data (any integer number): ";
       cin >> z;
       }

    void showdata()
    //Pre: Data for child is defined.
    //Post: Data is displayed.
       {
       mama::showdata();
       papa::showdata();
       cout << "\nThe child class data is: " << z;
       }
    protected:
    int z;
};                       //End of child class declaration

int main()
    {
    child c1;

    c1.setdata();
    c1.showdata();

    return 0;
    }
```

The only special thing in the above program is the declaration

```
          class child : public mama, public papa
```

The child class is derived publicly from both parent classes. The following program demonstrates how constructors are declared when using multiple inheritance. The

syntax of constructors for classes with multiple inheritance is a logical extension of
the syntax of constructors for classes derived by single inheritance.

```cpp
//Filename: mulinco0.cpp
//Demonstration of multiple inheritance with constructors

#include <iostream.h>

class mama
    {
    public:
    mama() {}        //No-argument constructor
    mama(int xx)     //Single-argument constructor
        {
        x = xx;        //Sets the mama class data
        }

    void showdata()
    //Pre: Mama data is defined.
    //Post: Data is displayed.
        {
        cout << "\nThe mama class data is: " << x;
        }
    protected:
    int x;
};                        //End of mama class declaration

class papa
    {
    public:
    papa() {}        //No-argument constructor
    papa(int yy)     //Single-argument constructor

        {
        y = yy;        //Sets the papa class data
        }

    void showdata()
    //Pre:  Data for papa is defined.
    //Post: Data is displayed.
        {
        cout << "\nThe papa class data is: " << y;
        }
    protected:
    int y;
};                   //End of papa class declaration

class child : public mama, public papa
    {
    public:
```

```
        child() : mama(), papa() {}        //No-argument constructor
        child(int xx, int yy, int zz) : mama(xx),papa(yy)
           {
           z = zz;        //Sets the child class data
           }

        void showdata()
        //Pre: Data for child is defined.
        //Post: Data is displayed.
           {
           mama::showdata();
           papa::showdata();
           cout << "\nThe child class data is: " << z;
           }
        protected:
        int z;
};                        //End of child class declaration

int main()
   {
   child c1;

   cout << "\nPrinting results from uninitialized object";
   c1.showdata();

   child c2(1,2,3);    //Initializing child object c2

   cout << "\nPrinting results from initialized object:";

   c2.showdata();

   mama m1 = c2;
   papa p1 = c2;
   mama m2 = c2;

   cout << "\nPrinting results from initialized parent classes:";

   m1.showdata();
   p1.showdata();
   m2.showdata();

   return 0;
   }
```

A sample output is presented below.

```
        Printing results from uninitialized object
        The mama class data is: 13729
        The papa class data is: 1716
        The child class data is: 3855
        Printing results from initialized object:
        The mama class data is: 1
```

```
The papa class data is: 2
The child class data is: 3
Printing results from initialized parent classes:
The mama class data is: 1
The papa class data is: 2
The mama class data is: 1
```

The constructor for the child class is declared as

```
child(int xx, int yy, int zz) : mama(xx),papa(yy)
```

The first two arguments in the argument list of child are passed on to the respective parent classes. The third argument is used within the child class to set the data of the child class. The variable names are chosen so that there is less confusion as to which variable should be passed on to the parent classes. If by mistake we had written mama(yy), the compiler would not complain, as the type and number of arguments match (which can be relaxed by using constructors with default arguments). The error would have been a logical one and would be harder to catch. Also, because of this reason, the statement mama m1 = c2 in the main program sends the first data in the child c2 to mama m1 and, similarly, the second data to the papa class in the statement papa p1 = c2, all using the default copy constructor provided by the compiler. Note that we could not assign a parent class object to a child class object.

In this example we have carefully chosen disjoint data for the parent classes. What if we have the same data member in both parent classes? Will there be double copy in the child class? This could happen if the mama and papa classes are both derived from another class. It could create a problem, but it can be overcome using the concept of virtual classes. This subject is outside the scope of this book.

DEFINING YOUR OWN HEADER FILES

When you start defining multiple classes and inheritance it becomes convenient to define your own header files. This can be done by (i) storing your class declarations in a filename ending with suffix .h and (ii) including these .h files in your source. Use the commands shown below in order to avoid multiple inclusions of the same header file.

```
#ifndef filename_h  //Checks if it is already defined
#define filename_h..//and defines it if it is not defined.
....
body of the class declaration
....
#endif
```

The three preprocessor commands define the variable filename_h declaration if it is not already declared. The header files are where we give information about the classes to the user, especially the interface information that the user needs. We hide their implementation in *.cpp source files. This is another systematic step to let users see only what they need.

MORE ON OBJECT-ORIENTED MODELING

Class invariants can be reinforced in derived classes. A derived class is a specialization and the base class is a generalization.

Inheritance is used to derive a new class from a base class. The base class is the superclass if we assume single inheritance. Note that we defined a class invariant as a property that no instance of a class can violate. In addition, make sure that no derived class instances disobey base class as well as derived class invariants. If *bird* is a base class and we defined it as animals that fly, then we cannot derive a new class called *ostrich* from our bird class. If we did, we would violate a base class invariant. However, a base class invariant can be reinforced by inheritance. For example, we have a `student` class which has been defined as a set of persons who are enrolled in a degree program at a university. Then a class of students chosen for the `deans_honor_list` reinforces the base class invariant because students in the dean's honor list must first be enrolled in a degree program. The derived class is a specialization and the base class is a generalization. Note that class invariants are properties of the classes and if any of the class invariants are violated, the model and the program that implements it are erroneous.

Pre- and Postconditions

You may remember that the preconditions of a method are conditions that are asserted to be true before calling the method and that postconditions are conditions that are asserted to be true after the method has executed correctly. A precondition can be further restricted in a derived class and a postcondition can be further reinforced in a derived class. For example, `setgraduate()` is a method of the `student` class and it puts a student on a graduating class list only if the average grade is 60 or above. Requiring the average to be 60 or above is the precondition of that class. If the `setgraduate()` method of the `deans_honor_list` expects the grade to be 80 or above, which is the precondition, then the precondition of the derived class is more restrictive than the base class precondition. This is allowed. On the other hand, the postcondition of the `setgraduate()` method in the `student` class is that the student's name will appear on the graduating list, which is reinforced by the postcondition of the `setgraduate()` method of the `deans_honor_list` class by putting the student's name not only on the graduating list but also on the dean's honor list. This is also allowed. In summary, class invariants, pre- and postconditions and their strict enforcement increase program reliability.

CASE STUDY (INHERITANCE AND OBJECTS' RELATIONSHIPS)

Multi-Reservoir System Simulator

You are aware of the single reservoir system simulator that was developed in Chapter 7. The program was useful to simulate the behavior of a single reservoir. We are now interested in simulating a multi-reservoir system where reservoirs are connected in some arbitrary manner, that is, either in series, or in parallel, or both. An example is

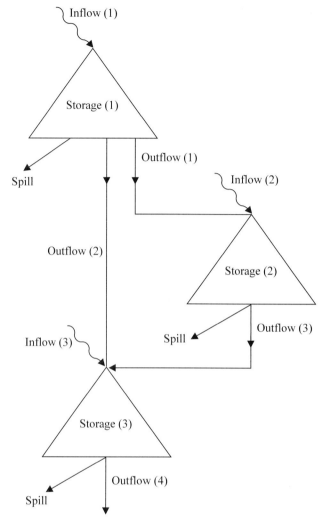

FIGURE 8.2
A three-reservoir system.

shown in Fig. 8.2. The problem has been chosen to be realistic yet simple. However, do not expect to understand the whole problem in a single reading. The advantage of studying this problem well is that many engineering systems in various fields such as electrical, mechanical, and structural, among others, can be solved similarly. The common concept behind all systems is that a system consists of one or many interrelated components connected together, thus defining the system topology, and that the components act together to form the system behavior. Understanding the system behavior is a major reason for modeling engineering systems.

Simulate the behavior of the above system for a single time period using C++ and object-oriented programming for the following data. The single period inflows for the three reservoirs are = {10, 5, 30}; the corresponding demands for water at each outflow for all four outflows are $= \{10, 5, 20, 30\}$. The initial storages in the three reservoirs are $= \{10, 5, 30\}$. For simplicity, you can assume that the reservoir storages have no minimum and maximum bounds; hence, there is no need to consider spills that are always zero, and the outflow values equal the demands of the respective outflows (see the Great Lakes problem in the exercises). The dynamics of reservoir i is now given as

$$\text{storage}(i) = \text{storage}(i) + \text{inflow}(i) + \sum_j \text{conmat}(i, j) * \text{outflow}(j)$$

where storage(i) on the left corresponds to the ending storage of reservoir i, storage(i) on the right corresponds to the starting storage, inflow(i) corresponds to the inflow in reservoir i, outflow(j) corresponds to the outflow value in outflow(j), and the last term with the summation corresponds to net flow to reservoir i due to various outflows in the system, where conmat(i, j) is a matrix that defines the connections between the reservoirs. For example, conmat(i, j) $= 1$ if the jth outflow is coming into reservoir i, conmat(i, j) $= -1$ if the jth outflow is going out of reservoir i. If the jth outflow is not connected to reservoir i, conmat(i, j) $= 0$. In the above system of three reservoirs, the dynamic equation for reservoir 2 is

$$\text{storage}(2) = \text{storage}(2) + \text{inflow}(2) + 1 * \text{outflow}(1) + 0 * \text{outflow}(2)$$
$$+ (-1) * \text{outflow}(3) + 0 * \text{outflow}(4)$$

because outflow(1) comes in, outflow(3) goes out, and outflow(2) and outflow(4) are not connected to reservoir 2.

1. Problem analysis

A multi-reservoir system is to be simulated using data on the system inflow values, demands at outflows, initial storages, and the connections between different components. The simulation is for a single period for which data for demand and inflow are known. The required results are the storages of all the reservoirs.

Problem statement: Simulate a multi-reservoir system with the given input.

Input/output analysis: The input required : The topology of the system (that is, which inflow is connected to which reservoir, which two reservoirs an outflow connects), initial storages; inflows and demands must be given for each period for each reservoir.

The outputs are final storage in each period.

2. Design

We will use class (object) based decomposition to solve the problem. Table 8.2 presents the objects identified (strictly speaking, classes), possible attributes, and methods (member functions) for each kind of object. We will assume that all objects require common functions to set and get data as well as constructors and destructors. Methods that are unique to any class/object are presented in the table.

Issues to consider while modeling the class hierarchy. Design a class hierarchy that considers (i) data visibility, that is, what each object needs in order to provide

TABLE 8.2
Objects in the multi-reservoir system simulator

Objects	Attributes	Methods
inflow	id, to reservoir, value	
outflow	id, to reservoir, from reservoir, value	
reservoir	id, storage	
system	id, inflows, outflows, reservoirs, connection matrix (conmat)	connect, process

the services expected of it, (ii) how closely you can model using the real-world relations, and (iii) reuse, which means that data and services common to more than one class should be separated and should be provided by base classes. When considering data visibility, consider data hiding as a protective device to hinder unauthorized access. By default we can assume that all data members are hidden (declared as private) and member functions should be provided for access to members outside the class members. There are many possible designs, each depending upon whether you consider single inheritance, multiple inheritance, *is-a* relation, *has-a* relation, and so on (see the exercises). Do not be afraid to go back to the beginning and iterate. There is no unique design. Designing is a creative activity, artistic as well as scientific. The authors, after many considerations and a couple of iterations, came up with the hierarchy shown in Fig. 8.3.

   Explanation of the class hierarchy and object relationships diagram. The boxes indicate the presence of classes and objects with their names, their respective data members and services (member functions). There are some recognizable patterns; for example, all components have constructors, member functions to set data, and member functions to get member data where they are allowed and necessary. The CComponent class (note the convention that all class names start with uppercase C) does not seem to be really necessary, but it gives help in terms of providing common data and services. We recommend it. The use of the convention that lets all classes originate from a single class is briefly discussed in Chapter 9 (in the section on static and dynamic binding) and is somewhat outside the scope of this book. *Is-a* relationships are shown with lines with a curved arrow, for example CInflow is a CComponent, COutflow is a CComponent, etc. The *has-a* object/class relationships (also called aggregate associations) are indicated with a straight-edged arrow. For example, a single CSystem *has-a* set of many CReservoirs and hence the diagram has a numeral 1 at the CSystem class and letter m (for many) at the CReservoir class. The relationships could be one-to-zero or one, one-to-one, one-to-many, or many-to-many. The first three are common and easier to model and implement than the last one.

   Note that the modeling of *has-a* relationships is explicit and is separated from the implementation done through data members of the particular class. For example, the association of CSystem object with CInflow objects is done with the inf[] array shown simply as inf in the CSystem class diagram. Similarly, the CSystem class has COutflow and CReservoir object arrays. After we learn pointers in Chapter

Design patterns:
Class pattern such as that used in the multi-reservoir problem is called composite by Gamma et al. and is probably the most prevalent pattern. Note that, using virtual functions described in Chapter 10, all the different objects such as inflows, outflows, reservoirs, and the system can be treated uniformly as simply component objects.

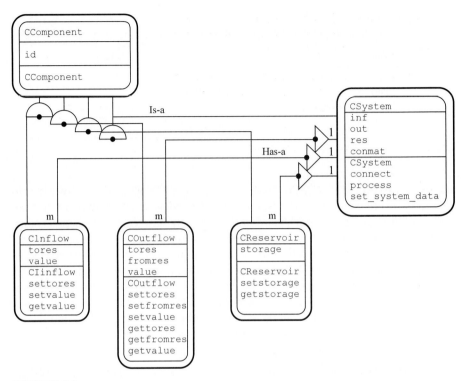

FIGURE 8.3
Class relationship diagram for a multi-reservoir problem.

9, they can be used to implement these associations efficiently. Lastly, an object diagram that is specific to the system solved could be drawn using the notations as above.

Hand example. So far, we have used hand examples for designing the functional model of the object-oriented modeling technique (whose usual duty is to get a result by transforming the input data; for example, sqrt(x) is a function whose result is the transform of x to $\sqrt{x}$). These hand examples help us design the algorithms necessary for providing the services required of the objects. In this multi-reservoir simulation example, all methods except connect() and process() of the CSystem class just correspond to data input or output and are quite straightforward to design. The process() function is simply the application of the reservoir dynamics equation given in the problem. Verify that the result you obtain for the storages of the three reservoirs for the given input data is 5, 0, 55, for reservoirs 1, 2, 3, respectively. We will concentrate here only on the connect() method and design an algorithm that performs the transformation which, in this case, is to build the conmat[][] matrix. For this transformation we will use the connection information stored in the COutflow objects. The objective of this method is to formulate the connection matrix of size number of reservoirs × number of outflows with appropriate element values from the set $\{0, 1, -1\}$ as explained before. If the problem is hard you may have to use the top-down design process on the data transformation required in any member function of interest.

> connect():   Initially set conmat $(i, j) = 0$, for all i, j.
>
>   For each column of conmat matrix
>
>   Set 1 or -1 depending upon the row number and
>
>   whether it is fromres or tores

The above pseudocode is further refined as below:

First refinement

connect():

```
//Initializing conmat (i, j) = 0, for all i, j
for i = 1 to maximum number of reservoirs
    for j = 1 to maximum number of outflows
        conmat (i, j) = 0
    endfor
endfor
// Setting the column elements to 1 or −1
for j = 1 to maximum number of outflows
    conmat (j.tores, j) = 1
    conmat (j.fromres, j) = −1
endfor
```

The above pseudocode was implemented, but we had a logic error involving outflows that did not connect to any reservoir, as in the outflow from reservoir 3 in our example. Therefore, two modifications to the program were done. We made sure that the `tores` data members of all outflows were set either with the corresponding reservoir number or -100. The -100 indicates that the outflow does not connect to any reservoir in the system. When setting the `conmat` matrix this information was used as shown below.

Second refinement

connect():

```
                    . . .

                    . . .
if (j.tores >= 0) conmat (j.tores, j) = 1 //otherwise = 0
                    . . .
```

3. Coding and debugging

At last we are ready to code. First we implemented the class diagram in C++ code and it is an easy and direct translation. Many Computer-Aided Software Engineering (CASE) tools exist that can do this work for you by creating appropriate header files to create the class declarations and corresponding definitions (stubs) in a source code file. We used one such CASE tool (see the annotated bibliography for details) to draw the diagram. But we wrote C++ code ourselves without using the CASE tool's code generator. Carefully go through our program, including reading and understanding the comments.

After the implementation of class declarations, we completed the definitions of all input (`set...`) functions and output (`get...`) functions, leaving

Csystem::set_system_data() until last. For pedagogical reasons we hard-coded the system initialization in the CSystem::set_system_data() so that it corresponds to the three-reservoir system we are solving. In the exercises, you will learn to modify this part of the program for any multi-reservoir problem. This is the only method that requires changes!

```cpp
//File mresych1.cpp
//Simulates a multi-reservoir system for a single period
//Currently the system data is hard-coded for a given example system.

#include <iostream.h>
#include <string.h>

const int MAXRES=3, MAXOUT=4;   //Maximum number of reservoirs
                                //and outflows
const int MAXCH=10; //Maximum number of characters in component id

//Component class declaration
//This is a base class for all the derived classes in this problem.
class CComponent
    {
    public:
        CComponent() {    //No-argument constructor
          strcpy(id, "");
        }
        CComponent(char lid[MAXCH]) {
          strncpy(id, lid, MAXCH); //This data is never really used
                            //in this program and hence is not
                            //set for any of the objects.
        }
    protected:
        char id[MAXCH];
    };        //Omitting the semicolon is a common error and
              //creates compiler error messages!

//Inflow class declaration
class CInflow : public CComponent
    {
    public:
        CInflow() : CComponent(){}  //No-argument constructor
        void settores(int);
        void setvalue(int);
        int getvalue();
    private:
        int tores;  //Connected to tores reservoir
        int value;  //Inflow value
    };

//Outflow class declaration
class COutflow : public CComponent
```

```cpp
    {
    public:
       COutflow() : CComponent(){}  //No-argument constructor
       void settores(int);
       void setfromres(int);
       void setvalue(int);
       int gettores();
       int getfromres();
       int getvalue();
    private:
       int tores;     //Flows into reservoir tores
       int fromres;   //Flows from reservoir fromres
       int value;     //Outflow value
    };

//Reservoir class declaration
class CReservoir : public CComponent
    {
    public:
       CReservoir() : CComponent(){} //No-argument constructor
       void setstorage(int);
       int getstorage();
    private:
       int storage;
    };

//System class declaration
class CSystem : public CComponent
    {
    public:
       CSystem() : CComponent(){}  //No-argument constructor
       void set_system_data();
    private:
       CInflow inf[MAXRES];        //has-a relation to inflows
       COutflow out[MAXOUT];       //has-a relation to outflows
       CReservoir res[MAXRES];     //has-a relation to reservoirs
       int conmat[MAXRES][MAXOUT]; //Connection matrix
       void connect();
       void process();
    }; //end of system declaration


//The declarations of classes end here!

//The definitions of class methods start here!

//This runs the simulation
void CSystem::process()    //Having a semicolon here will
                           //create compiler error
                           //messages
```

```
//Pre: The system is set (call set_system_data()!)
//Post: The system is run for a single period
{
   int tmp;
   for (int i=0; i<MAXRES; ++i) {
       //Find the total outflow for res i
       int totoutfl = 0;
       for (int j=0; j<MAXOUT; ++j)
           totoutfl += conmat[i][j] * out[j].getvalue();
       tmp = res[i].getstorage() + inf[i].getvalue() + totoutfl;
       res[i].setstorage(tmp);   //Set tmp as storage value
       cout << "RESERVOIR " << i << " storage = " << tmp << endl;
   }
   cout << endl << "THE END OF SIMULATION\n";
}


void CSystem::connect()
//Pre: The system outflows must have been created with valid
//data for their tores and fromres data members. Valid data
//for fromres is 0 to MAXRES-1 and for tores is
//0 to MAXRES-1 or -100.
//Post: Row by row the connection matrix conmat will
//be set with +1 corresponding to the tores index
//and -1 corresponding to the fromres index.
{
   for (int i=0; i<MAXRES; ++i) {
    for (int j=0; j<MAXOUT; ++j)
       conmat[i][j]=0;
   }

   for (int j=0; j<MAXOUT; ++j) {

      /*
       * Without the if condition below you will have a logical error!
       * The authors had this error and it was debugged using
       * trace (simple cout and cin statements; cout for getting
       * the results of operations to check for expected results and
       * cin to make a pause, thus marking the line). If you have
       * integrated debuggers use them! The trace was done starting
       * with main and going down to each function, block
       * and line!
       */

      if (out[j].gettores() >=0 ) conmat[out[j].gettores()][j] = 1;
      conmat[out[j].getfromres()][j] = -1;

      /*
       * The following 3 lines were used during debugging
       * cout << "i=3,j,conmat[3][j] " << conmat[3][j] << endl;
       * char ch;
```

```
        * cin >> ch; //Pausing to analyze the results
        */
    }


}

void CSystem::set_system_data()
//Pre: None
//Post: The entire system, namely, inflows, outflows, and reservoirs
//are set with their data. The connections are established and the
//process function is then called and the final storages are output.
{

    cout << "\nWelcome to the multi-reservoir simulator\n";
    cout << "You have to supply data for " << MAXRES
         << " reservoirs, inflows\n"
         << "and " << MAXOUT << " outflows\n";
    cout << "Here the required data has been hard-coded\n";
    //We will hard-code the system topology and other information
    //topology
    inf[0].settores(0);    //Connected to reservoir 1
                           //The index number is one less
                           //due to C++ array indexing!
    inf[1].settores(1);    //Connected to reservoir 2
    inf[2].settores(2);    //Connected to reservoir 3

    out[0].settores(1);    //Flows into reservoir 2
    out[1].settores(2);    //Flows into reservoir 3
    out[2].settores(2);    //Flows into reservoir 3
    out[3].settores(-100); //Does not flow to any reservoir
    out[0].setfromres(0);  //Flows from reservoir 1
    out[1].setfromres(0);  //Flows from reservoir 1
    out[2].setfromres(1);  //Flows from reservoir 2
    out[3].setfromres(2);  //Flows from reservoir 3
    //Initial storages of reservoirs are set
    res[0].setstorage(10);
    res[1].setstorage(5);
    res[2].setstorage(30);

    /*
     * If we do not want to hard-code, the
     * above block should be in
     * the form that gets input from the
     * user for a particular system.
     */

    //connect function is called to set up the conmat matrix.

    connect();

    //The topology has been set!
```

```
        cout << endl << "\nTHE START OF SIMULATION\n\n";

        /*
         * If there are many periods then a loop for the period should
         * start here!
         * Outflow values are equal to demands and hence...
         */
        out[0].setvalue(10);
        out[1].setvalue(5);
        out[2].setvalue(20);
        out[3].setvalue(30);

        /*
         * We will simulate the system just for the one period.
         * First set the inflow values in inflow objects.
         * Once again we hard-code that!
         */

        inf[0].setvalue(10);
        inf[1].setvalue(5);
        inf[2].setvalue(30);

        //Call the process function from here.
        process();

} //End of set_system_data() function.

void CReservoir::setstorage(int lstorage)
//Pre: None
//Post: A reservoir storage is set with the value input in lstorage
{
    storage = lstorage;
}

int CReservoir::getstorage()
//Pre: Reservoir storage has been set
//Returns: The current storage value
{
    return storage;
}

void COutflow::settores(int ltores)
//Pre: ltores is 0 to MAXRES-1 or -100
//Post: tores is set to the reservoir flowing into
{
    tores = ltores;
}

void COutflow::setfromres(int lfromres)
//Pre: lfromres is 0 to MAXRES-1
```

```
//Post: fromres is set to the reservoir flowing from
{
    fromres = lfromres;
}

void COutflow::setvalue (int lvalue)
//Pre: None
//Post: value is set with lvalue
{
    value = lvalue;
}

int COutflow::gettores()
//Pre: tores has been set
//Returns: tores
{
    return tores;
}

int COutflow::getfromres()
//Pre: fromres has been set
//Returns: fromres
{
    return fromres;
}

int COutflow::getvalue()
//Pre: value has been set
//Returns: value
{
    return value;
}

void CInflow::settores(int ltores)
//Pre: ltores is 0 to MAXRES-1
//Post: tores is set to the reservoir flowing into
{
    tores = ltores;
}

void CInflow::setvalue (int lvalue)
//Pre: None
//Post: value is set with lvalue
{
    value = lvalue;
}

int CInflow::getvalue()
//Pre: value has been set
//Returns: value
```

```
    {
        return value;
    }

    //The definitions for class methods end here!

    //The main function

    int main()

    {

     CSystem sys1;

     cout << "\nSystem is constructed\n";

     sys1.set_system_data();    //Will create and run the simulation!


     return 0;
    }
```

The following is the output of the above program.

```
        System is constructed

        Welcome to the multi-reservoir simulator
        You have to supply data for 3 reservoirs, inflows
        and 4 outflows
        Here the required data has been hard-coded


        THE START OF SIMULATION

        RESERVOIR 0 storage = 5
        RESERVOIR 1 storage = 0
        RESERVOIR 2 storage = 55

        THE END OF SIMULATION
```

4. Integration

Read the first two paragraphs of the coding and debugging section again. Despite being a fairly large and complex problem, the integration step was quite simple. This is another advantage of good object-oriented modeling, design, and implementation. The general guideline for integration is to consider only the set and display functions of all classes first (horizontal and vertical integration). This considers a large number of inter-class relationships. Thereafter use a depth-first strategy along some easy branches of the inheritance hierarchy. This of course means that some *is-a* inheritance relationships are implemented. Lastly, carry out a depth-first strategy along the harder branches of the hierarchy. Do carry out testing at all intermediate steps as described below.

5. Testing and validation

At the outset, the result corresponds to the result of the hand example, which is happy news. However, as noted before in the hand example, this was achieved after testing the problem and finding a logic error when setting up the `conmat` matrix. See also the comments in the `connect()` function. From discussions in previous chapters, we know that control structures introduce program complexity. In order to test control structures we need the three kinds of test cases, namely, valid (including boundary cases), special, and invalid test cases. Similarly, we can create test cases for objects that will fall in the domain of valid boundary, unusual, and invalid data corresponding to the class invariants and the pre- and postconditions of the methods.

In the above program, none of the methods make sure that only valid data is input. One way to do this is to violate the preconditions of some of the methods and see what happens to the program and the results it produces. For example, in the `COutflow::settores()` member function the precondition is that the `settores` data should be between 0 and MAXRES − 1 or −100. If we have data outside this range, the program will fail. Therefore, for the program to have high reliability, we should check that all input parameters are in the valid range. One common method is to use `assert (test condition)` which produces a diagnostic and aborts the program when this assertion fails, that is, when the assert condition results in `false`. This macro can be disabled after the testing of the program is complete. Similarly, in the `CSystem::connect()` method we should make sure that the preconditions are true for all the input cases. Use `assert()` macros. Do not forget that testing and validation is an ongoing and iterative process that is part of the maintenance activity of the software management process.

In summary, the problem was solved satisfactorily with little difficulty and further improvements have been identified. The authors have previously solved the same problem using procedural languages and have found that the OOP approach definitely made the development not only easier but also easily extendible (see Exercise 6). The program was more reliable and it was easier to identify parts that are susceptible to failure. This was mainly due to the localization of failures made possible by data hiding and encapsulation.

SUMMARY

Classes can be derived using the property of inheritance. This allows for extensibility and code reuse in object-oriented programming. Classes can be derived from base classes and will retain all the properties and functions of the base classes. When declared as private, only the objects of the class where they are declared can access the private data directly. Classes can be derived as public or protected or private, with public derivation being most common. Multiple inheritance is possible in C++ and is especially useful when deriving classes from disjoint parent classes. The syntax for constructors of classes derived under inheritance allows derived class data to be passed directly to base classes.

REVIEW QUESTIONS

1. Inheritance is to OOP languages as functions are to procedural languages. Why?

2. Reuse of design and code in OOP is primarily done using _____ .

3. Inheritance allows you to _____ new classes from _____ classes.

4. Inheritance also allows you to build a _____ of classes.

5. Draw an inheritance hierarchy from animal to Indian tigers.

6. Class diagrams help you understand class interrelationships. True or false?

7. Fill in the following table describing data accessiblity:

Derivation type	Access from own class?	Access from derived class?	Access from others?
—	—	—	—
—	—	—	—
—	—	—	—

8. The deeper the inheritance tree (i) the easier it is to program, (ii) the more reliable are the programs, and (iii) the complexity of the program increases. Discuss.

9. Write C++ statements for Question 5.

10. What are class invariants?

11. Add at least one data member, and functions to set data and show data, to each of the classes in Question 9.

12. The preconditions of a method in a derived class can be more restrictive than in the base class method. True or false?

13. Add the necessary constructors to Question 11.

14. The postconditions of a method in a derived class can reinforce the postcondition of the base class method. True or false?

15. A bat is a mammal and it flies. A whale is a mammal and lives in water. Use multiple inheritance to model bats and whales.

16. What does `CParent : public CPerson` mean?

17. Where do Ostrich and Platypus fit in Question 15? If necessary, redesign your classes in Question 15.

18. What does CMother : public CParent, public CWoman mean?

19. The *is-a, has-a, uses-a,* and *knows-a* relationships go from the strongest to the weakest. Discuss.

EXERCISES

1. Modify the reservoir simulation program to consider any system topology up to a specified maximum number of reservoirs and outflows.

2. Identify all class invariants, pre- and postconditions in the reservoir problem.

3. Modify the program in Exercise 1 to consider the results of Exercise 2 explicitly. That is, the program should stop if there is any violation and should indicate where it stopped. If your compiler has the assert() macro, use it.

4. Design a class for storing information on food; for example, name of the food, type of the food (meat, vegetable, etc.), and calories per serving. Write appropriate member functions. Write a C++ program to answer the following questions: (i) What is the total weight of a hamburger (you can choose to add as many (the number may have a fractional part as well) tomatoes, meat patties, etc. as you wish)? and (ii) What is the total calorific value of the hamburger you made in (i)? Use the following class design pattern: tomato is a food, lettuce is a food, bun is a food, meat patty is a food, and hamburger is a food. Hamburger has lettuce, tomato, bun, and meat. The data is given in Table 8.3.

5. The objective of this problem is to design a hierarchy of random number generators like uniform, normal, exponential, and DBPDF. ANSI C functions srand() and rand() are available in C++ and can be used to generate a sequence of uniformly distributed numbers. The prototypes of the two functions are void srand(unsigned int seed) and int rand(). The srand() function uses the argument seed to start a new sequence of pseudo-random integers in the range 0 to RAND_MAX = 32767 to be returned by subsequent calls to rand(). These numbers can be further scaled to the range 0 to 1 (simply divide it by RAND_MAX) and is denoted as U(0,1). These U(0,1) numbers can be used to generate random numbers from other distributions. Example pseudocodes and the required parameters are given in Table 8.4.

Design a hierarchy of classes as in Fig. 8.4.

Write a C++ program for the above classes with necessary data and methods. As an example, you can see how a uniform random number is used in the pseudocode.

TABLE 8.3
Data (from *Health and Welfare Canada Food Guide*)

Name	Measure	Weight (g)	Energy (kcal)
Lettuce	250 ml	59	11
Tomato	1 medium	123	23
Bun	1 bun	60	179
Meat patty	2 oz	98	245

TABLE 8.4
Details of random number generators

Distribution	Parameters	Pseudocode	
Normal	m and s where m is the mean and s is the standard deviation	uniform u(717)	//Sets the uniform random number //seed
		rand = 0	
		for i=1 to 12 do	
		rand = rand + u.rand() //u.rand() returns U(0,1)	
		enddo	
		rand = m + (rand-6)*s	
Exponential	m where m is mean	uniform u(717)	//Sets the uniform random number //seed
		rand = -m*ln(u.rand())	//u.rand() returns U(0,1) //ln is natural logarithm
Double Bounded Probability Density Function (DBPDF)	a, b are shape parameters zmax = maximum bound, zmin = minimum bound	uniform u(717)	//Sets the uniform random number //seed. //u.rand() returns U(0,1)
		$x = [1 - (1 - u.rand())^{1/b}]^{1/a}$	
		rand = x*(zmax-zmin) + zmin	

6. Rename the CSystem class defined in Exercise 3 or in the chapter as class hydrosystem. Derive a new class called hydro_electric using the hydrosystem class that includes a method energy() that estimates hydro-energy productions. For simplicity, you can assume that energy produced at a reservoir = outflow * storage/10 of the corresponding reservoir.

7. Design the inheritance hierarchy for instantiating objects from the following groups. You may choose to do just one of the questions and provide only one data member and one method for each class. The details in your methods can be few but try to understand the class invariants (depends on your definitions of the classes) and the pre- and postconditions of any methods you define.

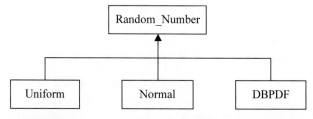

FIGURE 8.4
Inheritance hierarchy for random number generators.

   (i) hamburger, chocolate milk, veggie pizza

  (ii) red sedan, blue convertible, black formula 1

 (iii) encyclopedias, handbook of mathematics, a C++ primer

 (iv) F15, Boeing 747, helicopter

  (v) baseball event, 100m sprint event, 100m butterfly event

 (vi) gas stove, electric kettle, coal-fired barbeque

 (vii) bullock cart, bicycle, a motor car

(viii) a pen, a pencil, a chalk

8. Simulation of the Great Lakes system. The Great Lakes system is a system of very large freshwater lakes shared by Canada and the USA. They consist of five main lakes where water flows from the most upstream lake Lake Superior through the middle lakes to the most downstream lake Lake Ontario. From Lake Ontario the water flows via the St Lawrence Seaway to the sea. Lakes Michigan-Huron, Lake St Clair, and Lake Erie are the middle lakes (Where is Niagara Falls?). There are two man-made controls, one each at Lake Superior and Lake Ontario, which allow water to be released in any prescribed manner. The middle lakes are controlled naturally by the levels of lakes. For simplicity, we will assume that all lakes are fully controllable and the problem is the simulation of lake levels given the natural inflows into the lake, the expected outflows from each lake as demand at each outflow, and the initial storage levels. The equation that relates the different variables for a given lake is *storage at the end of a period = storage at the end of the previous period + natural inflow to the given lake during the period + outflow from the upstream lake during the period − outflow from the given lake during the period.* This equation is to be applied for all the time periods of interest. Assume that there is only one natural inflow into the lake, and one outflow from any lake. Most lakes and reservoirs have lower and upper bounds on storages and outflows. The required data is supplied on the accompanying diskette. Can you reuse the `Csystem` class from the text to simulate this system?

Note that the following problems can be solved at various levels of details. Choose an appropriate level according to the time allowed to solve.

 9. Simulate a two-story elevator system.

10. Simulate a home alarm system.

11. Simulate an Automated Teller Machine (ATM).

CHAPTER 9

Pointers to Aid
Efficient Implementation

Pointer constants are memory addresses. Pointer variables hold pointer constants.

Pointers allow a programmer to efficiently access data, functions, structures, and objects stored in a computer memory. When invoking a function, a pointer variable can be used to pass arguments, simulating a call by reference. The function can then have direct access to the value of the parameter of any type: variables, arrays, structures, functions, or objects. Most importantly, pointers are used to create and manipulate dynamic data structures such as linked lists, queues, stacks, or trees. These are data structures that can grow and shrink at execution time, unlike arrays whose size is determined at compile time. The efficiency issue will become clear when you see examples later that manipulate potentially large objects such as matrices by simply manipulating the pointers to such objects and not the objects themselves.

COMPUTER MEMORY ARRANGEMENT AND POINTERS

The memory in a computer is arranged in units called bytes. You may remember that character type variables `char` are stored using one byte, `int` type integers using two bytes (depending on the computer), `float` variables using four bytes, and so on. Your program and its variables are stored somewhere in this memory. Normally, you are interested only in the variables defined in your program. Their addresses can be found by using the ampersand sign (&) in front of the variable name. When the ampersand sign is used to get the address of a variable it is called the *address of* operator. Recall that the ampersand is also used to pass arguments by reference and the meaning there is different. For example, in a program where you have defined a variable `var1`, you can get its address, a pointer constant (printed in hexadecimal notation), using the following statement:

```
cout << &var1;        //Prints out the address of variable var1
```

We seldom need to know the actual value of the address. So don't worry if you do not know how to read a hexadecimal number! But what we really need are the *pointer variables* that can store these address values.

The following are examples of declarations of pointer variables:

```
char*   chptr;          //Pointer to char
int*    intptr;         //Pointer to int
float*  flptr;          //Pointer to float
vector* vecptr;         //Pointer to vector type variables
                        //(could be objects or structures)
void*   ptr             //This pointer variable can point to
                        //any data type!
```

It is important to realize that pointers should point to valid addresses. Trying to access an invalid memory location can cause you great trouble! A common convention is to set pointers to NULL when they are not pointing to anything in particular. Such a pointer is called a *null pointer.*

ADDRESS OF OPERATOR AND THE INDIRECTION OPERATOR

We noticed above that the *address of* operator can be used to find the address of a variable. This address can be assigned to a pointer variable of an appropriate type as follows.

```
int var1 = 100;     //Initializes int variable var1 to 100
int* intptr;        //Definition of pointer to int
intptr = &var1;     //Assigns the address of var1 to intptr
```

Figure 9.1 illustrates the relationship between the pointer variable `intptr` and the variable `var1`.

Now suppose we want to assign a new value to `var1`. We have two choices. We can simply use the variable `var1` directly, or use the pointer to indirectly access the memory where `var1` is stored and change it to a new value. The choices are as shown below.

```
var1 = 200;     //Assigns a new value 200 to var1
                //using direct addressing
```

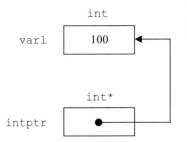

FIGURE 9.1
The convention for showing a pointer variable, the memory location it points to and its contents.

As soon as a pointer variable is defined, make it point to a valid address or else make it point to NULL.

```
*intptr = 200;    //Does the same but uses the indirection operator.
                  //This is called indirect addressing
```

The indirection operator * (also known as the *dereferencing* operator) reads as "the value of the variable pointed to by."

ARRAY NAME IS A POINTER CONSTANT

In Chapter 5 we mentioned that arrays are passed to functions by passing the start address of the array. This is because the array name is the memory address (a pointer constant) where the array storage starts, as shown in Fig. 9.2. Consider the following example.

```
//Filename: arrpoint.cpp
//Demonstrates that the array name is the address
//where the array storage starts.

#include <iostream.h>


int main()
    {
    const int MAX = 5;

    int age[] = {19,17,18,20,18};

    //Accessing the array using the pointer notation
    for (int i=0; i<MAX; i++)        //Each element is
        cout << "\n" << *(age+i);    //printed out using the
                                     //dereferencing operator
    return 0;
    }
```

Two important points to note are: (i) the array name age is the start address of the array, and (ii) array elements are stored in consecutive storage locations corresponding to the array type; for int types the addresses increment by sizeof(int) bytes. Therefore, *(age+i) refers to the element age[i]. Why is it not possible to use

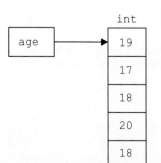

FIGURE 9.2
An array name is a pointer constant that points to the start address of the array.

$*$(age++) instead of $*$(age+i)? The increment operator ++ can work only on variables and not on constants; for example, 2++ is not possible. The address of the start of the array is a pointer constant and hence age++ has no meaning. However, you could assign a pointer variable, say int$*$ intptr, the address age and then increment it as $*$(intptr++). The following example demonstrates this point.

```
//Filename: strpoint.cpp
//Demonstrates that the array name is the address
//where the array storage starts and accessing the
//array using a pointer variable.

#include <iostream.h>

int main()
    {
    char str1[] = "Learning is not a spectator sport";
    char* str2 = "Learning is not a spectator sport";

    cout << "\n" << str1;    //Outputs str1
    cout << "\n" << str2;    //Outputs str2
                             //With strings this is possible
                             //because of the null character
                             //at the end of the string

//Accessing the array using the pointer notation

// str1++;                  //Not possible because str1 is the
                            //starting address of array str1.
    str2++;                  //Possible because str2 is a
                            //pointer variable

    cout << "\n" << str2;  //Prints starting with "earning is..."
    return 0;
    }
```

The output of the above program is

```
earning is not a spectator sport
```

because the pointer is now pointing to the second element in the array str2.

PASSING ARGUMENTS TO FUNCTIONS USING POINTERS

Earlier we saw that variables can be passed to functions either by copy or by reference. The third way to pass arguments to functions, that is, passing by pointers, is presented in the following program.

```
//Filename: paspoint.cpp
//Demonstrates the use of pointers for passing arguments
```

```
#include <iostream.h>

void display(int*,int*);    //Function prototype
                            //Parameters are integer pointers

int main()
   {
   int max = 5;
   int age[] = {19,17,18,20,18};

   display(&max, age);    //Passing the addresses
                          //&max is necessary to get the
                          //address where max is stored,
                          //age is the start address
                          //of the array age

   return 0;
   }
//Function definition
void display(int* intptr, int* arrptr)
   {
   for(int i=0; i < *intptr; i++)
     cout << "\n" << *arrptr++;    //Because arrptr is a pointer
                                   //variable initialized by the
                                   //array address age

   }
```

In order to pass only pointer constants in the function call display(), we used the ampersand operator to get the address of max; because the array name age is itself a pointer constant we simply passed it directly. In the definition of the display() function we use the indirection operators for both cases. Note that cout << "\n" << *arrptr++ is carried out left to right, so the indirection is done first and then the postfix. The output you get is what you expect but try to use arrptr[i] instead of *arrptr++ to maintain clarity in your program. In fact, most compilers will produce the same object code for both.

AN ARRAY OF POINTERS

We can form an array whose elements are pointer constants. A not-so-useful modification of one of the programs above demonstrates this point. See Fig. 9.3 for the corresponding memory allocation.

```
//Filename: pntrarr.cpp
//Demonstrates the use of an
//array of pointers.

#include <iostream.h>
```

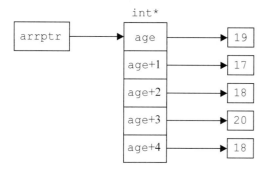

FIGURE 9.3
An array containing pointer constants which point to other data.

```
int main()
  {
  const int MAX = 5;

  int age[] = {19,17,18,20,18};
  int* arrptr[MAX];

  //Accessing the array using the pointer notation
  for (int i=0; i<MAX; i++)          //Each element is ...
     {
     arrptr[i] = age+i;              //Element addresses are stored.
     cout << "\n" << *arrptr[i];     //...printed out using the
                                     //dereferencing operator

     }
     return 0;
  }  // End of main
```

The contents of the array `arrptr` are pointer constants due to the program statement `arrptr[i] = age+i`.

We have seen so far how to pass variables and arrays to functions. The following example shows how a function can be passed to a function using pointers!

POINTERS TO FUNCTIONS

Functions are also accessible indirectly through pointers. A function name is a pointer constant or the start address in the memory where it is stored. Pointers to functions help to pass a function as an argument to another function. The following example illustrates the use of these pointers. Suppose we want to have a choice of calling any one of a number of functions and we want to operate on these functions in the same manner irrespective of which function is called. We can use function pointers to do this very efficiently.

```
//Filename: mfuncall.cpp
//Shows how to pass functions to functions
//using pointers!
```

```
#include <iostream.h>

double reciprocal(int ); //A function to calculate a reciprocal
double cube(int );       //A function to calculate a cube

//funcsum() will calculate a sum of reciprocals or cubes
//depending upon what function is passed as an argument.

double funcsum(int, double (*)(int) );      //Works! The second
                                            //parameter is a
                                            //pointer to function
//double funcsum(int, double* (int) );      //Does not work!!

int main()
   {
   cout << "Sum of five reciprocals: "
        << funcsum(4, reciprocal) << endl; //Pointer to reciprocal()
                                           //is passed.
   cout << "Sum of three cubes: "
        << funcsum(3,cube) << endl;        //Pointer to cube()
                                           //is passed.

   return 0;

   }    //End of main

double funcsum(int n, double (*f)(int k))
   {
   double sum=0;
   for (int i=1; i<=n; i++)
       sum += f(i); //Depending upon the function pointer
                    //passed an appropriate function is called
   return sum;
   }

double reciprocal(int k)
   {return 1.0/k;}

double cube(int k)
   {return double (k)*k*k; //Type casting result to double
   }
```

Note that the function name is passed as the pointer in the main() function. Both in the function declaration and in the definition the function pointer is used with the following syntax for the function prototype.

```
double (*f)(int k) //example
```
*function return type (*variable name)(function arguments with types)*

In the function prototype, only the function argument type is needed. Next we will see how objects can be accessed using pointers.

POINTERS TO OBJECTS OR STRUCTURES

Consider the following example which is a modification of the simple class from Chapter 7. Here we use pointers to access the object data and object functions.

The following example uses a new type of operator, the operator ->, used to refer to a member of a structure variable or object, when the address of the structure variable or object is stored in a pointer variable. The operator -> is a short notation for the expression:

(*ptr_structure)

where **ptr_structure* is a pointer to a structure variable or object. For example, if `vecptr` is defined as:

`vector* vecptr`

and if it contains the address of an object of class `vector`, we could refer to member x of the class `vector` using the following notations:

`(*vecptr).x` or `vecptr->x`

We can also use this notation to refer to a member function:

`(*vecptr).setdata(1.5,2.5)` or `vecptr->setdata(1.5,2.5)`

The following program demonstrates the above use.

```
//Filename: ptrsimob.cpp
//Demonstrates a pointer to a simple object

#include <iostream.h>

class vector          //Specifies the class
   {
   public:
     void setdata(float x, float y)  //Member function to
                                     //set data
        { xCo=x; yCo=y; }
     void showdata()        //Member function for display
        { cout << "\n(X,Y) = " << "(" << xCo << ","
              << yCo << ")"; }
   private:
     float xCo, yCo;  //Class data hidden from all except
                      //member functions
   };                      //end of specification (note semicolon)

int main()
   {
   vector v1;    //Object v1 is defined
   vector* vecptr;

   vecptr = &v1; //Stores the address of object v1
   v1.setdata(1.5,2.5);  //Calls member function to set data
                         //using dot operator
```

```
(*vecptr).showdata(); //Calling showdata() of v1
vecptr->showdata();    //Calling showdata using alternative
                               //notation
return 0;
}                      //End of main
```

The display function of the object v1 is indirectly accessed through the pointer as vecptr->showdata where -> substitutes for the dot operator and vecptr has the address of the object v1. This notation is equivalent to the less elegant and less preferred method (*vecptr).showdata, which uses the indirection operator.

THE this POINTER

The this pointer is a pointer to the object itself and is provided so an object can know its own address. The this pointer can be used to access both member data and member functions. Obviously, the type of the object decides the type of the this pointer. Most new compilers now support RTTI (Run Time Type Identification) which can be used to identify the object type while executing the program. The typeid(*this) statement will return information about the type (this facility may not be available in some compilers).

```
//Filename: vecasov.cpp
//Demonstrates the use of the "this" pointer and the
//overloading of the assignment operator

#include <iostream.h>

class vector         //Specifies the class
    {

    public:
      vector() { }          //No-argument constructor
                            //Same name as class
      vector(float x, float y)  //Two-argument constructor
                                //to initialize with data
          { xCo=x; yCo=y; }
      void getdata()  //Get coordinates from the user
          { cout << "\nEnter X-Coord.= "; cin >> xCo;
            cout << "\nEnter Y-Coord.= "; cin >> yCo;
          }
      void showdata()       //Member function for display
          { cout << "\n(X,Y) = " << "(" << xCo << ","
                << yCo << ")" << endl; }

      vector  operator = (const vector&); //Assignment operator
//    vector& operator = (const vector&); //Assignment operator     I
```

```
    ~vector() {cout <<"Destructed\n";}  //Destructor.
                                        //Same name as class
                                        //but with tilde
                                        //as a prefix.
  private:
    float xCo, yCo;   //Class data hidden from all except
                      //member functions
  };                  //end of specification (note semicolon)


vector vector::operator = (const vector& u)
//vector& vector::operator = (const vector& u)   II
   {
   xCo = u.xCo;
   yCo = u.yCo;
   cout << "\nassignment operator called: \n";
   return vector(xCo,yCo);
   //return *this;                               III
   }

int main()
   {
   vector v1, v3;       //Objects v1 and v3 are defined
   vector v2(3.5,4.5); //Object v2 is initialized
   cout << "Get info from user: \n";
   v1.getdata();        //Calls member function to get
                        //data from the user.

   v3 = v1;     //Assignment with overloaded operator

   v3.showdata();

   return 0;
   }
```

Sample output from this program is as follows.

```
              Get info from user:

              Enter X-Coord.= 1

              Enter Y-Coord.= 2

              assignment operator called:
              Destructed

              (X,Y) = (1,2)
              Destructed
              Destructed
              Destructed
```

Returning pointers to member data in public member functions breaks data hiding!

The assignment operator here does not do anything more special than the default assignment operator; both do bit-wise copying. See the example in Chapter 10 on why and how to define your own copy constructor and assignment operator for classes that have pointer variables as data members. In order to get rid of the temporary object created during the assignment operation, remove the // from lines I, II, and III, as marked, and appropriately comment out the redundant headers and the return statement. Be careful if you are returning pointers to member data in public member functions, as this breaks data hiding!!

DYNAMIC MEMORY MANAGEMENT

One of the features of the C++ language is the ability to allocate and release memory when needed during execution; this was not available in some older languages like Fortran. Instead of using data structures of fixed size such as arrays, structures, and objects, we can create and manipulate dynamic data structures that grow or shrink at execution time, such as a linked list. Typically, arrays and objects (or structures) can consume large amounts of memory. Also, the required amount of memory is often unknown before execution time. To address these two problems, C++ has two operators called new and delete. The new operator fetches the start address of the memory (in number and type) requested. The delete operator prevents further access to this memory by deleting the start address. Let us use the following example to understand these operators. Of course, the program itself does nothing profound!

```cpp
//Filename: newdel.cpp
//Demonstrates the use of new and delete operators

#include <iostream.h>

int main()
   {
   int max = 5;      //max is a variable. Can have different
                     //values at execution time.
   int age[] = {19,17,18,20,18}; //5 spaces found at compilation
   int* age2 = new int [max];
   if(!age2)
   {
       cout << "\nNot enough memory!!";
       return -1;              // Return an error code
   }

//Copying the array using the pointer notation

for (int i=0; i<max; i++)       //Each element is
   {
   age2[i] = age[i];             //accessed and
```

```
cout << "\n" << *(age2+i);   //printed out
}

delete [] age2;   //Releasing the memory for the array age2
age2 = NULL;       //This is a safe programming style
return 0;
}   //End of main
```

Remember that anything as powerful as pointers and the `new` and `delete` operators should be used with extreme care. If you use a lot of `new` and create memory, then do use `delete` to delete the memory when it is no longer needed. Otherwise you create a *memory leak* and you can easily swallow up the entire memory in no time at all. If you are using objects, the destructors should be used to deallocate memory. Do not delete memory if there is more than one pointer pointing to that location unless you make sure that the additional pointers are given valid addresses (or NULL) to point to. Otherwise, you cause *dangling references (pointers)*! Dangling references can point anywhere in the memory and can cause great pain and sorrow!!

In the above example, note the line

```
if(!age2)
{
    cout << "\nNot enough memory!!";
    return -1;
}
```

If the `new` operator is unable to allocate a block of memory, it will return a null pointer (a pointer to the address 0). It is good practice to check pointers returned from `new` to ensure that they are not null. However, this can become tedious if the operator `new` is used frequently. For this reason, C++ provides a way to define a global function which will be invoked whenever the `new` operator fails. This is illustrated below.

```
#include <stdlib.h>              // Needed for abort()
#include <new.h>                 // Needed for set_new_handler()

void handle_out_of_memory()
{
    cerr << "Out of memory!" << endl;
    abort();
}

int main()
{
    set_new_handler(handle_out_of_memory);
    ...
    ...
}
```

The function `set_new_handler()` takes a pointer to a function, and stores it. If the `new` operator fails, this function is called.

Dynamic Matrices

Until now, when we wanted to create matrices, we used the following types of statements in our programs.

```
...
const int ROWS = 4, COLS=4;
...
float mat1[ROWS][COLS];
...
```

Note that ROWS and COLS cannot be variables if they are used in array definitions! However, by using an array of pointers we can dynamically create matrices whose size becomes known only at execution time, as in the following example. In the example, a dynamic two-dimensional array is created (a matrix), and some input operations to this matrix and swapping of the rows are demonstrated.

```cpp
//Filename: dynmatrx.cpp
//Demonstrates the creation of a matrix at execution time!

#include <iostream.h>
#include <new.h>
#include <stdlib.h>

void handle_out_of_memory()
{
    cerr << "Out of memory!" << endl;
    abort();
}

int main()
    {
    set_new_handler(handle_out_of_memory);
    int rows, cols;   //rows and cols are integer variables
    float** mat;      //mat is a pointer to pointers of float variables

    cout << "\nPlease input the matrix size: Rows and Columns";
    cin >> rows >> cols;

//Create the matrix mat[rows][cols] dynamically

    mat = new float *[rows]; //new creates a vector of pointers
                             //of size rows to float type variables

    for(int i=0; i<rows; i++){
       mat[i] = new float [cols];   //Each row gets cols amount of
                                    //memory
    }
```

```
//matrix mat[rows][cols] is now created
//Input to the matrix by the user.
    cout << "\nPlease input the matrix by rows";

    for(i=0; i<rows; i++)
        for (int j=0; j<cols; j++)
            cin >> mat[i][j];  //Accessing the matrix as usual!

//Display the matrix
    cout << "\nThe matrix input is:";

    for(i=0; i<rows; i++){
        cout << "\n";
        for (int j=0; j<cols; j++)
          cout << mat[i][j] << " ";
    }

//Swapping the first row with the last row
    float *temp = mat[0];
    mat[0] = mat[rows-1];
    mat[rows-1] = temp;   //Incredible!!
                          //Only the pointers are swapped!!
//Display the swapped matrix
    cout << "\nThe swapped matrix is:";

    for(i=0; i<rows; i++){
        cout << "\n";
        for (int j=0; j<cols; j++)
          cout << mat[i][j] << " ";
    }

//deleting the matrix
    for (i=0; i<rows; i++)
        delete [] mat[i];   //Reverse of what was done with new
    delete [] mat;

    return 0;
    }  //End of main
```

Carefully examine the code. Note the new syntax `float** mat` which is a pointer of pointers. The number of asterisks depends upon the number of dimensions! Once the array has been dynamically created it can be used like a normal array with loop indices. An entire row swapping is done by just swapping the corresponding pointers which, of course, leads to great efficiency. This is shown in Fig. 9.4.

Lastly, the matrix is deleted responsibly. We used `cerr` instead of `cout` for error handling. If we use a matrix class to do the above, then the destructor will have the responsibility for deallocating matrices. Next we describe a class for a simple data structure that uses pointers.

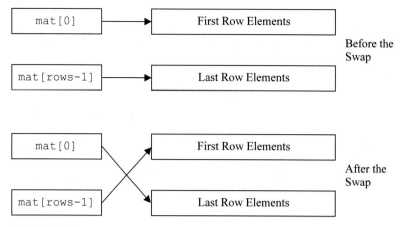

FIGURE 9.4
Swapping row pointers to get the same effect as swapping rows.

Linked Lists

Linked lists are simple data structures. They are alternatives to arrays for storing data. A singly linked list is a sequence of nodes where each node is linked to the node following it. We will discuss the implementation of singly linked lists using pointers. Figure 9.5 shows a singly linked list for storing three integers.

In the figure, head is a pointer that is pointing to a link that has two pieces of information: one is an integer and the other is a pointer that points to the next link. The last link points to the zero (null) address and is denoted by the crossed box. The following program can be used to implement the linked list.

```
//Filename: simplist.cpp
//A program to demonstrate a simple linked list structure

#include <iostream.h>

//Declare a structure link which contains one data and pointer to
//the next link of the same structure
struct link
    {
    int data;        //Actual data stored
    link* nextlink;  //Pointer to the next link,
                     //a self-referential pointer
    };
```

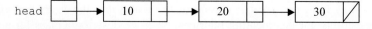

FIGURE 9.5
A singly linked list.

```
//Declare a simple linked list class with
//member functions to display and insert a new link
class simplelist
    {
    public:
      simplelist(){ head = 0; }   //No-argument constructor
      ~simplelist();
      void insertlink(int);        //Member function to insert
                                    //at the head
      void showlistdata();         //Traverses the list to print
                                    //out the data
    private:
      link* head;     //Pointer that points to the head of the list
    };

//Displays the data of the entire list
void simplelist::showlistdata()
//Pre: None
//Post: Traverses the list and prints out the data of each link
    {
    link* currlink = head;          //Gets the pointer stored in
                                    //head that points to
                                    //the first element in list
    while (currlink != 0)    //Exit when last link has been reached
      {
      cout << currlink->data << endl;      //Prints out the data
      currlink = currlink->nextlink; //Places the nextlink address
      }
    }

//Inserts a new link at the head of the list
void simplelist::insertlink(int ldata)
//Pre: None (if ldata has a limited range mention it here)
//Post: Inserts at the head a new link with ldata as its data
    {
    link* newlink = new link;       //A new link is created
    newlink->data = ldata;          //Initializes the data
    newlink->nextlink = head;       //Points to whatever the head was
                                    //pointing to previously
    head = newlink;                 //Head points to the address
                                    //of new link
    }

simplelist::~simplelist()
{
    link* currlink = head;
    while (currlink != 0)
    {
        link* prevlink = currlink;
        currlink = currlink->nextlink;
        delete prevlink;
```

```
      }
   }

int main()
   {
   simplelist list1;              //Defines a simple list with
                                  //only the head

   list1.insertlink(30);          //Inserts the first link with data
   list1.insertlink(20);
   list1.insertlink(10);          //Note that head points
                                  //to the link with data 10

   list1.showlistdata();
   return 0;
   }
```

We used a structure to define the link but we could also have used a class. A better choice would be to define the structure within the link list class. (The link list is implemented as a class.) Go through the code for detailed explanations. The key point to notice is that the insertion is done at the head and hence in the `main()` function, the data is inserted in reverse order! It is fairly simple to add new member functions to insert at the tail.

Time complexity. Flexibility in memory management brings a higher time complexity. In order to access any element in an array of N elements we use `age[i]`, a single operation and hence the time complexity is O(1). However, for a singly linked list, a traversing function has to be used to find any individual element, typically requiring O(N) operations. Therefore, we gain in memory management and lose in CPU time if we used linked lists instead of arrays.

SUMMARY

Pointer constants are memory addresses that can be stored and manipulated using pointer variables. A pointer variable is defined according to the type of variable it is pointing to. Because of this feature, the pointer variable when incremented can point to the correct address of the next element of an array. Use pointers and dynamic memory allocation in large problems to improve the storage and execution efficiency. But use them responsibly, as they can be disastrous if improperly applied.

REVIEW QUESTIONS

1. A pointer constant is an _____ in the computer memory.

2. How would you print out the address of the variable `float variable1`?

3. Go back to Chapter 2 and memorize the number of bytes required for each type of the variable on your platform.

4. The term "pointer" is synonymous with "pointer variable." True or false?

5. Define a pointer variable `char_ptr` that points to `char`.

6. In a single program statement define two pointers, one pointing to `float` and another to `char`.

7. How would you use an indirection operator to assign a value `5.0` to `variable1`?

8. An array name is a pointer constant. Explain.

9. If `a` is an array, is `a++` allowed in C++?

10. `Apple` is a float. `Bananas` is an array of integers. How would you pass these to a function `dummy()` using pointers.

11. Assuming `void` type for `dummy()` in Question 10, write the function header.

12. Write a declaration for a pointer that points to a function of type `float` and has two arguments of type `int` and `float`.

13. What is a `this` pointer?

14. When we sort an array of objects according to some criterion (assume each object needs a large amount of memory), if we use pointers, we do not need to physically move the object in the memory. Discuss.

15. Pointers are efficient implementation tools. Discuss.

16. Can pointers sometimes slow program execution? Discuss.

EXERCISES

1. Write a program with a one-dimensional array using the pointer notation. The array is used to read a set of numbers and find the average.

2. Use `new` and `delete` operators in Exercise 1 to create the array dynamically and delete the array after the average has been calculated.

3. Develop a string class with operator overloading.

4. Develop a stack for integers. A stack is a linked list where the last element added is the first element deleted. A new element is added to the head of the list. The linked list program in the text can be modified easily to program a stack. Name the function that adds the element as `push()`. To the class add a function `pop()` to return the last element added to the list and delete it from the stack. Name the new class `my_stack`!

5. Develop a queue for integers. A queue is a linked list where the first element added is the first element deleted. A new element is added to the tail of the list by the `enqueue()` method. `Dequeue()` method returns the first element and deletes it.

6. Convert the programs for matrix operations in the exercises of Chapter 7 so that they use pointers. Make sure the destructor deletes the allocated memory. The sizes of the matrices should be dynamically adjustable.

7. Write a program for the merging algorithm in Exercise 8 of Chapter 5 using pointers and compare its efficiency when using arrays.

8. Solve the reservoir problem in Chapter 8 using pointers.

9. Solve the mesh problem in Chapter 7 (Exercise 15) with pointers.

*10. Traffic simulation in a highway segment. Assume that you are considering just single-direction traffic in a highway with two lanes. You may have to model only the traffic of cars and trucks. The highway segment will have a certain length and road conditions (assume the same conditions for the entire segment), and a maximum speed limit. The cars and trucks enter at one end of the segment and leave at the other end. Cars and trucks enter randomly and are controlled by the random inter-arrival times. Assume that cars have more frequent arrivals and a smaller inter-arrival time than trucks, both entering at speeds which are also random. The speeds will be the speed limit plus or minus a small random deviation. Assume that each vehicle knows its position in the segment, has an estimate of the speed and the distance to the vehicle in front in the same lane and the speed and the distance to the vehicle behind in the other lane. If the distance to the car in the same lane becomes less than a prescribed limit, there are two choices: (i) reduce speed or (ii) change to the other lane if the car behind is a safe distance away. Crashes can occur if two vehicles are at the same position, with the following results: (i) some vehicles are out of the highway (they do not move and should be cleared off the highway) and (ii) the speeds of the vehicles behind the crash are reduced by a certain amount for a certain length of time. The amount and the time depends on the number of vehicles involved in the crash. The problem here has many objects, communication between objects, and some functions. You may need linked lists as well.

CHAPTER 10

Miscellaneous Topics in C++

In this chapter, we will see a potpourri of topics that are necessary to take advantage of the full capability of C++. The topics include virtual functions, abstract classes, friend functions and friend classes, templates, copy constructors, and calling external functions, including functions written and compiled in other languages such as Fortran and C.

VIRTUAL FUNCTIONS

Suppose you have a mammal class and have derived other animal classes such as tigers, elephants, etc. One of the member functions in these classes could be `make_a_warning_noise()` which an animal makes to ward off others. You have written the following code to test the function for various animals.

```
    . . .
    mammal* mamptr[3]; //An array of pointers to mammal objects

    //Assign mamptr[1] to a tiger object
    . . .
    //Assign mamptr[2] to an elephant object
    . . .
    //Assign mamptr[3] to a lion object
    . . .
    //Test the warning noise function of all the animals

    for (int i=0; i<3; ++i) {
        mamptr[i]->make_a_warning _noise();
    }
    . . .
```

That is, at execution or run time, different functions are called by the same statement! This is a good example of polymorphism where the same operation has different meanings. In order for the above code to work, we have to use inheritance for deriving the various animal classes from the mammal class, but we also have to declare the make_a_warning_noise() function as virtual in the base class. The next example describes the C++ mechanisms for using virtual functions.

Virtual functions are used to extend polymorphism when using inheritance. We will use an example to understand this concept. The example declares two base classes, namely stat and dyna. In the stat class there is a function f() and a similar function is declared as virtual in the dyna class. There are derived classes, namely statchild and dynachild, derived from the stat class and the dyna class, respectively.

```cpp
//Filename: virtualf.cpp
//Demonstration of Static Binding and Dynamic Binding(virtual
functions)

#include <iostream.h>

class stat
   {//Base class
   public:
     void f(){cout << "Base: Stat\n";}

   private:
     int i;
   };

class dyna
   {//Base class
   public:
   //Note the reserved word virtual
     virtual void f(){cout << "Base: dyna\n";}
   private:
     int i;
   };

class statchild : public stat
   {//Derived class
   public:
     void f(){cout << "Derived: Statchild\n";}
   };

class dynachild : public dyna
   {//Derived class
   public:
     void f(){cout << "Derived: Dynachild\n";}
   };
```

```
int main()
   {
   cout << "Class sizes in bytes using sizeof(): " << endl;
   cout << "Static binding: Base Class " << sizeof(stat) << endl;
   cout << "Dynamic binding: Base Class " << sizeof(dyna) << endl;
   cout << "Static binding: Derived Class "
        << sizeof(statchild) << endl;
   cout << "Dynamic binding:  Derived Class "
        << sizeof(dynachild)<< endl;

   statchild sc;
   dynachild dc;
   stat* stptr =&sc;
   dyna* dyptr =&dc;
   cout << "stptr->f() calls ";
   stptr->f();
   cout << "dyptr->f() calls ";
   dyptr->f();
   return 0;
   }
```

The output from this program is as follows.

```
Class sizes in bytes using sizeof():
Static binding: Base Class 2
Dynamic binding: Base Class 4          The value might depend on the compiler
Static binding: Derived Class 2
Dynamic binding: Derived Class 4       The value might depend on the compiler
stptr->f() calls Base: Stat
dyptr->f() calls Derived: Dynachild
```

Static binding requires fewer resources but is less flexible. Note that the base class pointer can be used for derived class objects. Note also that we used base class pointers to access the child class objects. This is not possible if you have derived the child class in private and not in public, as above. Virtual functions are very important for the practical implementation of polymorphism.

ABSTRACT CLASSES

Suppose we were designing a set of classes to model animals. Near the top of the hierarchy, we might have "Mammal," which we might model as an *abstract* class because there is no animal called the mammal. Tiger is derived from the mammal class but is a concrete class. Another example: circle and square are concrete classes derived from an abstract class called the shape class. An abstract class in C++ is a class with at least one pure virtual function. Pure virtual functions are functions that have no body in the base class and are defined as

```
virtual function_name() = 0;
```

If you try to create an instance of an abstract class, the compiler will report an error.

FRIEND FUNCTIONS AND FRIEND CLASSES

This is a concept that should be used sparingly. Friend functions and classes have access to private members of classes where they are declared as friends. Obviously, this breaks the idea of data hiding and hence could be dangerous. Yet, there are situations where friend declarations can make programming simpler. To declare a friend function or class, simply place the reserved word `friend` in front of the type declaration of the function or the reserved word `class`, respectively. The next example uses this concept.

A SIMPLE STRING CLASS AND THE OVERLOADING OF THE << OPERATOR

The following is a simple string class (most compilers now have a built-in string class and you should use it instead of trying to write your own; the following program is for demonstration only!).

```
//Filename stringcl.cpp
//Demonstration of a simple string class

#include <iostream.h>
#include <string.h>


const int MAX = 80; //Size of the string array

class s_string //A simple string class
   {
   public:
     s_string(char lstr[] = "") //Null string initialization
       {strncpy(str,lstr,MAX);}
     void display()
       {cout << str << endl;}
     void setdata()
       {
       char lstr[MAX];
       cout << "Input the string please:";
       cin >> lstr;
       strncpy(str,lstr,MAX);
       }
     s_string getdata()
       { return s_string(str);}
     char getdata(int lindex)
       {
       return str[lindex];
       }
```

```
    private:
      char str[MAX];
    };


int main()
    {

    char str1[] = "Learning is not a Spectator Sport"; //A string
                                                        //constant
    s_string string1(str1); //Initialization of string

    string1.display();

    s_string string2 = string1;

    string2.display();

    s_string string3;
    string3.setdata();
    string3.display();
// if (string3.getdata() == "secret\0") //Won't work as ==
                                         //not defined!
//      cout << "TRUE\n";


    return 0;

    }   //End of main
```

In order to display strings using the cout operator, we need to overload the <<
operator in our simple string class. This operator, when used with cout, belongs to
another class, namely the ostream class. Until now, we have used data hiding to
deny direct data access to nonmembers. How can we allow these operators of another
class to access the string array in a string class? C++ will allow this violation of data
hiding if those classes are declared as friend classes/functions. That is, modify the
class declaration as given below.

```
    . . .
    class s_string      //A simple string class
       {
       . . .
       //Only a single line modification and can be placed
       //anywhere in the class declaration!
       friend ostream &operator<< (ostream &, const s_string &);
       public:
    . . .
       private:
         char str[MAX];
       };
```

The statement `friend ostream` ... declares that the insertion operator `<<` of the `ostream` class is a friend of the `s_string` class and hence has access to all the data of the `s_string` class. For this reason, in the implementation of this function shown next, the data member `str[]` of the local object `lstr` is available to this friend!

```
//The definition of the << operator
ostream &operator<< (ostream &out, const s_string &lstr)
    {
    out << lstr.str;
    return out;
    }
```

Note the last line `return out;` this allows us to use the chaining of `cout << string1 << string2` because the result `out` is returned by reference. Lastly, the `<<` operator can be defined as a global function, thus avoiding friend functions.

TEMPLATES

Templates can be used to make the compiler do a lot of code generation for you. If you have already built and tested a function or a class for a certain data type and you would like the same function or class for another data type, then you should consider templates. A simple example: You have built an absolute value function for `int` types. If you want to build the same function for other data types like `long`, `float`, `double`, etc., then, without templates, the only choice you have is to hand-code the function again for the various types. If the function (or class) is fairly large then there is a good chance that the work is very large and error prone. Fortunately, by using templates, you can reuse code written for one type to be converted to any other type, where the type becomes the parameter. The following example demonstrates the use of function templates, where the data type parameter (`class T`, here) is specified with angle brackets after the reserved word `template`. The function template is written to calculate the average of an array of numbers.

```
//Filename: functeml.cpp
//Demonstration of function  templates
#include <iostream.h>
// Function template to compute the average value
//of an array of data of any data type specifed as
//parameter T. See the main().
template<class T>              //T is the class type
T average(T* data, int n)      //data is the array,
                               //n is # of elements
    {
    T sum = 0;
    for (int i=0; i < n; ++i)
        sum += data[i];
    return sum / n;
    }
```

```
// Test program
int main()
{
    float rainfall[] = { 12.0, 13.0, 14.0, 15.0 };
    cout << "The average rainfall is "
        << average(rainfall, 4) << endl;      //Instantiates
                                              //average<float>()
    int class_size[] = {10, 8, 6};
    cout << "The average class size is "
        << average(class_size, 3) << endl;    //Instantiates
                                              //int<float>()
    return 0;
}
```

In the syntax `template<class T>`, the template parameter T specifies the data type on which the function defined below will be specified. In the `main()` function the statement `average(rainfall, 4)` generates code for instantiating an `average()` function that takes a `float` data array as input and returns a `float` as its return value. In the second case `average(class_size, 3)` is another function instantiated which takes an `int` data array as input and returns an `int` value as its output. In the template function definition we used the data type T

```
    T average(T* data, int n)        //data is the array,
                                     //n is # of elements
    {
        T sum = 0;
    ...
    }
```

wherever a data type parameter is necessary. In the next example, we describe class templates where a vector class is parametrized to be of any data type. The class also demonstrates the use of a copy constructor and overloaded assignment operator for classes using pointer variables as member data.

```
//Filename: template.cpp
//Demonstration of function and class templates
#include <iostream.h>
#include <new.h>
#include <stdlib.h>

void handle_out_of_memory()
{
    cerr <<"Out of memory!" << endl;
    abort();
}

// Function template to compute the average value
//of an array of data of any data type specified as
//parameter T
template<class T>                //T is the class type
T average(T* data, int n)        //data is the array,
                                 //n is # of elements
```

```cpp
{
    T sum = 0;
    for (int i=0; i < n; ++i)
        sum += data[i];
    return sum / n;
}


// A template vector class.
template<class T>
class Vector {
public:
    Vector(int n)
    {
        size = n;
        data = new T[n];
    }

    //Copy constructor
    Vector(const Vector&);

    //Overloaded assignment operator
    Vector& operator=(const Vector&);


    ~Vector()
    { delete [] data; }    //Note the word data!

    T& operator[](int i)   //Overloaded [] operator.
    { return data[i]; }


    T average();


private:
    Vector() { }        //Making the default constructor private
                        //prevents Vector from being created with
                        //no size parameter
    T* data;            //Vector of data
                        //with pointer notation.

    int size;           //Number of elements
};


// Member function declared outside of the
// class -- special syntax
template<class T>
T Vector<T>::average()
{
    // :: indicates that average() is outside the
```

```
      // class (in global scope)
      return ::average(data, size);    //Calls template
                                       //function average()
}

//Copy constructor definition
template<class T>
Vector<T>::Vector(const Vector& loc)
{
    size = loc.size;
    data = new T[size];
    for (int i=0; i<size; ++i)
        data[i] = loc.data[i];


}



//Overloaded assignment operator definition
template<class T>
Vector<T>& Vector<T>::operator=(const Vector& rhs)
{
    if( &rhs != this ) { //Checking it is not a self-assignment
      delete [] data;
      size = rhs.size;
      data = new T[size];
      for (int i=0; i<size; ++i)
          data[i] = rhs.data[i];
    }
    return *this;
}


// Test program
int main()
{
    set_new_handler(handle_out_of_memory);
    float rainfall[] = { 12.0, 13.0, 14.0, 15.0 };
    cout << "The average rainfall is "
        << average(rainfall, 4) << endl;        //Instantiates
                                                //average<float>()


    int groupSize[] = { 6, 7, 8, 6, 6 };
    cout << "The average class size is "
        << average(groupSize, 5) << endl;

    Vector<double> x(3);            // Instantiates Vector<double>

    x[0] = 1.3;
    x[1] = 2.0;
    x[2] = 3.0;
```

```
        cout << "The average is " << x.average() << endl;

        Vector<double> y(x);            //Testing copy constructor
        cout << "The average is " << y.average() << endl;

        Vector<double> z = x;           //Testing assignment = operator
        cout << "The average is " << z.average() << endl;

        return 0;
    }
```

The output of the program is

```
                The average rainfall is 13.5
                The average class size is 6
                The average is 2.1
                The average is 2.1
                The average is 2.1
```

The template for classes is similar to the function templates but note the syntax for defining the member functions outside the class declaration. The syntax is

```
            template<class T>
            T Vector<T>::average()
```

where <T> is added to the class name Vector. Otherwise the syntax is as seen before. The statement return ::average(data, size) in the function definition of T Vector<T>::average() indicates that a template function defined outside the class scope is called. In the main() function, a Vector object is instantiated by passing an appropriate type, double here, as the template argument. The statement Vector<double> x(3) instantiates a Vector object of type double. Note (3) and not [3] because 3 is simply the argument for the constructor of the Vector class. However, we have overloaded the [] operator in the Vector class, and we can conveniently use x[i] to access the ith element of the object x.

COPY CONSTRUCTOR AND THE OVERLOADED ASSIGNMENT OPERATOR

In previous chapters we noted that the compiler gives us a default copy constructor; that is, an object can be initialized with another object of the same type (for example, Vector<double> y(x) in the above program). However, unlike in the above program where a copy constructor was provided, if you use a default copy constructor, the copy made is simply bit-wise. That is, in the above example, the pointer data of the object x(x.data) with the address it is pointing to would simply be copied into the member data of the object y(y.data). This is sometimes called a *shallow copy*. To get a proper copy of the elements that this pointer is pointing to as well, we have to provide our own copy constructor as above. In that case the copy made is sometimes called a *deep copy* which anyway is the proper copy. In the same manner, we have to provide an overloaded assignment operator for all classes that use pointers as their data members as well as destructors which delete memory as in the above program.

In the next section, we present details on how to use existing Fortran or C code in an object-oriented framework provided by C++.

CALLING EXTERNAL FUNCTIONS

In the true sense of reuse, you can use your existing Fortran, C, or any other "legacy" code (code from the past) in C++ by wrapping these other functions as external functions. But you have to be careful about compiler vendor compatibility. Generally, the same vendor compilers are preferred. For example, if you want to use a Fortran number cruncher routine, then do the following in your C++ program.

```
extern "FORTRAN" {
void FORTRAN_number_cruncher_(argument1, argument2, ...)
                            //Pass all arguments by reference
}
```

In some environments you may have to use the word "C" instead of "FORTRAN."

The following example shows how a Fortran subroutine foo.f is used in a C++ class definition data. The Fortran subroutine is used to multiply the input arguments by 2. The first parameter a is of double type in C++ and the second parameter b is of type int. A UNIX environment was used in the following example.

```
C       Filename:numcru.f
C       Fortran number cruncher routine
        subroutine foo( a, b)

        double precision a
        integer b

        a=2*a
        b=2*b
        return
        end
```

The C++ class where the Fortran function foo.f is used is as following. The class is very simple but one of the member functions, double_it(), calls the Fortran subroutine foo.f to do the actual work.

```
//Filename: main.C
//Demonstration of C++ wrappers for "legacy" code

#include <iostream.h>

//Uses extern C instead of extern FORTRAN
//Needs the underscore after the name foo for Fortran linkage
```

```
extern "C" {
void foo_(double* a, int* b); //Fortran function prototype
}
class data {
  public:
      data(){ }   //No-argument constructor

      data(double one, int two)
         { a = one; b = two; }

      void double_it()
         { foo_(&a, &b); } //Call to Fortran subroutine
                           //must pass arguments using pointers
      void display()
         {
         cout << "a= " << a << ","
              << "b= " << b << endl;
         }
  private:
      double a;
      int b;

}; //End of data class definition

int main()
   {
   double a=3.14;
   int b=2;
   data data_obj1(a,b);

   cout << "before Fortran call\n " ;
   data_obj1.display();
   //Double it using Fortran function

   data_obj1.double_it();

   cout << "after Fortran call \n";
   data_obj1.display();

   return 0;
   }   //End of main
```

The following is the actual session. The first command line statement
(ponnu@dial[1]% f77 -o foo.f) is for compiling the Fortran subroutine
to create the object code foo.o. The second statement compiles the C++ code
and links it with the object code of the Fortran routine foo.f. The third statement
simply runs the executable code to produce the desired result.

```
ponnu@dial[1]% f77 -o foo.f
ponnu@dial[2]% CC main3.C foo.o
CC main3.C:
```

```
cc -L/.software/arch/c++3.0/lib main3.c foo.o -lC
ponnu@dial[3]% a.out
before Fortran call
a= 3.14,b= 2
after Fortran call
a= 6.28,b= 4
```

The main point is that the data passed from C++ always has to be passed by pointers. The second point is that the name of the Fortran routine in C++ is slightly changed by adding the underscore after the name. However, these changes depend on a particular environment. Otherwise, the syntax and the use are quite intuitive.

SUMMARY

Virtual functions extend polymorphism to inherited classes. Friend functions and classes break data hiding and hence should be sparsely used. Templates help code reuse by generating code for a specific data type at compile time from a code written for a generic data type. Calling external functions in Fortran, C, etc. is possible and this feature can help in the reuse of legacy code.

CHAPTER 11

Java for C++ Programmers

Java is a recent development in object-oriented programming and is creating great excitement in the computing world today. C++ programmers are easily poised to take leading roles in Java programming because Java is a close relative of C++ with significant improvements towards simplicity and portability, and with a good set of class libraries (called packages) to do advanced computing. The objective here is to make a C++ programmer understand the essential features of Java at a beginner's level. We will also present the case study from Chapter 7 written in Java to understand the similarity of Java to C++.

The major differences between C++ and Java are:

(i) Java, like Smalltalk, is truly object-oriented in the sense that there are no global functions. Recall that a global function in C++ can stand alone, does not belong to any class and can be called from anywhere (except for `main()`). Global functions are a feature left in C++ to make it compatible with C and structured programming [Chapters 2 to 6].

(ii) There is no operator overloading [Chapter 7] but function overloading [Chapter 4] is allowed.

(iii) There are no (explicit) pointers [Chapter 9] but references [Chapter 4] are allowed.

(iv) There is no multiple inheritance [Chapter 8] although other easier to use features called multiple interfaces can be used to fill in, to a large extent, where they may be needed.

There are also differences such as availability of "garbage collection," multithreading, features that are specifically designed for worldwide computer networks, etc.

Note that the syntax of Java is quite similar to C++ and would not require much introduction to readers of this book. Java is highly portable; that is, programs developed in one computer and operating system can be run without changes or recompilation in another computer using a different operating system. This is an important feature for developers of applications and is especially suitable for distribution via worldwide networks.

We will introduce Java by using some examples to understand the language features; the first two examples demonstrate simple output and input, respectively, the third demonstrates the use of arrays, and the fourth is the presentation of the single reservoir problem [Chapter 7] in Java. Lastly, we introduce Graphical User Interface (GUI) programming in Java using a simple applet, a Java program that can also run in network browsers and so can be easily distributed through the Internet. This is a feature not covered in the book because GUI programming in C++ depends on compilers and available class libraries as these class libraries are not features of the C++ language specification. However, the Java class libraries for GUI programming are available across most platforms and operating systems as they are part of the Java language.

SIMPLE INPUT AND OUTPUT

Example 1 (The Hello Program). The first example we present is commonly used and is called the hello program. It simply prints a HELLO message on the monitor screen which, in C++, might have been written with a simple (global) function. But there are no standalone global functions in Java where everything has to be an object. In order to instantiate an object we need a class and in order to make the program know where to start we have a single method called main() which is of static type. Note that static data and functions are instantiated only once, as in C++.

```
//Filename: hellojava.java
//Hello in Java
//Java application

public class hellojava {
   public static void main(String args[]) {
    System.out.println("HELLO!");
   }
} //End of class definition
```

Comment lines are similar to C++ and both forms (// and /* ..*/) can be used. The program name suffix always ends in "java." Note that the program name and the class name are the same. The first executable line clearly indicates that the class name is hellojava, and the class accessibility is public. Within the class definition starting with { and ending with } are the various methods (member functions) and member data. Here we have just a single function main() which is of static type and accessibility is public. For now, ignore the function argument String args[] which is explained in the next example. The function body is enclosed between curly brackets { } with a single program statement, namely, the function call System.out.println("Hello!"). This member function is part of a huge number of classes and associated services available in Java. Of course, it is clear that this function is used to simply output HELLO! ending with a linefeed indicated by the "ln" following "print." This function is similar to cout in C++. The Java compiler in command line mode is simply invoked as

`javac hellojava.java`

and the end result is a file **hellojava.class**. This is the code that the Java interpreter will interpret and execute.

If hellojava.class has been created, then you can execute the program using

`java hellojava`

at the command line. The result will be output to the monitor.

Example 2 (Inputting to Java at the command line). To input data at the command line the following is used. This assumes that the program input.java has been compiled and the file input.class has been created.

`java input 1 2 6.8 Velan`

and the output is

```
Arguments input are 0 : 1
Arguments input are 1 : 2
Arguments input are 2 : 6.8
Arguments input are 3 : Velan
```

The program is

```
//File: input.java
//Shows how to input data to a Java program
//at the command line!

class input {
  public static void main(String args[]) {
    for (int i=0; i<args.length; ++i) {
      System.out.println("Arguments input are " + i + " : " + args[i]);
    }
  }
} //End of input class
```

The program simply reads anything delimited by space as a string and prints it out to the monitor. The reading is done at the command line and the input parameter is the string array String args[] in the header of main(). The strings "1", "2", "6.8", and "Velan" are stored in the array args[]. Note that the for loop is identical to a C++ for loop. The variable args.length is available because length is a public member data of the array class. The next example explores Java arrays further.

ARRAYS AND CONSTRUCTORS

Example 3 (Array Objects). The following program demonstrates how to create objects with member data and many methods, some of which are constructors of that class. Note it is customary that individual methods and data are preceded by their corresponding accessibility indicators. The syntax therefore is somewhat different from C++. The following intArray class has two constructor methods (function overloading, of course!) to create intArray objects, two setArray() methods to set array data, and one display method printArray() to display the intArray object contents, especially those stored in the array referenced by the member data int integers[]. In Java all objects have to be created dynamically (recall that in C++ we use pointers and new operators for that purpose) using a reference which works similar to a pointer variable. The reason Java is more secure than C++ is that these reference arguments are not pointers and so cannot point to memory addresses arbitrarily.

```java
//Filename: intArray.java
//Demonstration of Java array objects
//and their manipulations

class intArray {
  public intArray(int max){ //Constructor 1 for initialization
      MAX = max;
      integers = new int[MAX]; // Arrays have to be created dynamically!
      for(int i=0; i < MAX; ++i) {
         integers[i] = 0;
      }
      printArray();
  }

  public intArray(int max, int vals[]){ //Constructor 2
      MAX = max;
      integers = new int[MAX];
      for(int i=0; i < MAX; ++i) {
         integers[i] = vals[i];
      }
      printArray();

  }

  public void setArray(int i, int value) { //Set function 1
    integers[i] = value;
  }
  public void setArray(int vals[]){
      for(int i=0; i < vals.length; ++i) { //Set function 2
         integers[i] = vals[i];
      }
  }
```

```
      public void printArray() { //Display function
        for(int i=0; i < MAX; ++i) {
          System.out.println(integers[i]);
        }
      }
      public static void main(String args[]) {

        intArray intArray1 = new intArray(3); //Dynamic array creation
        intArray1.setArray(0,1);
        intArray1.setArray(1,2);
        intArray1.setArray(2,3);
        intArray1.printArray();

        int arr1[] = {1, 2, 3, 4};

        //intArray1.setArray(arr1); //Will create an error
                                    //because arr1 size is > 3
                                    //which is the size of intArray1

        intArray intArray2 = new intArray(4,arr1);

        int arr2[] = {-100, -200, -300, -400};
        intArray2.setArray(arr2);
        intArray2.printArray();
      }

//Member data of intArray class hidden here!
  private int MAX;
  private int integers[]; //Reference to an array of integers

} //End of intArray class!
```

The output of this program is simply

```
                              0
                              0
                              0
                              1
                              2
                              3
                              1
                              2
                              3
                              4
                            -100
                            -200
                            -300
                            -400
```

Unlike in C++, array bounds cannot be exceeded and if tried it will cause an error or exception. An error at execution time causes the creation of an object of the type exception. An exception handler is used to deal with exceptions. Exception handling is not covered in the book but Java and C++ have identical functions for that purpose. The major aspect of Java which is different from C++ is that all arrays and objects are created dynamically. This feature is equivalent to C++ where pointers and new operators are used for that purpose. However, there is *no* delete operator and no destructors because, in Java, such actions are taken automatically as and when possible. This feature is called "garbage collection" and is of great convenience to programmers. The disadvantage of garbage collection may be an unexpected pause in the execution of programs, which may not be acceptable in certain applications. Overall, the above program is quite close to a C++ program and you will notice these common ideas also in the next example.

COMPARING C++ WITH JAVA

Example 4 (Single reservoir simulation). This is the single reservoir simulation example from Chapter 7. Except for the way in which the data is input to the program, the program is identical to the C++ program. In fact, we simply copied the C++ program and converted it to Java using ideas from Examples 1 to 3 above. The following shows how we can interact with the program.

`java res 4 1 2 1 2 -1 -1`

The output of the program is

```
MAX. STOR. = 4   MIN. STOR. = 1   INITIAL STORAGE = 2
Inflow  Demand Outflow Spill Fin.Stor.
1   2    2   0   1
```

The program is as follows.

```
//Program res.java
//Program will simulate a single reservoir system for a given
//demand and inflow series input by the user.

import java.lang.Float;

public class res {
     public void errormsg() {
       System.out.println("Input data again");
     }
     public res() {
       float maxsto = args[0];
       float minsto = args[1];
       float stor = args[2];

       if ( (maxsto < minsto ) ||
            ( stor > maxsto ) ||
            ( stor < minsto ) ||
```

```
                      ( maxsto < 0 ) || ( minsto < 0 ) ) {
                errormsg();
                output_system_charac();
          }
          else {
                max_storage = maxsto;
                min_storage = minsto;
                storage = stor;

                output_system_charac();
          }
    }   //End of constructor
    public void output_system_charac()
    //Precondition: max, min, and initial storages should have values and
    //preferably should be called before process().
    //Postcondition: max, min, and initial storages are output

    {
     //cout << "MAX. STOR. = " << max_storage
     //      << "   MIN. STOR. = " << min_storage
     //      << "   INITIAL STORAGE = " << storage << "\n\n";
     System.out.println("MAX. STOR. = " + max_storage +
                        " MIN. STOR. = " + min_storage +
                        " INITIAL STORAGE = " + storage);
    }
    public void process()
    //Pre: max, min and storage should have been set.
    //max >= min; max, min, storage >= 0;
    //Post: outflow, spill, and storage would be calculated
    //for each user input

    {
    //Read user data for each period

    read_a_period();

    //Calculate outflow, spill, and new storage for each period

    while ( (inflow >= 0 ) && ( demand >=0 ) ) {

       calc_a_period();

        //write output for each period

        write_a_period();

        read_a_period();

    } //End of while loop

    } //End of function process
```

```java
private void read_a_period()
//Pre: None
//Post: Inflow and demand are read from the user

{
  timeind += 2;
  inflow = args[timeind];
  demand = args[timeind+1];

}


private void write_a_period()
//Pre: Outflow, spill, and storage have been calculated.
//Call this after calling calc_a_period().
//Post: Outflow, spill, and storage are output to the monitor
{
  //Print out results

  System.out.println("Inflow Demand Outflow Spill Fin.Stor.");
  System.out.print( inflow + "    " + demand + "    ");
  System.out.println( outflow + "    " + spill + "    " + storage);
}



private void calc_a_period()
//Pre: Storage,inflow and demand have non-negative values
//Post: Outflow, spill, and new storage will be calculated

{

  float temp_storage;
  temp_storage = storage + inflow - demand;

  if ( ( min_storage <= temp_storage ) &&
     (temp_storage <= max_storage) ) {
       outflow = demand;
       spill = 0;
       storage = temp_storage;
  }
  else if (min_storage > temp_storage) {
       outflow = storage + inflow - min_storage;
       spill = 0;
       storage = min_storage;
  }
  else { //This corresponds to max_storage < temp_storage
       outflow = demand;
       spill = storage + inflow - demand - max_storage;
       storage = max_storage;
  }
  //End of the three cases
```

```
      } //End of process

  public static void main(String arginp[]){
     int Max_time = (arginp.length - 3)/2;
     args = new float[3+2*Max_time];
     for(int i=0; i<args.length; ++i) {
       args[i] = (Float.valueOf(arginp[i])).floatValue();
                                        //String to float
                                        //conversion
                                        //through a Float
                                        //object!
     }
     res res1 = new res(); //The reservoir object is created here!
     res1.process();

   } //End of main

//Member data of res class hidden here!
     private float max_storage;
     private float min_storage;
     private float storage;
     private float demand;
     private float inflow;
     private float outflow;
     private float spill;
     private int timeind = 1;
     private static float args[]; //Reference


} //End of res class
```

As you can see, the major difference is in the `main()` function which is used in Java to get the input data; this is explained below. From the `input.java` example described earlier you may have noticed that passing data to a Java program at the command line is different from C++ where we could have simply used appropriate `cin` statements. In Java the input is passed through the string array argument in the main program. The data passed to the program has the following format, corresponding to the input required in the reservoir problem:

Maximum storage Minimum storage Initial Storage Inflow for period 1 Demand for period 1 ... − 1 − 1

Using this string of arguments we first find out how many time periods (`Max_time`) are passed by the user in the statement

```
        int Max_time = (arginp.length - 3)/2;
```

The number 3 in the above expression corresponds to the maximum, minimum, and initial storages. Because for each period we require 2 pieces of data, namely inflow and demand, the above expression calculates the number of periods of data the user has passed to the program. The next statement is used to define an array `args[]` using the reference `static float args[]` of the member data. This array is used to store all the input information supplied by the user.

```
args = new float[3+2*Max_time];
```

Using a for loop the input strings are converted into float data. The expression `(Float.valueOf(arginp[i])).floatValue()` is used to first convert the input string to a `Float` object using `Float.valueOf()` method of the `java.lang.Float` class and then using `floatValue()` method of this object, the floating point value is returned as follows:

```
for(int i=0; i<args.length; ++i) {
    args[i] = (Float.valueOf(arginp[i])).floatValue();
```

The only other change required is in the method `process()` where the member data `time` keeps a track of the simulation time periods and is used for fetching appropriate inflow and demand data in the function `read_a_period()`. As this program shows, there is good correspondence between C++ and Java programs giving some advantage to C++ programmers over others when learning Java. Note that in Java you can initialize the class variable `timeind = 1` which is something you cannot do in C++. The `java.lang.Float` class library is imported into the program using the import statement at the very top (always must come before any class definition), roughly equivalent to the `include` statement in C++, in order to use methods such as `Float.valueOf()`, etc.

APPLETS AND GRAPHICAL USER INTERFACE PROGRAMMING

Applets are Java programs that can be embedded in network browsers. The following example is an applet that is used to demonstrate Graphical User Interface (GUI) programming in Java. However, the Java Development Kit includes an applet viewer which can be used to run applets without connecting to a network or a browser. Applets are embedded in **html** (Hyper Text Markup Language) documents, an example of which is given below. Detailed discussions of `html` programs or networks or browsers are outside of the scope of this book.

An example html file (`entry.html`*).*

```
<title>GraphicsApplet</title>
<applet code="textentry.class" width=200 height=300>
</applet>
```

As you can see, the `html` file here simply allows us to see the textentry applet that we have created as below. The following command runs the applet viewer

```
appletviewer entry.html
```

and the output seen on the monitor is as shown in Fig. 11.1.

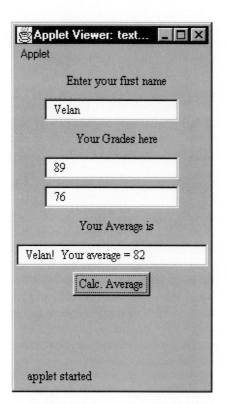

FIGURE 11.1
An example GUI produced using Java.

If the GUI is user-friendly then just by studying the various forms or windows, associated menus, textfields, and buttons, one should be able to understand what the program does. In the program above, the first textfield is where you type your first name, in the next two textfields you type your grades (only two allowed here) and then if you click the "Calc. Average" button it will provide the average of the two grades in textfields above the button. Therefore, this simple applet can be used to understand GUI programming in Java with input and output. The class diagram is shown in Fig. 11.2 and the Java program is listed below.

```java
//Filename: textentry.java
//Demonstration of GUI textentry

import java.awt.*;  //Forward reference to Java packages we need
import java.applet.Applet;

//textentry class is derived from base class java.applet.Applet
//Note keyword "extends"

public class textentry extends java.applet.Applet {
  public int calcAverage(){
    //Pre: mathGrade and scienceGrade should be set with
    //valid values
    //Post: Calculates the average of two grades in
    //mathGrade and scienceGrade
```

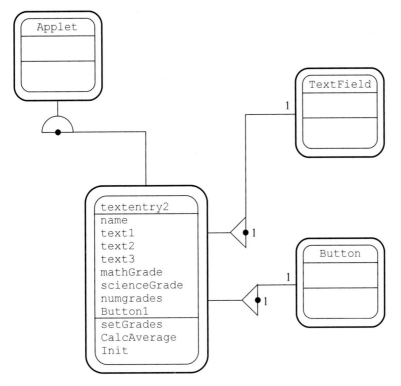

FIGURE 11.2
The class diagram depicting various classes used in this example.

```
    int sum = 0;
    sum = mathGrade + scienceGrade;
    int ave = sum/numgrades;
    return ave;
  }
public void setGrades() {
    //Pre: Enter first name in first textfield
    //and the two grades in the next textfields
    //Post: Parses the text from text1 and text2
    //textfields to mathGrade and scienceGrade, respectively.
    //Calculates average and sets the value as text in text3

    String s1 = text1.getText();
    String s2 = text2.getText();
    mathGrade = Integer.parseInt(s1);
    scienceGrade = Integer.parseInt(s2);
    int average = calcAverage();
    text3.setText(name.getText() + "! Your average = " +
                  String.valueOf(average));
```

```
        }
        public void init(){
          //Pre: None
          //Post: Initializes the textentry2 object created
          //by CalcButton object. Displays the form with the
          //initialized values

          add(new Label("Enter your first name"));
          name = new TextField(20);
          add(name);
          name.setText("Velan");

          add(new Label("Your Grades here"));

          text1 = new TextField(20);
          text1.setText("Your Math. grades here");
          add(text1);
          text2 = new TextField(20);
          text2.setText("Your Science grades here");
          add(text2);

          //Set default values
          text1.setText("100");
          text2.setText("80");

          add(new Label("Your Average is"));
          text3 = new TextField(30);
          add(text3);

          //Create button set label
          button1 = new Button("Calc. Average");
          add(button1);

          setGrades(); //Average for the default data
        }

        public boolean action(Event evt, Object arg){
            if ( evt.target == button1 ) {
                setGrades();
            }
            return true;
        }

    //Member data hidden here!
      private TextField name;  //Output text field
      private TextField text1; //For first name
      private TextField text2; //For grade 1
      private TextField text3; //For grade 2.
      private int mathGrade;    //Variable to store grade 1
      private int scienceGrade;//Variable to store grade 2
      private int numgrades=2;
```

```
    private Button button1; //Calc. Average button

} //End of textentry class
```

Note we have imported the Java class libraries `java.awt.*` and `java.applet.Applet`, where the first is the abstract windowing toolkit (`awt`) class which is used for instantiating the various GUI components in our program. The `java.applet.Applet` class is itself derived from the `awt` class and is mainly used for launching applets (to start, to initialize, to stop, and to destroy). Our `textentry` class is derived from the `Applet` class as in `public class textentry extends java.applet.Applet {..}` where the reserved word `extends` indicates the derivation relationship. The `textentry` class also contains *(has-a)* a `textfield` class and a `button` class as the diagram indicates.

Notice that we have used the `new` operator many times to create objects of various types dynamically and the function `add()` puts the created object in the form. We used the default layout to place the various objects in the form. The function `action()` is an event function that catches the event objects automatically created in the form by mouse movements or keyboard actions; we can write code to take an appropriate action depending upon the type of the event as in

```
if ( evt.target == button1 ) {
            setGrades();
}
```

which executes the `setGrades()` function when someone clicks the button in the form. The return value `true` indicates that we have taken appropriate actions and the base class need not bother taking any default actions. Go through the comments in the program to understand some of the details.

SUMMARY

Java programming is very close to C++ programming despite some differences. Java is a truly object-oriented language with many easy-to-use class libraries, including the ones for the development of GUIs. It is not difficult to convert some C++ programs to Java as shown above with the reservoir example.

ASCII Character Set (Character Codes 0–127)

Dec	Hex	Char	Code†	Dec	Hex	Char	Code†
0	00		NUL	31	1F		US
1	01		SOH	32	20	(space)	
2	02		STX	33	21	!	
3	03		ETX	34	22	"	
4	04		EOT	35	23	#	
5	05		ENQ	36	24	$	
6	06		ACK	37	25	%	
7	07		BEL	38	26	&	
8	08		BS	39	27	'	
9	09		HT	40	28	(	
10	0A		LF	41	29	)	
11	0B		VT	42	2A	*	
12	0C		FF	43	2B	+	
13	0D		CR	44	2C	,	
14	0E		SO	45	2D	-	
15	0F		SI	46	2E	.	
16	10		SLE	47	2F	/	
17	11		CS1	48	30	0	
18	12		DC2	49	31	1	
19	13		DC3	50	32	2	
20	14		DC4	51	33	3	
21	15		NAK	52	34	4	
22	16		SYN	53	35	5	
23	17		ETB	54	36	6	
24	18		CAN	55	37	7	
25	19		EM	56	38	8	
26	1A		SIB	57	39	9	
27	1B		ESC	58	3A	:	
28	1C		FS	59	3B	;	
29	1D		GS	60	3C	<	
30	1E		RS	61	3D	=	

(continued)

Dec	Hex	Char	Code†	Dec	Hex	Char	Code†
62	3E	>		95	5F	_	
63	3F	?		96	60	`	
64	40	@		97	61	a	
65	41	A		98	62	b	
66	42	B		99	63	c	
67	43	C		100	64	d	
68	44	D		101	65	e	
69	45	E		102	66	f	
70	46	F		103	67	g	
71	47	G		104	68	h	
72	48	H		105	69	i	
73	49	I		106	6A	j	
74	4A	J		107	6B	k	
75	4B	K		108	6C	l	
76	4C	L		109	6D	m	
77	4D	M		110	6E	n	
78	4E	N		111	6F	o	
79	4F	O		112	70	p	
80	50	P		113	71	q	
81	51	Q		114	72	r	
82	52	R		115	73	s	
83	53	S		116	74	t	
84	54	T		117	75	u	
85	55	U		118	76	v	
86	56	V		119	77	w	
87	57	W		120	78	x	
88	58	X		121	79	y	
89	59	Y		122	7A	z	
90	5A	Z		123	7B	{	
91	5B	[		124	7C	|	
92	5C	\		125	7D	}	
93	5D	]		126	7E	~	
94	5E	^		127	7F	DEL	

†The Code column is meaningful only for characters 1–31.

C++ Reserved Words or Keywords

WARNING: Some of the reserved words may not be available or somewhat different depending upon the compiler. There may also be additional reserved words in some compilers. Consult the compiler manuals!

C LANGUAGE RESERVED WORDS

```
asm
auto
break
case
char
const
continue
default
do
double
else
enum
extern
float
for
goto
if
inline
int
```

```
interrupt
long
register
return
short
signed
sizeof
static
struct
switch
typedef
union
unsigned
void
volatile
while
```

C++ LANGUAGE RESERVED WORDS

```
bool
catch
class
delete
friend
inline
new
operator
private
protected
public
template
this
throw
try
virtual
wchar_t
```

Some Important Header Files and Their Uses

WARNING: Some header file names could be different depending upon the compilers used!

Filename	Brief Description
ASSERT.H	Assert debugging macro. Use it for `assert()`
CTYPE.H	Character classification. Use it for `isalnum()`,...
FLOAT.H	Constants needed by math functions
FSTREAM.H	Functions used for opening files using `file.open()`,...
IFSTREAM.H	Functions used for file input
IOMANIP.H	Definitions/declarations for iostream's manipulators like `setw()`,...
IOS.H	Functions used by the `ios` class
IOSTREAM.H	Functions used by the `iostream` classes. Use it for `cout`, `cin`,...
ISTREAM.H	Functions used by the `istream` class
LIMITS.H	Ranges of integers and character types. For example, `INT_MAX` for maximum value of `signed int` type,...
MATH.H	Floating-point-math routines. Use it when you need `sin()`,...
OSTREAM.H	Functions used by the `ostream` class for file output.
STDARG.H	Macros for variable-length argument-list functions
STDIO.H	Standard I/O header file. To use `printf()`,...
STRING.H	Functions for string handling like `strncpy()`,...
STDLIB.H	Commonly used library functions. Use it for `rand()`,...
TIME.H	General time functions

Precedence and Associativity of Operators

The following table presents C++ operators and their precedence levels and associativity. The highest precedence level is at the top of the table and the lowest at the bottom of the table. In rows where there are more than one operator, the operators have equal precedence and the associativity decides which ones get executed first. In the table, each level of precedence is separated from the next by spacing.

Operator Symbol	Description	Associativity
`::`	Scope resolution	Unary has right to left and binary has left to right
`++`	Postfix increment	Left to right
`--`	Postfix decrement	Left to right
`( )`	Function call	Left to right
`[ ]`	Array indexing	Left to right
`->`	Pointer to class member	Left to right
`.`	Class or union member	Left to right
`++`	Prefix increment	Right to left
`--`	Prefix decrement	Right to left
`!`	Logical NOT	Right to left
`~`	Bitwise NOT	Right to left
`-`	Unary minus	Right to left
`+`	Unary plus	Right to left
`&`	Address	Right to left
`*`	Indirection	Right to left
`sizeof`	Size of … (in bytes)	Right to left
`new`	Allocate memory	Right to left
`delete`	Deallocate memory	Right to left
`.*`	Pointer to member of objects	Left to right
`->*`	Pointer to member	Left to right

(*continued*)

Operator Symbol	Description	Associativity
*	Multiply	Left to right
/	Divide	Left to right
%	Modulus with remainder as the result	Left to right
+	Add	Left to right
–	Subtract	Left to right
<<	Left shift	Left to right
>>	Right shift	Left to right
<	Less than	Left to right
<=	Less than or equal to	Left to right
>	Greater than	Left to right
>=	Greater than or equal to	Left to right
==	Equal	Left to right
!=	Not equal	Left to right
&	Bitwise AND	Left to right
^	Bitwise exclusive OR	Left to right
|	Bitwise OR	Left to right
&&	Logical AND	Left to right
||	Logical OR	Left to right
? :	Conditional	Right to left
=	Assignment	Right to left
*=, /=, %=, +=, -=, <<=, >>=, &=, ^=, |=	Compound assignment	Right to left
,	Comma	Left to right

APPENDIX E

Software Engineering

Until about a decade ago, software was produced (engineered) in a more or less haphazard manner, unlike other engineered products. It is still very much a cottage industry with no industry-wide production guidelines and product standards. However, there is a general realization that software is so omnipresent that it impacts basically all aspects of modern living like alarm clocks, bread toasters, TVs, medical equipment, cars, telephone networks, etc.; code sizes range from 100 lines to millions of lines. Due to increasing complexity, software should be engineered as other engineering products which are governed by standards and regulations.

In order for us to call a product an engineered product, it should have the following properties: (i) a publishable production process has been followed adhering to a minimum set of standards set by a national or international body, and (ii) the process can be repeated and essentially the same quality product can be obtained. The first property concerns the process and the second concerns the result of the process, namely, the product. Although software is yet to be a truly engineered product, the field of software engineering is rapidly developing and gaining importance. Software engineering attempts to develop and specify (i) to achieve (ii). In general (i) involves both project management and the problem solving methodology but we will consider here mainly the problem solving methodology.

In software engineering, the problem solving methodology may be described as either a waterfall model or a spiral model. The waterfall model is shown in Fig. E.1.

The difficulty with this waterfall model is that the software developed is usually too fragmented and hence the integration does not provide what is required. Consequently, project managers lose confidence in the design and development process and also in the team. Therefore, the more common solution today is to follow the waterfall steps in a spiral, going from the solution of an easier version of the original problem to more and more detailed versions. This model is shown in Fig. E.2 where V1 means Version 1 etc., and implementation includes coding, debugging, and integration.

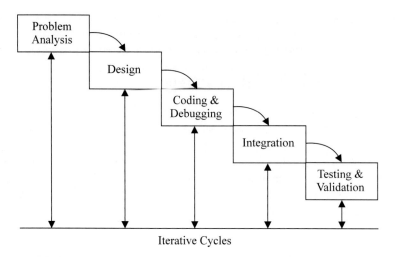

FIGURE E.1
The waterfall model for analysis, design, and development.

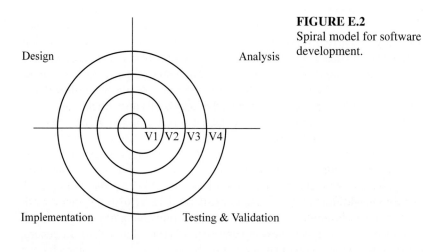

FIGURE E.2
Spiral model for software development.

SOFTWARE PRODUCTION AND MANAGEMENT

The five most important questions that define software and its quality are: (i) How easy it is to produce (including testing), (ii) how easy it is to use, (iii) how easy it is to maintain and modify, (iv) how reliable it is, and (v) how good its performance is. Performance includes how fast the program completes execution and how little memory it needs for execution. Some of the above questions can be answered directly; for example, testing the user-friendliness of the software at usability labs or counting the number of CPU seconds and amount of memory used (in bytes) to measure performance. If the software uses algorithms, the performance of the algorithms can be pre-calculated (or estimated) using mathematical techniques. The reliability of software (the number of successful runs and the ability to recover from failures), which may depend upon the structure of the software (discussed in Chapters 7 and 8), is an issue that is outside the scope of this book and will not be discussed further.

Questions (i) and (iii) are hard to answer directly. Therefore features of the software that can be measured are often used to answer them indirectly. These measurable quantities are called software metrics. The metrics can be useful during design to make a decision on an appropriate software structure. How we do that is an ongoing research topic. They can also be used to understand the advantages of object-oriented programming over traditional structured programming. Hence, some selected metrics will be described here.

SOFTWARE PRODUCTION AND TESTING

For quite some time, the number of executable lines of code (ELOC) in software has been used to indicate how difficult it is to produce software for a given problem, because the effort and cost involved has been found to be directly proportional to ELOC. The productivity of a programmer was also measured in terms of ELOC per unit of time. Although this metric is still used, there is less dependence on it due to its well-known disadvantages such as code bloat (unnecessary size increase) and lower performance, among others. Some extensions to this idea include calculating the number of operators and operands, number of functions, and number of modules (here, module is defined as an independently translatable program unit).

This section can be read after completing Chapters 2 and 3.

It was soon recognized that software control structures such as decisions and loops introduced program complexity and testing difficulty and hence some measure of the complexity of these structures was introduced. For example, the McCabe complexity number is a metric that measures the number of decisions, ands, ors, and nots plus one. Some empirical rules have been devised to indicate an optimal upper bound for the McCabe metric of each module. This number is somewhere between 10 and 15. The following code segment is from the reservoir case study of Chapter 3:

```
if (test1) &&
   (test2) {


         }
else if (test3) {


             }
else{
} //End of the three cases
```

The McCabe metric for this example is 4 because there are two `if`'s and one `&&`. Note that this number reflects the number of paths in the decision structure. Figure E.3 indicates the three possible paths.

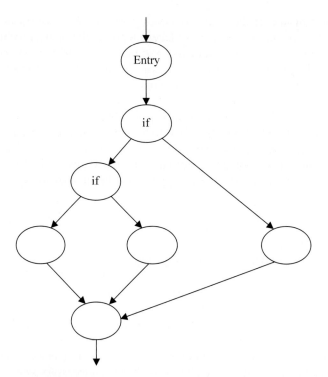

FIGURE E.3
A decision structure.

The fourth path, which is not shown in the diagram, corresponds to the condition that storage is less than the minimum and simultaneously greater than the maximum. This is a physically impossible condition that has been eliminated by checking for error conditions on the input data. Typically, a software testing strategy should test each of these independent paths to conclude that they are working properly. Compare this number with the test cases in Chapter 3.

In addition, if there is a loop, as in our case, the possible paths become very many. Suppose we had used a `for` loop that executes 10 times; the possible number of test paths would become 4^{10}, an enormous number. Therefore, we can conclude that measuring the control structures in some way would indicate how complex the software is. The disadvantage of the McCabe metric is that it does not differentiate nested loops from ordinary loops; research is continuing into finding a metric that indicates the complexity of software due to control structures more realistically.

SOFTWARE MAINTENANCE

This section can be read after Chapters 2 to 4.

The number of comment lines is a simple and indirect measure of the maintainability of software. Similarly, for doing the same work, software that has more modules (or functions) is preferable to software that has fewer functions. Because functions help modularize, they can be used to follow the top-down design process or the divide and conquer strategy closely in the implementation of the software. The advantages of modularization are that it becomes (i) easier to delegate work to different groups, increasing software productivity; (ii) easier to maintain the software, and localization of errors, that is, bugs are likely to be local to a few functions and can be removed quickly; and (iii) easier to modify the software because it is likely that only a few functions are affected by changes and not the entire software. The two major disadvantages of modularization is that software could become non-cohesive and data passed between functions could become a major source for error due to coupling. Understanding coupling and cohesion is a major study of software science because a good design is supposed to minimize coupling and maximize cohesion.

Consider the reservoir case study in Chapters 3 and 4, respectively, which perform the same work. In the first case we had a single `main()` function and in the second case we have seven functions, including the `main()`. In terms of modularity the second case is the clear winner. But the additional complexity introduced due to data passed to different functions must be considered, as discussed in the next section. In summary, higher modularization is good in general but has some associated disadvantages.

COMPLEXITY DUE TO DATA PASSED TO FUNCTIONS

Consider again the reservoir case study of Chapters 3 and 4 which perform the same work. In the first case we had a single `main()` function and there was no passing of data to any other functions. The passing of data to functions introduces an additional problem because of the possibility of unintentional modification. In addition, we have to consider the global data, that is, the data common to the entire function, in order to calculate the data complexity. In the reservoir problem, the data complexity equals 5, corresponding to minimum storage, maximum storage, initial storage, inflow, and demand. In the second case where we have used functions to modularize, the data we are interested in monitoring is that passed as arguments. For example, the `calc_a_period()` function alone has seven arguments, the arguments in the rest of the functions amount to 16 and, in total, the data complexity is 23. Of course, there are more sophisticated metrics such as Shepperd's IF4 metric which $= (\text{fan-in} * \text{fan-out})^2$, where fan-in and fan-out represent the number of information flows entering and emanating from a module, respectively. Whatever metric we use, the underlying conclusion is that modularization is good for production and maintainability but it comes with a higher program complexity due to data. In the next section we will show that object-oriented programming solves this problem: modularization can be increased without significant increase in program complexity due to data hiding and unification of data with functions in objects.

PROGRAM COMPLEXITY IN OBJECT-ORIENTED PROGRAMMING

This section can be read after Chapters 2 to 4, and Chapter 7.

Consider the reservoir case study in Chapter 7. The program we developed performs the same task as in Chapters 3 and 4. Therefore, the complexity due to control structures (McCabe metric) remains the same. (Check this for yourself.) We have increased modularity slightly (due to the constructor member function in the reservoir class) compared with the program in Chapter 4 which uses functions to modularize. However, the number of data items passed in the OOP structure is 3 (for the constructor) plus the member data in the reservoir object which equals 7, giving a total of 10. There is no data passing anywhere else in spite of the many member functions that have been used to maintain modularity. Therefore, it is possible to show that object-oriented programming is quite superior to structured programming when considering the same kind of metrics.

Another example. Suppose we have three integer variables x, y, and z with unequal values and we are interested in finding the maximum of the three. Here are three possible solutions: the first uses old-style programming, the second is based on structured programming and uses functions to modularize, and the last solution is based on object-oriented programming and uses objects.

```
Solution 1:  if (x > y)
                {
                if  (x > z)
                    cout << x;
                }
             else
                {
                if  (y > z)
                    cout << y;
                else
                    cout << x;
                }
```

```
Solution 2: cout << max(x,max(y,z));//Assumes max function exists
                                    //which takes two arguments and
                                    //returns the maximum of the two.
```

An example max function is:

```
int max(int first, int second)
{
if (first > second)
   return first;
else
   return second;
}
```

```
Solution 3: cout << x.max(y.max(z)); //Works when x,y,z are Integer
                                     //objects with a member function
                                     //that takes one argument and
                                     //returns an integer value as
                                     //shown below.
```

The minimum required member functions of the `Integer` class are shown:

```
void putvalue() { //Inputs object.value
   cout << "Please input the value\n";
   cin >> value;
}
int max(Integer lsecond){
   if (value > lsecond.value)
      return value;
   else
      return lsecond.value;
}
```

It is clear that the McCabe complexity numbers for solutions 1, 2, and 3 are 4, 2, and 2, respectively. Solutions 2 and 3 are more modular than Solution 1 but with the additional complexity introduced due to data passed as arguments. The data passing complexity number (simply the number of arguments) for Solutions 1, 2, and 3 are 0, 2 and 1, respectively. Once again, the object-oriented programming solution is nearly as good as the first solution in terms of data passing complexity but with a much better McCabe complexity number than Solution 1. In terms of clarity, both Solutions 2 and 3 are better than Solution 1.

However, if inheritance (which allows further structuring of solutions and code reuse) is used, then the complexity in OOP does increase. There is continuing research in this area to measure complexity due to inheritance structures and to devise guidelines for upper bounds on number of classes, member functions, instance variables (objects), etc. In summary, OOP can maintain simplicity as in the case of a single function program while simultaneously maintaining modularity as in the case of structured programming.

Answers to Selected Review Questions and Exercises

ANSWERS TO EVEN NUMBERED REVIEW QUESTIONS

Chapter 2

2. At `main()`.   **4.** Names of variables, objects, functions, and classes acceptable to the compiler.   **6.** T.   **8.** a semicolon.   **10.** F.   **12.** Object.   **14.** (i) 1.0e−04, 10e−05, .1e−03. (ii) 1.000001e+03, .1000001e+04.   **16.** (ii), (iv).   **18.** F.
20. F.   **22.** right-hand side, =, left-hand side.   **24.** `cin`.   **26.** Syntax errors are errors due to not using the compiler-accepted sequence of symbols and characters according to the rules of C++ grammar.   **28.** F.   **30.** F.   **32.** T.   **34.** 3, 1, 3, 0.
36. `pow(x,y)`.   **38.** `w`, `setprecision(d)`.   **40.** lower, higher

Chapter 3

2. compare, True, False.   **4.** T.   **6.** `>, >=, ==, <, <=, !=`.   **8.** 0.
10. Yes.   **12.** Infinite loop!   **14.** `for (float x = -pi; x <= pi; x += 0.6)`
`{cout << "x = " << x << " sin (x) " << sin(x) << endl; }`. Checking for equality of a float number!   **16.** F.   **18.** `if (temperature < -2) && (cloudy) { cout`
`<< "It will snow"; }`.   **20.** Valid (includes boundary), Special, and Invalid.

Chapter 4

2. defined.   **4.** T.   **6.** by value, by reference, and by pointer.   **8.** T.
10. header.   **12.** F.   **14.** last.   **16.** Conditions that are asserted to be true before a function is executed.   **18.** Conditions that are asserted to be true after a function has correctly executed.   **20.** These are contractual agreements between the function user and the function developer. Increases the chance of error-free programs.

Chapter 5

2. cout << rain[0] << " " << rain[9].   **4.** rain [7] [24].   **6.** F.
8. fstream infile ("Data.dat"); for (int i=0; i<10; ++i) {infile >>
x[i];}.   **10.** Arrays can be potentially large. Passing by reference means the same
memory allocated to an array is used everywhere in the program.   **12.** Steps taken to
solve a problem in a finite time.   **14.** T.   **16.** "Best" depends on the type of problem. Different problems may require different algorithms. But it also depends whether you
want speed, less memory, or simplicity.   **18.** Yes. Arrays can be used to store tables.
Row and column operations in a spreadsheet are similar to row and column operations in an
array.   **20.** (i) Copies "in" string to "out" string to a maximum of MAX characters, (ii)
Concatenates "add" string to the end of "orig" string.

Chapter 6

2. T.   **4.** a semi-colon.   **6.** T.   **8.** struct time_struct {int hour,
minute, second;};.   **10.** time_struct times[MAX].   **12.** struct
fpsunits {int feet; float inches;};.

Chapter 7

2. data hiding, encapsulation.   **4.** F.   **6.** private, protected, public.
8. class, float.   **10.** has, need not.   **12.** class time {private: int hrs, min,
sec;};.   **14.** ::.   **16.** public: int gethrs() {return hrs;}   **18.** time
times[MAX_TIMES];.   **20.** T.   **22.** time() {hrs = min = sec = 0;}.
24. assert ((hrs >= 0) && (hrs <= 24)); similarly for others.   **26.** See Fig. F.1.
28. scope resolution operator ::.   **30.** See Fig. F.2.

FIGURE F.1
Memory allocation for time_of_birth2 object data.

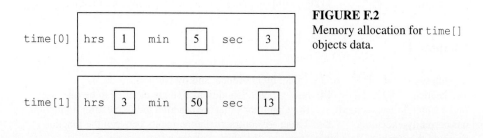

FIGURE F.2
Memory allocation for time[]
objects data.

32. tilde ~.   **34.** T.   **36.** ~time() {cout << "\nTime object destroyed";}.   **38.** F.   **40.** For easy use of objects and for intuitive implementation of mathematical algorithms.   **42.** T.   **44.** \.
46. T.

Chapter 8

2. Inheritance.   **4.** hierarchy.   **6.** T.   **8.** Hint: (i) What happens to the derived classes if the base class has to be changed? (ii) Reliability may increase with higher reuse of well-tested classes. (iii) To use a derived class do you need to know all the parent (base) classes?   **10.** A set of properties and methods that no instance of a class or classes derived from it can violate.   **12.** T.   **14.** T.   **16.** The CParent class is derived in public from the CPerson class.   **18.** The CMother class is derived in public from its base classes CParent and CWoman.

Chapter 9

2. cout << &variable1;.   **4.** T.   **6.** Not possible.   **8.** An array name is an address and addresses are pointer constants.   **10.** dummy (&Apple, Bananas);.
12. float (*) (int, float).   **14.** Just sort the respective pointers pointing to the start address of the objects.   **16.** Depends. If you use, say, a linked list to store arrays it may slow down. If you are sorting and you sort only the pointers of objects then it speeds up.

SAMPLES OF SELECTED EXERCISES (MORE ON THE ACCOMPANYING DISKETTE— SEE FILE READ_ME.1ST)

Chapter 2—Exercise 7(a)

1. Problem analysis

Problem statement: Determine the value of the hypotenuse of a right angle triangle

Input/output analysis:
    Input: Lengths of two sides
    Output: Length of hypotenuse

2. Design

See Fig. F.3.

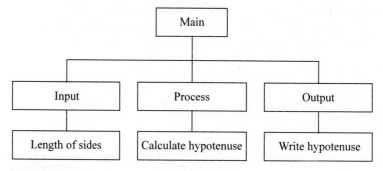

FIGURE F.3
Decomposition diagram.

Chapter 7—Exercise 8

1. Problem analysis

Problem statement: To write a program to store data on books. Print the titles of books costing less than $60.
I/O analysis:

Input: Book: title, author, subject, year, ISBN number, price ($)
Output: Store data in objects
Print the stored data
Print out books that cost less than $60

2. Class design

Hand example:

Sample object data:
> Title: C++ for Engineers
> Author: Tiuley
> Subject: Computers
> Year: 1995
> ISBN: 124792
> Price: 60.99

Algorithm design to find books that cost less than $60:
Pseudocode: for $i = 0$ to $MAX - 1$
>>> if (book price $<$ 60)
>>>> display title
>>> endif
>> endfor

Sample table of output.

Book #	Title	Author	Subject	Year	ISBN	Price
1	C++ for Engineers	Tiuley	Computers	1993	124792	60.22
2	Physics	Hiddler	Physics	1995	12127	74.30
3	Philosophy	Navak	Philosophy	1995	32173	22.00
4	Total Design	Hugh	Design	1994	93939	32.99
5	Calculus	Wright	Math	1993	72199	82.99

3. Coding and debugging

```
//*************************************************************
//
// Assignment No:
//
// Due:
// Author:
//
// Program Name: book_rec.cpp
// Description:  Contains class for Book_record
//               and a simple string class called s_string
//               (can set data, display, access data etc...)
//               Creates a book_shelf array to store book records
//*************************************************************

#include <iostream.h>
#include <string.h>
#include <iomanip.h>
#include <stdlib.h>
```

```cpp
const int MAX = 40;
const int SHELF = 5;

/************* Class definition for s_string ***************/
class s_string
{

    public:

            s_string(char str1[] = "No data\0")
                { strpcy(str,str1); }

            void display()       //Displays contents of str array
                //Pre: None
                //Post: Displays the contents of str with ios::right
                //No returns
                    { cout << setiosflags(ios::right) << str; }

            void setdata()       //Prompts user for data to store in str
                { strcpy(str,"\0");
                    cin.getline(str,MAX); }

            void setdata(char data[MAX])  //Allows data to be
                                          //passed in directly
                { strncpy(str,data,MAX); }

            s_string getdata()            //Returns a s_string object
                { return s_string(str); } //This allows us to
                                          //pass the str array

            int length()
                { return strlen(str); }

            char getdata(int index)   //Allows single character
                                      //from str to be accessed
                { return str[index]; }
    private:
            char str[MAX];
};/************* End of class definition for s_string ***********/

/*************** Class declaration for Book_record **************/
class Book_record
{
    public:
        Book_record();  //No-argument constructor
        void setdata();  //Function to set data
        void display();  //Function to display data
        void display_table_form();  //Function to display
                                    //in table format
```

```
        s_string get_name();   //Function to access author's name
        long get_isbn();       //Function to access isbn#
        float get_price();     //Function to access the price
        void display_title();  //Function to display the book title
    private:
        s_string title;
        s_string author;
        s_string subject;
        int year;
        long isbn;
        float price;

};/******* Declaration of Book_record class ends here *******/

int main()          //The main() function starts here
{

    Book_record book_shelf[SHELF];

    cout << "\nCreating Book shelf..............\n";
    for(int i=0; i<SHELF; i++) {
        cout << "\nEnter data for book number [" << i+1
            << "] --->\n";
        book_shelf[i].setdata();
        }
    cout << "\nThe book shelf now contains records for ["
        << i << "] books:";
      cin.get();
    for(i=0; i<SHELF; i++) {
        cout << "\nBook [" << i+1 << "] is: ";
        book_shelf[i].display_title();
          cin.get();
        }
    cout << "\nThe books that cost less than $60 are:";
    for(i=0; i<SHELF; i++) {
        if(book_shelf[i].get_price() < 60.0) {
        book_shelf[i].display_title();
        cout << ", ";
        }
    }
    cin.get();
    cout << endl << setw(50) << "TABLE FOR BOOKSHELF\n";
    cout << setiosflags(ios::left) << endl
        << setw(7) << "Book#" << setw(18) << "| Title" << setw(10)
        << "| Author" << setw(14) << "| Subject" << setw(9)
        << "| (c) Year" << setw(13) << " | ISBN#" << setw(8)
        << "| Price";
    for(i=0; i < 80; i++) {
        cout << "-"; }
```

```
        for(i=0; i<SHELF; i++ {
                cout << setiosflags(ios::left) << setw(7) << i+1;
                book_shelf[i].display_table_form();
                cout << endl;
                }


        return 0;
}

//Definition for constructor to initialize.
//Initializes with default data
Book_record::Book_record()
{
        title.setdata("C++ for Engineers\0");
        author.setdata("Tiuley\0");
        subject.setdata("Programming\0");
        year = 1995;
        isbn = 124792;
        price = 60.99;


}

//Definition for function to set data
//Pre: None
//Post: Prompts user for data and sets accordingly
//in private, no returns
void Book_record::setdata()
{
        cout << "Enter the title for the book: ";
        title.setdata();
        cout << "Enter the author of the book: ";
        author.setdata();
        cout << "Enter the subject of the book: ";
        subject.setdata();
        cout << "Enter the year the book was published: ";
        char temp[MAX];
        cin.getline(temp,MAX);
        year = atoi(temp); //String to integer conversion
        cout << "Enter the ISBN number: ";
        cin.getline(temp,MAX);
        isbn = atol(temp); //String to long conversion
        cout << "Enter the price of the book: ";
        cin.getline(temp,MAX);
        price = atof(temp); //String to float conversion


}
```

```
//Definition for function to display data
//Pre: None
//Post: Displays the private data contents of the book_record
void Book_record::display()
{
      cout << "\nThe data for this record is:\n"
           << "\n Title: ";
           title.display();
      cout << "\n Author: ";
           author.display();
      cout << "\n Subject: ";
           subject.display();
      cout << "\n Year: " << year
           << "\n ISBN Number: " << isbn
           << "\n Price: " << price;
}


//Definition for function to display record data in table form
//Pre: None
//Post: Displays the contents of a book_record in table format
void Book_record::display_table_form()
{
   cout << setiosflags(ios::right);
   cout << "| ";
   title.display();
   cout << setw(18 - title.length()) << "| ";
   author.display();
   cout << setw(10 - author.length()) << "| ";
   subject.display();
   cout << setw(14 - subject.length()) << "| " << year << setw(10)
        << "| " << isbn << setw(11) << "| "
        << setprecision(2) << price;
}


//Definition for function to access the ISBN number
//Pre: None
//Post: Accesses private isbn long and returns it
long Book_record::get_isbn()
{
return isbn;
}


//Definition for function to access author's name
//Pre: None
//Post: Accesses name in private and returns it using string object
s_string Book_record::get_name()
{
return author;
}
```

```
//Definition for function to access the price of the book
//Pre: None
//Post: Accesses the price in private and returns it
float Book_record::get_price()
{
return price;
}

//Definition for function to access the name of the book
//Pre: None
//Post: Accesses the title in private and displays it
void Book_record::display_title()
{
title.display();
}
```

4. Integration

The string class was developed first. The book_record class contains (*has-a*) the string class.

5. Testing

The hand example was tested and the results were as expected. Further random choices also passed. [Details not given here!]

C++ at a Glance—
A Student Help Sheet

Top-Down Design Process

1. Problem Analysis:

   - Problem statement
   - Input/output analysis

2. Design:

   - Decomposition
   - Class design
   - Hand example
   - Algorithm design

3. Coding and debugging:
4. Integration:
5. Testing and validation:

Header Files (have declarations)

`#include <iostream.h>`// for input/output
`#include <iomanip.h>`// for formatting
`#include <stdlib.h>`// for standard library
functions like `exit()`, `rand()`
`#include <math.h>`// for mathematical functions

Variable Definitions

`int num;`—integer
`char letter;`—character
`float num;`—real number
`long num;`—long integer
`double num;`—double precision float
`const int num=...;`—A constant

Input and Output Commands

`cout << variable;` (output)
`cin >> variable;` (input)
`cout << setw(n)`—set width
`cout << endl`—end line
`cout << setprecision(n)`
`cout << setf(ios::left)`—left justify field
`cout << setiosflags(ios::scientific);`
—scientific notation
`cout << setiosflags(ios::showpoint);`
—show decimal points to specified precision

Arithmetic Operators

+	$a + b$ (addition)
-	$a - b$ (subtraction)
*	$a * b$ (multiplication)
/	a/b (division)
%	$a \% b$ (modulus)

Arithmetic assignment operators
`a += b` means $a = a + b$
`a -= b` means $a = a - b$
`a *= b` means $a = a * b$
`a /= b` means $a = a/b$
Increment and decrement
`i++, ++i` both mean $i + 1$
`i--, --i` both mean $i - 1$
prefix $(++)$
`b = b*++a` means
$a = a + 1$
$b = b * a$
postfix $(++)$

b=b*a++ means
$$b = b * a$$
$$a = a + 1$$

Relational Operators

```
==   equal to
>    greater than
<    less than
>=   greater than or equal to
<=   less than or equal to
!=   not equal to
```

Mixing of Data Types

```
int salary;
long (salary) // converts to long
```
Lowest to highest conversion in an expression is done automatically. The order from lowest to highest: char, int, long, float, double, and long double.

Selection

```
if (condition with relational
operator) {
...
}
else if (condition ...) {
...
    }
else {
...
}
switch (variable_name) {
  case 'possible_condition1':
   ...
  break;
  case 'possible_condition2':
   ...
  break;
}
```

Repetition

For loop

```
for (i=0; i<MAX; ++i) {
...
}
```

While loop

```
while (condition) {//when true
...
}
```

Do loop

```
do {
...
} while (condition); //when true repcat
```

Logical Operators

```
&&   means and
||   means or
!    means not
```

Functions

Syntax:

function_type function name (parameters);

Declare function before use

```
void func();
int main()
{
...
 func(); //function call
...
}
//Function func() definition
void func()
{
...
}
```

Function with argument passing

Passing by values:
```
type0 funcname (type1);
int main() {
  type0 var1 = funcname (arg1);
  return 0;
  }
type0 funcname (type1 par1) {
//par1 is a copy of arg1
...
  return type0(...);
}
```
Passing by reference:
```
type2 funcname (const type3&);
int main(){
  funcname (arg2); //no ampersand
  return 0;
}
type2 function (const type3& par2) {
    //par2 and arg2 are the same
    //because of const this function
    //cannot modify par2. Safe way!
```

```
  return type2 (...)
}
```
Overloaded functions
```
//The compiler
//will know which function to call by
//the type/number of arguments passed
function_type funcname (parameter
list1) {
...
}
function_type funcname (parameter
list2) {
...
}
int main() {
...funcname (argument_list1);
```
  //if `argument_list1` is the same type and
  //number as `parameter_list1` then
  //the first function is called.

```
}
```

Storage Classes

- automatic (local)—visible only inside { } in which it was defined
- external (global)—visible throughout entire program, many declarations allowed but only one definition
- static—like automatic but retains value on leaving scope, one initialization only

Inline Function

- for very short often used functions
- reduces function calls

e.g., `inline type function_name (parameters) {...}`

Arrays (Examples)

Definition: `int age [MAX];`
Initialization: `int age[]={19,20,21,22}`
Accessing: `age[i]` ←index
               ↑ array name
—an array of max size 3 will have array indices 0,1,2

Multidimensional Arrays

```
int matrix [ROWS][COLS];
or: int matrix [][COLS]={{1,2,3},
{4,5,6}};
```
Note: ROWS not necessary if initializing; COLS is necessary.

Passing Arrays

function call:
`show_matrix (matrix);`
                    ↑ array name
                      without [...][...]

Defining function for passing arrays

//declaration
```
void show_matrix (int [ROWS][COLS]);
or: void show_matrix (int [][COLS]);
```
//definition
```
void show_matrix (int matrix
[ROWS][COLS]) {...}
```

Character Arrays (Strings—Examples)

```
char str1[MAX];
char str2[]="string here";
```
Note: last character of string is always a null character (`'\0'`)
Note: when entered at keyboard, a space or return generally signals the end of the string. Use `cin.getline(str1,max)` if an entire line is desired.

Classes

Declaration (reserved words: class, private, public, protected)
```
class class_name
{
public:
 //data and methods
...
private:
 //data and methods
...
  }; //semicolon here
```

Definition of an Object

`class_name v1;` //v1 is an object identifier

Dot Operator

To access the individual member data of a function use the dot operator
`v1.method_name();`

Scope Resolution Operator (::)

To define a function outside the class declaration (preferable)
`type class_name::method_name(...)`
is the header for the member function `method_name()` of the class `class_name`

Operator Overloading

Most operators can be overloaded except `.`, `::`, `.*` and `?:`.

e.g., Change the `method_name` to `operator+` for defining the + operator

Inheritance

```
//Single inheritance
class derived_class : public
base_class
{...};
```
Constructor
```
derived_class(...) : base_class(base
class arguments)
```
```
//Multiple inheritance
class derived_class : public
base_class1, public base_class2
{...};
```
Constructor
```
derived_class(...) : base_class1(base
class1 arguments),
base_class2(base class2 arguments)
```

Pointers

Just add an asterisk after the type of the variable the pointer is pointing to.

e.g., `int* intptr;`
`float* floatptr;`

To define a pointer to an array of pointers used to define matrices use
`int** matrix;`

Dynamic Memory Allocation/Deallocation

```
int* intptr = new int; //allocates memory
//for one integer variable
delete intptr; //releases the integer variable
//memory
intptr = NULL; //for safety
int* intptr = new int[max];
//allocates an integer array of size max
delete [] intptr; //releases the memory
//allocated for the array
...
```

Miscellaneous

The following modifications are done in class declarations:

To make a member function virtual add the reserved word virtual to the front of the member function.

To make a class abstract make at least one member function pure virtual: `virtual function_name() = 0;`

To make a function or class a friend add the reserved word `friend` to the front of the function or class name.

Function template:
```
template<class T> //T is class type
T function_name(...){...}
```
Class template:
```
template<class T>
class class_name {...}
```
To define outside the declaration
```
template<class T>
T class_name<T>::method_name() {...}
```
A copy constructor declaration:
```
class_name(class_name&);
```
A copy constructor definition:
```
class_name::class_name(class_name&)
{...}
```
To declare an external function:
```
extern "FORTRAN" { //or "C"
function_type function_name_(arg's)
//Pass by reference or pointer
```

Object-Oriented Programming

Is-a relation: A kind-of relation that describes base class-derived class relationships.

Has-a relation: A containership relation seen when one class is contained in another class.

Uses-a and *knows-a* relations are weaker relations or associations that are often implemented in similar manners.

Class invariants: A set of properties and methods that no instance of a class or classes derived from it can violate. Base class is a generalization and derived classes are specializations.

Preconditions: The conditions that are asserted to be true before a function or method is executed. Preconditions in derived class methods could be more restrictive than in base class methods.

Postconditions: The conditions that are asserted to be true after a function or method has correctly executed. Postconditions in derived class methods can further reinforce the postconditions of base class methods.

Index